The Backstage of the Care Economy

"*The Backstage of the Care Economy* reveals the causes and consequences behind the explosion of migrant care work. It is a remarkable accomplishment and contribution from one of the leading social scientists of gender, care and migration in Europe."

—Rhacel Salazar Parreñas, Princeton University

"A tour de force distillation of radical social thought on domestic labour grounded in critiques of global capitalism. This prodigiously researched book strikes a perfect balance between theory and empirics, examining the entanglement of migrant women's lives in former-socialist republics as they shuttle between wage employment abroad and their homes."

—Heidi Gottfried, co-editor of *Global Labor Migration: New Directions*

"A powerful, systemic analysis of the outsourcing of care in Western Europe and the transnational social inequalities underpinning these processes. With remarkable precision and insight, Lutz brings the contemporary "private" relations of care to the front stage of theory and debate on capitalism and society – emboldening us all to engage vigorously with the centrality of care."

—Isabel Shutes, Associate Professor, Department of Social Policy, London School of Economics and Political Science

"Lutz tackles one of the most important issues facing us today: transnational care migration. Based on over 14-years of research and focusing on East-to-West European migrations of care workers, this book is an absolute must-read for anyone interested in gender, migration and care work."

—Ito Peng, Professor of Sociology and Public Policy, University of Toronto

The Backstage of the Care Economy

Transnational Perspectives on the Commercialisation of Care

Helma Lutz

First published 2025 by Pluto Press
New Wing, Somerset House, Strand, London WC2R 1LA
and Pluto Press, Inc.
1930 Village Center Circle, 3-834, Las Vegas, NV 89134

www.plutobooks.com

British Library Cataloguing in Publication Data
A catalogue record for this book is available from the British Library

ISBN 978 0 7453 4536 9 Paperback
ISBN 978 0 7453 4540 6 PDF
ISBN 978 0 7453 4538 3 EPUB

This book is printed on paper suitable for recycling and made from fully managed and sustained forest sources. Logging, pulping and manufacturing processes are expected to conform to the environmental standards of the country of origin.

Typeset by Stanford DTP Services, Northampton, England

Simultaneously printed in the United Kingdom and United States of America

EU GPSR Authorised Representative
LOGOS EUROPE, 9 rue Nicolas Poussin, 17000, LA ROCHELLE, France
Email: Contact@logoseurope.eu

Contents

Acknowledgements

As this book is based on research conducted between 2007 and 2021, the list of those I want to thank is very long.

First of all, I want to thank the migrant women who were willing to share their life stories and who persuaded their family members to be interviewed, too.

For her great and sensitive interviewing of the Polish care workers and their relatives, for contributing her extensive knowledge and for constantly providing new references to relevant debates in Poland, I would like to thank Ewa Palenga-Möllenbeck. I have always benefited from her patience, care and practical wisdom, regardless of whether it was about problems arising in the research process or issues with colleagues, foundations and third-party funders: I learnt from her to become more patient. Together, we have organised three major international conferences over the past 16 years, and worked on 15 publications (books and journal articles) to date. We have drawn up many applications and were successful in obtaining funding for two large research projects that allowed us to continue our collaboration.

I am also deeply indebted to researchers Myroslava Keryk, Viktoriya Volodko and Oksana Kis who conducted the interviews with Ukrainian care migrants and their relatives, and Iga Obrocka and Tatiana Jewsiejewa who conducted interviews with migrant care workers from Poland.

My thanks go to Petra Pommerenke, Anna Proc and Yevgeniya Wirz for their excellent cooperation in analysing German, Polish and Ukrainian press articles on the subject of care and migration. Wirz also translated interviews, materials and articles from Ukrainian into German. In 2020, she successfully defended her dissertation on the reconstruction of social networks of Ukrainian labour migrants.

The data I present in this book comes from two research projects, "Landscapes of Care-Drain: Care Provision and Care Chains from the Ukraine to Poland and from Poland to Germany" (2007–10), and "Decent Care Work? Transnational Home Care Arrangements" (2017–21). For the financing of the German part of both projects I thank the German Research Foundation (DFG). While the first project was part of a European joint project within the EUROCORES line of the European Science Foundation (Migration and Networks of Care in Europe: A Comparative European Research Project), the second was a D-A-CH* cooperation. The collaboration with my colleagues Brigitte Aulenbacher, Michael Leiblfinger and Veronika Prieler from the Austrian team and Karin Schwiter, Jennifer Steiner and Anahi Villalba from the Swiss team was not only an extraordinarily successful project in terms of output, but above all a particularly enjoyable experience of collegial cooperation that continues to this day. The Frankfurt team, consisting of Ewa Palenga-Möllenbeck, Aranka Vanessa Benazha, Iga Obrocka and Amanda Glanert, was a really successful collaboration for which I continue to be very grateful.

The many years of scientific exchange with our partner projects in Amsterdam (NL), Leeds (UK) and Cork (Ireland) have enriched the analyses and expanded the knowledge production in a transnational framework. Fiona Williams (Leeds), Linda Connolly, Siobhán Mullally and Caitríona Ní Laoire (Cork) and Sarah van Walsum (Amsterdam) have given me hugely important food for thought. The early death of Sarah van Walsum, with whom I shared a decades-long friendship and collaboration, is still hard to bear. Her commitment and her intelligent questions always inspired me; she has left a big gap in my network of colleagues and friends.

Other institutions that have contributed to the realisation of this book and to which I am deeply indebted include the Swedish Riksbanken Foundation (Stockholm), which honoured me in 2012 with the award of the Alexander von Humboldt Prize, thus enabling me to spend six months at REMESO (Institute for Research on Migration and Ethnic Relations) at the University of Linköping; Torbjörn Eng from the Riksbanken offered me much support. Anders Neergaard and Jeff Hearn, who invited me to Sweden, Carl-Ulrik Schierup, Alexandra Alund, Stefan Jonsson, Anna Bredström, Peo Hansen and Zoran Slavnic (all at Linköping University) and Diana

---

*   D-A-CH: Germany-Austria-Switzerland.

Mulinari (Lund University) made my stay in Linköping and Norrköping a very special experience. I still remember their hospitality and the many great discussions we had.

This book would not have been possible without a nine-month fellowship from October 2012 to June 2013 at the Woodrow Wilson International Center for Scholars (WWC) in the heart of Washington DC, which not only provided me with the most beautiful office I have ever had, but also gave me the luxury of direct access to the Library of Congress. Sonya Michel, who supported me during the application and throughout my time at WWC, not only gave me advice but also opened her home, shared her love of art and gave me access to her feminist network, family and friends. I owe more to her than I can express here.

I also owe the WWC an illuminating insight into the stimulating atmosphere of US universities. I have been friends ever since with Claudia Kinkela, my landlady in DC and Yohanna, her daughter.

Without the support of my wonderful transatlantic network of friends, Gül Ozyegin (Williamsburg), Sherri Grasmuck and John Landreau (Philadelphia), Kathy Davis and Barbara Henkes (Amsterdam), Barbara Waldis (Cressier, Switzerland), who supported the book's development process with their intelligent enquiries and great advice, I would not have persisted with the book project. To my colleague Anna Amelina I owe many new insights into transnational migration and inequality research; the three years in which we occupied neighbouring rooms at the Westend Campus of Goethe University Frankfurt made all the difference to me.

My Frankfurt team members Ina Schaum, Aranka Benazha, Ewa Palenga-Möllenbeck, Marija Grujić, Minna Ruokonen-Engler, Anna Krämer, Annette Erzinger and Heike Strohmann have repeatedly provided me with important suggestions. I thank them all, as well as Lotte Rahbauer and Ulla Wischermann for their caring and supportive assistance. It was a privilege to work with them.

I am very lucky that Jakob Horstmann, who worked as an editor at Zed Books 15 years ago, and at that time supervised the publication of my book *The New Maids: Transnational Women and the Care-Economy*, is now working with Pluto Press. Over the past few years, he has repeatedly encouraged me to complete this new book. I thank Jakob very much for his support. Pluto Press can consider itself fortunate to have such a committed collaborator. The same applies to Naira Antoun, who edited and greatly improved the entire English text.

My partner, Rudolf Leiprecht, has had a lasting influence on my work over the past 34 years.

He has not only relieved me of doubts that are part of every writing process, but also read every single line of this book; he gave me much important feedback throughout the entire process. Rudi not only took care of my emotional and physical well-being, but above all, his humour and accurate assessments put the small and big worries of life into perspective. He should, actually, appear here as a co-author, because I owe him many sensitive and inspiring comments and insights that opened my eyes, for example on the subject of masculinity and care.

It is a pity that my mother, Hedemarie Lutz, to whom I dedicate this book, cannot see its publication as she passed away in August 2023. In autumn 2016, when she was no longer able to live independently in her house in a small town in Lower Saxony, she had to decide whether, as her friends and neighbours suggested, she should be cared for by a migrant woman from Eastern Europe in her own home or move into assisted living at a home for the elderly in Frankfurt. I am very grateful that she chose the latter, but with this choice, unfortunately, she had to accept the loss of her personal network and surroundings. The associated dilemma for me as her daughter – taking her out of her familiar environment, in which she was able to orientate herself – often left me sad. Nevertheless, I am glad about the years in which I could visit and look after her as often as possible. Although she was confronted with the ongoing development of dementia during these years, there were still many wonderful moments when we could go for walks, watch the birds and the flowers, laugh and cry together. With the exception of the period during the height of the pandemic when we were not allowed to visit her but tried to keep in contact by singing for her and chatting via her raised ground floor balcony, the three of us – she, myself and Rudi – would play Rummy Cup or do crossword puzzles every Sunday. I thank her for her love, understanding and trust in me and my work.

Frankfurt, April 2024

Preface
Frontstage and Backstage – A Brief Overview

Since the start of the century, the international debate about transnational migration of care workers has developed rapidly and has spread across disciplines. Care migration is now a common practice around the globe, whether formal, informal, state-sponsored or tolerated with complicity. The diversity of this service market as part of the new care economy has taken on a scale that was hardly imaginable 20 years ago. Worldwide, this market – which promotes the feminisation of migration – has become the most important labour market for migrants, in particular migrant women. At the same time, the expansion of this phenomenon is being investigated and documented on a larger scale, and studies on transnational care migration are now being carried out in most parts of the world. In addition, researchers in German-speaking countries – which is the geographical focus of this book – have paid increased attention to live-in care.[1]

It is clear that the issue will not lose its relevance for the demographically ageing societies of the twenty-first century; on the contrary, it will become even more relevant. It is thus no surprise that the figure of a caregiver from Central and Eastern Europe has become a theme of documentaries and even a component in German and Austrian political cabaret shows (see, for example, Markus Hirtler as Ermi Oma[2]).

The majority of studies conducted so far deal with what I call the frontstage, namely the situation in the private households of care recipients. In contrast, research that examines the transnational lifestyle and biographies of migrant women, focusing on the situation of relatives left behind (children, husbands, mothers and fathers) and investigating the family implications of temporary or long-term absences of mothers, continues to be rare (but see Wirz 2021; Solari 2017).

This book focuses on what I call the backstage. I use the metaphor of frontstage and backstage not so much in the sense of Erving Goffman's (1952) symbolic interactionism, which is concerned with the definition and staging of social roles according to predetermined rules, but rather as perceptual templates localised in geopolitical power relations. These templates suggest a certain perspective on an everyday phenomenon, in this case care migration. I use these terms in order to shift the gaze from the situation of the live-in carer in the homes of care recipients (the frontstage) to the social and societal situation of migrants' family members who remain behind in their hometowns (the backstage). The lives of migrant women move within and between these two spheres, and it is important to understand their entanglement.

In international research, it is usually assumed that care migrants come from the Global South. However, this is not the case in Europe, where the majority of employees are women from "Central and Eastern Europe". This book aims to make a contribution to the understanding of commonalities and differences with regard to their work and life situations. Here, I put "Central and Eastern Europe" in quotation marks to draw attention to the complex history of the characterisation of these territories as Western Europe's "Other".

International analyses of the global care supply identifying "global care chains" (Hochschild 2000; Parreñas 2001) assume that the Global South functions as a sending or origin region, while the Global North is regarded as a destination region for care migrants. Apart from the fact that there is no precise definition of either term, it is unclear where the Central and East European countries are to be placed in this schema. From the end of the 1940s until the collapse of the socialist system in the early 1990s, Eastern Europe historically figured as part of the so-called Second World, as communist/socialist states that were in alliance with the Soviet Union. In the three-world model that dominated until the collapse of the Soviet Union, the First World was regarded as the territory of the rich industrialised nations, while the designations First and Second World primarily referred to the different political systems (capitalist versus communist/socialist). The Third World was initially the self-designation of 118 non-aligned countries that advocated for the disarmament of military blocs formally established in Belgrade, Yugoslavia, in 1961 under the leadership of Josip Broz Tito.[3] Regions in Africa, Asia and Latin America, formerly subjugated and exploited by European colonial powers, were subsumed under this term. Their economic development after decolonisation was dependent on Western industrial nations and they were considered poor according to the criteria of the World Trade Organization (WTO).

The collapse of the Soviet Union and the socialist regimes contributed to the rejection of the three-world model and it has now been replaced by a global division into two parts. Only a quarter of the world's population lives in the prosperous Global North, primarily located in the northern part of the hemisphere, but Australia, New Zealand, Japan, Hong Kong, Singapore, South Korea and Taiwan are also included. Four-fifths of the world's income and ownership of 90 percent of industrial production facilities are concentrated here (Mimiko 2012). The term Global South initially encompassed all regions with massive economic, social and political problems in the southern hemisphere, previously considered a characteristic of the Third World. It is now increasingly being used to refer to the exploitation of natural and human resources, and describes inequality as an economic and social problem on a global scale. An answer to the question of whether the post-socialist countries of Central and Eastern Europe belong to the category of the Global South is complex. As will be demonstrated in this book, after the system transformation following the collapse of the Soviet Union, the economic dependence of the region on Western foreign currency, and relatedly on migrant remittances, is comparable to the situation in many countries of the Global South. This also applies to the exploitation of (human) resources and the survival strategies of a considerable proportion of the population living on or below the poverty line. The situation of the middle classes is also comparable with that in the Global South: despite high levels of education, they are unable to generate incomes that enable them and their families to maintain their status. As with the Global South, a discursive narrative that fulfils the function of the fictitious "Other" in relation to the identity and self-presentation of citizens in the Global North is also assigned to citizens of Central and Eastern Europe (Safuta 2018). Within the EU, the countries of "old" Europe see themselves as the civilised, democratic, developed and progressive part of the union of states, whereas the "new" Europe embodies the opposite. Notwithstanding the commonalities, the integration of many post-socialist countries into the EU offers financial and socio-political opportunities that most countries of the Global South do not have.

In post-socialist transformation processes since the 1990s, the incorporation of Central and Eastern Europe into the late capitalist economies of the world market took place through price and trade liberalisation, the privatisation of state property, the establishment of private companies and a drastic dismantling of public services. The disastrous loss of millions of jobs in the course of the dismantling of state socialism, which affected men and even more so women, can be seen as the driving force behind the high motivation of the population to be mobile. Large segments of these populations discovered that their good education would not protect them from sliding into poverty. At the same time, it can be assumed that the level of education is key to understanding people's migration strategies: members of the middle classes, whose formal qualifications and professions were devalued or rendered superfluous in their home countries, still had certain forms of cultural and human capital at their disposal, including foreign language skills, manual skills and so-called care skills, which they could use as migrants to compensate for the fall into poverty. Ultimately, they contribute their professionally acquired expertise without this being officially recognised or remunerated. As a rule, they employ migration as a short-term strategy to ward off social decline, and not so much as a long-term, systematic solution to financial problems.

Overall, the mobility of Central and Eastern European citizens has led to tremendous outmigration. In some countries more than 50 percent of the population emigrated. For example, four million Albanians live outside the country, and the remaining population is only two million.[4] In 2023, a total of around 1.55 million Polish citizens were living in another member state of the European Union (EU-27). With around 784,224 people, Germany had the highest number of Polish citizens living in the EU in 2023.[5] Interestingly, in the Polish case the extent of emigration has decreased, as it was much higher in earlier years. The 2011 census shows that 3.5 million Polish citizens out of 38.3 million inhabitants (9%) were absent for up to 12 months (Anacka et al. 2014: 12). One reason for the decline is undoubtedly the introduction of Brexit, as for many years Britain was the main destination country for Polish migrants. In comparison, the rates of migration from Ukraine was already higher than that of Poland before the Russian invasion in February 2022: an estimated 14.4 percent (around six million people) of the country's 46 million inhabitants lived abroad (Ambrosetti et al. 2014; Ratha et al. 2011). At the time of writing, almost six million (5,930,400) Ukrainian refugees are living in European countries, most of them in Germany and Poland.[6] This mobility not only affects the route from Central and Eastern Europe to Western, Northern and Southern Europe, but also includes a migration pattern between East European countries, such as that between Ukraine and Poland, whereby Ukrainian women work as nannies, domestic workers or caregivers for the elderly in private households of upwardly mobile Polish citizens in urban regions.

RESEARCH QUESTIONS AND RESEARCH DESIGN

The research project "Landscapes of Care Drain: Care Provisions and Care Chains from the Ukraine to Poland and from Poland to Germany" (2007–10) was dedicated to researching the migration movement from (Western) Ukraine to Polish private households and from Poland to German households, while the project "Decent Care Work? Transnational Home Care Arrangements" (2017–21) studied the transnational recruitment by home care agencies of migrants as live-in caregivers in private households. Focussing on recruitment to the global cities of Frankfurt am Main, Vienna and Zurich, it examined 24-hour care carried out in the destination countries of Germany, Austria and Switzerland.

"Landscapes of Care Drain" was guided by the following questions: How do migrant women organise their transnational lifestyles and what goals do they associate with migration? How do these goals change over time and how do their families at home react to this situation? What are their future prospects? How do the respective migration regimes affect working conditions and the individual's scope for negotiation? How do these migrant women cope with their situations and what networks do they fall back on? How do significant others experience the periods of absence of migrant women? How are care migration and the transnational lifestyles of women addressed in public debates in Poland, Ukraine and Germany? Are there connections between the narratives of the (relatives of the) women and the media debates on the topic of migration? Between 2007 and 2009, a total of 63 qualitative interviews were conducted, including 22 biographical interviews of care and domestic workers from Poland (ten) and Ukraine (twelve), as well as 41 guided interviews with their family members, including partners, parents, children, siblings and friends, who stayed behind in the country of origin during the migrants' absence (21 with Ukrainians and 20 with Poles). In addition, a discourse analysis was carried out on a total of 969 newspaper articles published in the German, Polish and Ukrainian press on the topic of care and migration between 1997 and 2008. Furthermore, other relevant materials, such as documentary films, were taken into account and analysed.

The second project, "Decent Care Work? Transnational Home Care Arrangements" (2017–21) had an even more complicated design, as it took place in the three German-speaking countries of Austria, Germany and Switzerland. This collaborative project investigated and compared the development of agency-brokered live-in care in the three countries, and focused on the following questions: In what way is live-in care embedded in and regulated by care regimes on the supra-, inter-, trans-, and national level? What requirements, demands and claims are asserted by each of the involved parties? How does the live-in care arrangement take shape, and what types of existing or newly emerging social inequalities and power relations are relevant for the understanding of this phenomenon?

For the German part of the project, a total of 42 guided interviews with owners and representatives of Polish and German brokering agencies and with care workers were conducted by native speakers in the respective languages of the interviewees, and then transcribed and translated into German. The interviews were analysed narratively or content-analytically, informed by the analytical steps of grounded theory (see Lutz et al. 2018; Müller and Skeide 2018; Spies 2018). In addition to the analysis of brokering agencies' websites, we conducted interviews with managers and owners of brokering agencies and with other relevant stakeholders, including NGO workers, directors of professional associations and trade union organisations. At the same time, the focus was primarily on care workers and their experiences. The results of the project have been published in many articles and two books (see Aulenbach et al. 2021; Aulenbacher et al. 2024; Lutz and Benazha 2024). The outbreak of the coronavirus pandemic also led us to interview many care workers for a second time by telephone in the summer of 2020, which is analysed in Chapter Seven.

As I have not included a chapter on methodology, I would like to make a few comments here on the methods of data collection and analysis. All of the interviews were conducted in the language of origin, then transcribed and finally translated into German. Unfortunately, I was not able to conduct any of the interviews myself, but I accompanied the data collection process closely and, above all, worked on the analysis. Together with my colleagues Ewa Palenga-Möllenbeck and Yegeniya Wirz, we analysed the interviews in the form of hermeneutic case reconstructions and worked on a critical discourse analysis of the press articles. A detailed description of our collaboration on the material would require its own chapter, which is not possible here. I have also refrained from discussing a large number of questions that we faced, such as how to deal with the diversity of the data material, issues around the adequate translation of interviews (which can give rise to various problems and misunderstandings), and the many suggestions that emerged from the joint interpretation of the data. At this point, I refer to an important article by Palenga-Möllenbeck (2018) in which she describes the methodological challenges that arise when translating transcriptions of transnational biographies: translation as a method, she contends, implies reflecting the role of the (invisible) translators, as well as contextualising the narratives of the interviewees. Questions also repeatedly arise about how to deal with the diversity of meanings of narratives and life stories (that have to be) clarified in the translation process. Palenga-Möllenbeck argues that in societies with an increasing number of transnational (family) biographies, methodological considerations on how to adequately record their life stories are becoming increasingly urgent.

For this book, I have selected the ideal-type representation of contrasting cases that enables the emergence of theoretical building blocks in an empirically guided way. This approach is less about the representation of frequency than about a theoretical understanding of the (structural) conditions that shape the lives of care migrants and their relatives, as well as how these conditions are dealt with raising the question of resistance and the shaping of subjective spaces of possibility under precarious working conditions. The concept of intersectionality served as a methodological tool (see Lutz 2018a), and was used to trace and analyse transnational life courses between the workplace and families of origin.

THE STRUCTURE OF THE BOOK

This book is conceived of both as a contribution to the academic debates on care and migration and an intervention in a neoliberal political discourse that sees the marketisation of care work as an acceptable solution to care gaps. This prevailing discourse refuses to address the question of the ongoing devaluation (Müller 2016) of care work in the twenty-first century and its long-term social implications. The book is divided into seven chapters.

The first chapter, "Uncaring Care Economies", provides an overview of the many contradictions in current debates on the care crisis. It begins with an introduction to the global scope and significance of care migration, presents an overview of the development of the transnational care economy on a global scale, and ends by describing the developing live-in care regimes of Germany, Austria and Switzerland.

In Chapter Two, "On the Road: The Supply Chain of Care Workers Between Germany and East European Countries," I investigate the transnational connections of the care regimes of Poland and Ukraine. This is followed by an examination of "othering" and racialisation processes of Central and East European carers in West

European receiving states. I then discuss three theoretical concepts that classify the phenomenon of care migration. First, the global care chain concept (GCCC) is presented, followed by the concept of care circulation (CCC), and finally the concept of transnational social inequality (TSI) which is still under development.

In the following chapter, "Distance and Proximity: Transnational Mothering and Emotional Inequality", I describe how care migrant women mother their children, whom they (have to) leave at home while working abroad. Unlike male migrants, their absence conflicts with individual and societal ideals of good motherhood. How do mothers and children deal with experiences of loss, and how do women shape their motherhood from a distance? What substitute care arrangements are established, and how do family members practise their management of emotions transnationally? Three case studies of two Polish women and one man, all of them working in Germany, demonstrate differences between the situation of female and male care migrants. This chapter also considers normative discourses of motherhood and how these women do transnational motherhood or mothering from a distance showing that emotional inequality is a core dimension of transnational social inequality.

Chapter Four, "Euro-orphans: Transnational Motherhood Under Pressure", discusses the sensationalist media coverage of the physical absence of mothers who leave their children in the care of family members. This debate, primarily conducted in the media of Central and East European sending countries, is today a transnational one. Children left behind in their countries of origin are referred to as Euro-orphans or social orphans, and their suffering has become the core of a societal debate on the social consequences of migration. I present the results of a comprehensive media analysis of Polish and Ukrainian newspapers between 1997 and 2008, a period in which a radical change in the public perception of female migration took place. Parents began to be accused of educational incompetence and irresponsibility, and mothers in particular were accused of being bad parents. The last part of the chapter analyses the media discourse on Euro-orphans through complementary explanatory models: moral panic, transnational motherhood as a deficient motherhood practice, and the role of transnational (aid) organisations.

The fifth chapter, "Masculinity and Care in Post-socialism: The Fatherhood of Stay-behind Partners", deals with an aspect of circular migration that has hardly been investigated to date: the care practices of husbands of transnational migrant women. The chapter begins by examining the current debate on the relationship between masculinity and fatherhood, before going on to present three case studies of fatherhood practices by men whose wives work abroad. These three fathers deal with the dilemmas of fatherhood and combining care and paid work very differently. Although there are no comparable disciplinary public discourses in the case of stay-behind fathers as there are for migrant mothers, these men have to negotiate hegemonic notions of masculinity, which in the post-socialist context entails being a main breadwinner.

Chapter Six, "From Socialist Utopias to the Global Commercialisation of Care: New Answers to an Old Question", deals with the utopias of emancipatory movements, the gender history of socialism and post-socialism, and the critical feminist debates currently being conducted on gendered care asymmetries, the care economy and the transnational commercialisation of care. From the re-reading of the works of socialist utopians and their implementation (to some extent) in real state socialism to the feminist critique of capitalism of the 1970s and 1980s in Western industrialised countries, in particular the texts of the Socialist Feminists, an arc is drawn to the contemporary feminist critique of capitalism in the early twenty-first century. This chapter seeks to bring together debates about the commodification of care work and the associated transnational migration of care workers with the current feminist critique of capitalism and discussions about gender-equitable alternatives to dominant care regimes, with which they are rarely linked.

Chapter Seven, "The Care Economy after COVID-19: Vulnerability and Resilience", focuses on the impact of the pandemic on an employment field which depends on the mobility of migrants. Using interviews conducted with migrant caregivers in the summer of 2020, I ask whether public interest in care work during this period may have led to greater recognition and appreciation, improved working conditions or even better payment of migrant care workers. It finishes with reflections on the pandemic's consequences for the transnational care economy.

If, by the end of this book, I have succeeded in convincing readers that care as a pressing issue cannot only be considered within national containers, that the transnational dimensions of the question are of growing importance, and that companies and governments, activists and theorists should include the *back-stage* of care migration in their considerations, I will have made a humble contribution to further debates.

1

Uncaring Care Economies

The capitalist economy relies on – one might say, free rides on – activities of provisioning, caregiving and interaction that produce and maintain social bonds, although it accords them to non-monetised value and treats them as if they were free. (Fraser 2022: 55)

Migrants from Central and Eastern Europe are increasingly working as live-in caregivers for the elderly in private households in European receiving countries. Based on two extensive research projects that spanned 14 years,[1] the book seeks to describe the evolution and commercialisation of care work under current European finance capitalism. I will first look at the care economy, a sector that has been established – or rather has established itself indirectly and in an undocumented way – over the past two to three decades. To a certain extent, this development follows the path of countries such as the US, Canada and the UK, where little or no state support has long meant that the care of children, disabled people and elderly citizens has been subject to the market. A rapidly growing care economy has developed in Europe, spawning an array of organisational forms including migrant domestic and care workers' placement agencies, agency associations, businesses and corporations. This economy functions according to the so-called cash-for-care principle (Williams 2010), whereby the state pays a care allowance to those in need of support who then use it to buy care labour from the market. This chapter begins with an overview of the evolution of the transnational care economy, before turning to the development of the live-in care economies in the three German-speaking countries of Austria, Germany and Switzerland.

THE CARE ECONOMY

In the twenty-first century, neoliberal transformation in many (welfare state) countries has entailed a focus on the responsibility of citizens. This turn implies so-called "demand and encourage" policies that promote measures that, for example, encourage the unemployed to be proactive in finding jobs rather than rely on unemployment benefits paid by the state. These modes of governmentality have been analysed in terms of a shift "from employee to entreployee" (Pongratz and Voß 1998) or the rise of the "entrepreneurial self" who is driven to constantly improve, change and adapt (Bröckling 2007). Processes of marketisation and the dissolution of boundaries in the workplace deeply impact gender relations not least in terms of how caring for others and for oneself can be realised under these economised conditions. Subjects are faced with new demands connected with the formation of consumer behaviour and the emergence of complex care relationships. Care risks must now be solved in new ways. It is important not to overlook the fact that the transfer and the payment of care responsibilities to people outside the family brings with it a host of risks and dilemmas. Ultimately, the transition from the male breadwinner model, in which women were responsible for all care activities related to children and the elderly (the so-called "housewife marriage"), to the "adult–worker model", in which all adults are seen as potential workers, must be understood as a welfare state paradigm shift from welfare to workfare (Esping-Andersen et al. 2002; Giddens 1991).

While many European welfare states have social investment policies in certain areas related to social reproduction (such as childcare), care for elderly and sick family members remains a critical area with large gaps. The long path from Fordism to finance capitalism has changed society in a number of ways, and care services formerly provided free of charge – mostly by women – are now commodified and commercialised. In her book on the evolution of capitalism in the twenty-first century, Nancy Fraser argues that finance capitalism is devouring democracy, care and the planet. She describes this new form of capitalism as "a progressive neoliberalism, which celebrates 'diversity', meritocracy and 'emancipation' while dismantling social protections and re-externalising social reproduction" (Fraser 2022: 69). Social reproductive work was already commonly externalised by the bourgeois classes in the eighteenth, nineteenth and early twentieth centuries (see Lutz 2011). Its re-externalisation under conditions of finance capitalism takes the shape of commercialised outsourcing of the care and relationship work of the private sphere and an increasing individualisation of responsibility for social reproductive work (Fraser 2022; Hochschild 2012). In addition, Jennifer Jihye Chun and Heidi Gottfried (2018) rightly argue that "shifting its policy priorities, the state has withdrawn, retreated, and devolved responsibilities (and risks) for care, but also has pursued reforms fuelling the marketisation of care and intimate labour."[2] Seen from a global perspective, there is an observable expansion of economised care in the private household. Brigitte Aulenbacher, Maria Dammayr and Fabienne Décieux call this development, which leads to the marketisation of care work, the "structural 'carelessness' of capitalist economic activity" (Aulenbacher et al. 2015b: 7).

Despite many commonalities in neoliberal welfare policies, there is significant diversity of care regimes. In contrast to most West European welfare states, the US and Canada have never regarded care for children and the elderly as a public task, but first and foremost a private one. Accordingly, policies in these countries continue to be geared towards families organising care for seniors and children privately. Households with the means to do so employ care workers, often those who are excluded from other segments of the labour market. In North America, these are primarily black women and migrants from Latin America, Asia and the Caribbean (see Boris and Klein 2012; MacDonald 2010; Romero 1992; Parreñas 2001). Characteristic of this care regime is a substantial and largely informal labour market, whose working conditions are barely regulated by the state. The externalisation of social reproductive labour has thus largely led to a precarious labour market for migrants and marginalised workers.

In European welfare states, responsibility for those in need of care has long laid primarily with the (female members of the) family, although over the last three decades this has been somewhat cushioned by state institutions or state subsidies. These offers – such as publicly funded day centres and subsidised mobile care services – barely make a dent in meeting demand, however. The need for care has increased due to the ageing of the population, while the expansion and intensification of gainful employment for all genders has reduced the care resources formerly available within families. The current development of welfare state services does not take this problem sufficiently into account, and in the course of neoliberal restructuring, services are reduced rather than expanded. Publicly funded nursing homes and mobile care services, for example, are subject to increasingly tight cost and time constraints (Schwiter et al. 2018). In combination, these developments are leading to a "care crisis" (Dowling 2022).

Following the logic of a "careless" capitalism, the state is increasingly withdrawing from its responsibility for care, while intensified gainful employment deprives working people of time to care for their relatives or their own social reproduction. As a result, middle-class and upper-class families are increasingly seeking relief by externalising care activities. Care work has become a hot commodity, and a growing market of profit-oriented care companies is emerging for those who can afford these services. But how exactly can care be understood and analysed as a commodity? (How) Is it possible that an activity previously seen as a labour of love or intergenerational responsibility has become a commodity? The contradictions and dilemmas of the commodification of care work go to the roots of modern economic thinking.

ON THE (SUPPOSED) PRODUCTIVITY OF WORK

Adam Smith's 1776 work *The Wealth of Nations*, considered the birth of classical economics and economic liberalism, rests on a conceptual separation of productive and unproductive labour. In this schema, labour is productive if it makes something that generates an exchange value or price on the market (Smith 1999: 429–30). For Smith, productivity was not linked to the creation of social benefit, but rather to social utility defined in terms of accumulating capital. In contrast, unproductive labour is that in which production and consumption coincide in time, and so no value can be conserved. Smith pointed to the labour of the servant classes as exemplary of unproductive labour (ibid.: 429–30). This value abjection of household and care work (Müller 2016) was shared in the nineteenth century by another important economist, Karl Marx. As Hannah Arendt argues, Smith and Marx share the asymmetrical valuation of gainful (productive) and domestic (unproductive) work, making a distinction between low and highly valued labour and separating the private from the public sphere, a division that is fundamentally gendered (1958). The legacy of the nineteenth century bourgeois servant society can be seen in the post-Fordist adult–worker and service society of the twenty-first century (Lutz 2010: 26). Feminist historians Gisela Bock and Barbara Duden have demonstrated that domestic work, disguised as a labour of love, was closely interwoven with the emergence of capitalism in the seventeenth and eighteenth centuries charting how it was not until the nineteenth and twentieth centuries that the bourgeois nuclear family model extended to other classes to become the dominant household structure (Bock and Duden 1977: 122). Bock and Duden argue that this social model of gendered power asymmetries can only be dismantled "when the production and reproduction of labour power is remunerated like any other work" (ibid.: 185).

Over the past three decades it has become evident that the contemporary adult–worker model has led to an increase in female employment, but by no means to an equal division of care and household labour. Ruth Lister and colleagues observe: "As citizen-earners, mothers and fathers are becoming more equal; as citizen-carers, the inequality remains pronounced" (Lister and Williams 2007: 134–5). With care work in the private sphere increasingly outsourced, it is most often migrant women who contribute to reducing the conflict between family responsibilities and gainful employment for middle-class women. The low prices of these services (which accompanies the feminisation of migration) expands the possibility and scope of the labour market participation of qualified middle-class women in care-receiving countries, as well as enabling them to realise their (potential) desire to have children without giving up their careers (ibid.: 1–2). Care and household labour remains in female hands, but it is now in those of ethnically and socially "other(ed)" women (Lutz 2011). In the early

1970s, a feminist campaign launched by Italian activists – notably Silvia Federici – demanded "wages for housework" (Toupin 2018) and protests rallying behind this call were seen in several countries of the Western world. At the beginning of the twenty-first century, household labour is indeed often renumerated; it is a perverse fulfilment of the 1970s feminist call, one that does not upgrade the activity itself because the scale of values of "productive" labour remains untouched.

OUTSOURCING CARE WORK

The care economy is one of the fastest-growing markets globally (see Peng 2019; Michel and Peng 2017). Western welfare states have been undergoing far-reaching economising processes limiting public social expenditure under the banner of new public management since the 1980s (Pierson 2001: 456). This trend is manifested in many welfare states' marketisation and privatisation of formerly state-run healthcare services now geared to high economic profitability, with correspondingly high costs (Madörin 2011: 57–8). In other words, the market does not replace the welfare state but moves into it, with the consequence that social risks generated by the market come to be compensated for by welfare markets (Nullmeier 2004: 646–7). Citizens become consumers, with the effect of not only deepening existing social inequalities but also simultaneously creating new ones. The strengthening of consumer choice mainly benefits the upper and middle classes which is particularly evident in the domain of long-term care.

Care and/on the Market

The growth of the care economy has driven forward commodification, marketisation and privatisation. Privatisation, reflected in a growing market not only for childcare but in particular care for the elderly, is leading to a rapidly growing number of people in upper- and middle-class households taking on the status of employers.

Following the analysis of the sociologist and economist Ito Peng, the care economy refers to paid and unpaid activities "related to the provision of social and material care, which contribute to nurturing and supporting the present and future populations" (Peng

2019: 2). Peng highlights the contradiction that comes from the invisibility of care work in economic theory. On the one hand, statistics on national Gross Domestic Product (GDP) exclude care activities, and on the other, there is a growing recognition that care is not only essential for the well-being of society but also an economic necessity (see also Folbre 2006; Sen 1993). Nancy Folbre (2006) has demonstrated that with regard to social reproductive care, state provision of services are crucial for the maintenance of the well-being, capability and efficiency of individuals and the functioning of societies. Care services are now on the way to becoming the largest and fastest-growing labour market in the twenty-first century. The service sector economy has been expanding over the last 50 years in the OECD[3] member countries of the Global North, accounting for over 70% of total employment: approximately 435 million people are employed, twice as many as the 227 million workers in manufacturing and industries (Peng 2019: 4). With regard to the US, "it is projected that by 2026 not only will there be more people working in care-services than in retail, the two occupational sectors of 'healthcare support' and 'healthcare practitioners and technical occupations' alone will contribute about one-fifth of all new jobs" (ibid.: 4).

This development has radical implications as the care economy not only "produces" large numbers of employees in these new fields of activity, but also undermines the logic used as the basis of economic calculation. These jobs are fundamentally different from manufacturing and industrial work in that they require conceptualising production differently. As Peng argues: "Not only is it *not* possible for care services to be produced and stored for later use, as in the case of manufacturing of goods, each unit of care services must also accommodate to the preferences and tastes of the clients served" (ibid.: 7, emphasis in original). With person-related care work, it is possible to establish efficiency criteria only to a limited extent, in contrast to the production of goods. In particular, the interpersonal dimension challenges economic valuation principles such as productivity gain or quality gain. Peng writes: "Such quantity-quality trade-off and other difficulties associated with productivity gain inherent in care work in turn depress the market value of care work under the existing economic equation postulated on the manufacturing and industrial economic conditions" (ibid.).

Traces of the "gender care difference" characterise the care economy. Women are more likely to be channelled into this labour market; in other words, it is work that has a low occupational status and is often poorly paid. Moreover – and this is definitively important for the development of the sector – women are also in the majority on the users' side of the care economy: a woman is usually the main person responsible for employing and managing the care workers (Peng 2019: 7). Even in families where women work full time, they are more likely to manage the household, childcare and care for ageing relatives. This implies that they seek relief from the work that continues to be expected of them, a clear sign that the growing entry of women into the workforce by no means leads to gender parity with regard to care work.

Over the last decade, there have been efforts by economists to generate models for more gender-sensitive approaches to measuring GDP, for example by making a list of indices that include the work of care. Uncertainties remain, however: unpaid care done outside the market is mostly excluded from the calculation of GDP. The findings of an International Trade Union Federation study on high income and emerging economies, indicate that "the direct effect of public investment in the health and care sector would lead to a greater number of the newly created jobs going to women than if the same level of investment were made in construction" (2017: 7). The report argues that this job creation generates multiplier effects in other economic sectors.

These analyses, however, often do not take into account the poor working conditions faced by care workers in a transnational division of labour that has been called the "global care chain" (Hochschild 2000; Parreñas 2001). Saskia Sassen (1991), Nicola Yeates (2009) and Bridget Anderson (2000) have demonstrated that those who benefit are members of the "upper circuit", while the service providers are migrants, imported from countries whose economies have collapsed for various reasons (see also Lutz 2011). Yeates finds the connections between service providers and recipients to be "textured by wider socio-economic inequalities, resulting from hierarchies of states, classes (castes), gender and ethnic groups" (Yeates 2009: 42). She argues that the global care chain can be compared with the global manufacturing system, since the care sector similarly involves many actors on different levels: caregivers and their families, care receivers and their families, networks, brokers, social welfare and care regimes, and migration regulations. Like goods produced transnationally, care can be seen as a commodity that is distributed, marketed and consumed and "materially connects economies, firms, workers and households" (ibid.). As I argued in my earlier work, however, various factors make it difficult to simply conceptually map care onto goods production (Lutz 2011: 22). One significant difference between care and the production of goods is that the profit and surplus from care provision flows primarily to individual actors and not national economies – except indirectly, through the reproduction of labour power. It is important to quantify and make visible the value of care and emotional work, but to consider care as a commodity is problematic because the value and the costs of emotional work accrue not only to the person performing that work and the person for whom is it performed, but are also relevant for those deprived of it. The latter group consists primarily of the children and family members left behind by migrant women in their countries of origin. The social costs of the care drain manifest over longer periods of time, often after many years of people living apart from each other (see Chapters Three, Four and Five).

Senior Care from the Market in German-speaking Countries

The care economy in Europe has undergone major changes and has now expanded into a substantial economic sector. While for a long time the placement of live-in caregivers for senior care was done informally through word-of-mouth among friends and colleagues or individual internet portals, the role of placement agencies has become increasingly pronounced. These agencies have become major actors in the field of care and engage in intensive lobbying so that politicians treat them as indispensable market players. In the following section, I will briefly describe the legal regulations and their impact on the care economy in the three German-speaking countries. In all three, the brokering of "live-in care" has developed into a lucrative business, though there are differences in how the field is organised, legally regulated and socially contested (see also Aulenbacher et al. 2024).

Unlike some first world countries, notably the US and Canada, where the majority of migrant care workers come from the Global South, in many states of (western and southern) Europe the externalisation and commodification of care work was facilitated by the fall of the Iron Curtain (Lutz 2011; Lutz and Palenga-Möllenbeck 2014). From the early 1990s onwards, workers in the post-socialist countries of Central and Eastern Europe – women in particular – lost their jobs and were forced to urgently look for work. Given the paucity of employment opportunities in their own countries, women started to work in private households as cleaners and caregivers in western and southern Europe (see also Lutz 2011). The recruitment of caregivers is carried out by placement agencies that operate transnationally, whereby an agency in the sender country recruits the workers and another one in the receiver country finds the clients. These agencies have become powerful players in a rapidly growing market, but their activities have so far been controlled and regulated only to a very limited extent (Aulenbacher et al. 2021a). A care model for seniors has emerged that is referred to as "live-in care", also known by the problematic term "24-hour care". This implies that a caregiver lives in the household of an elderly person and is responsible for their well-being and any care needs that arise around the clock. After a few weeks or months, the caregiver is replaced by a new worker on a rotation schedule.

Board and lodging in the households of the recipients of care are prerequisites for the emergence and establishment of this form of senior care. Recruited migrants from Central and Eastern Europe often accept the difficult terms of the live-in model out of economic necessity as they do not earn enough to cover the cost of living in an apartment outside of their workplace. For the clients this is convenient because many seniors often require night-time assistance. Living in the household of the employer drastically restricts the migrant's own scope of action, however, and creates a high level of dependency. Caregivers often live and work in such a way that they have to conform entirely with the existing household's rules (see Lutz and Benazha 2024). In addition, the private household is difficult to subject to regulation and control. Notwithstanding the formalisation and professionalisation of live-in care through agency-mediated commercialisation, the conditions of caregiving are usually informally negotiated with the clients, and in particular with their adult children who generally organise this care arrangement and are the contact persons for the care workers. The divergence and contradiction between the promise of good care and its provision on the basis of good work is thus a core contradiction inscribed in the live-in arrangement.

The main characteristics of the live-in care markets in the German-speaking countries of Germany, Austria and Switzerland are described below.

THREE CARE REGIMES

Prevailing gender-specific, culturally anchored ideals in the German-speaking countries of Germany, Austria and Switzerland have long prescribed that ageing people should remain in their own households as long as possible and be cared for by (female) family members. While this model of a "home-care society" (Pfau-Effinger 2005) continues to leave its mark, it is dissolving as care of seniors is transferred to migrant women. In all three countries, this arrangement involves undercutting labour standards that apply in other care sectors, including regulation of working hours, payment, and occupational health and safety. Despite many commonalities, there are important differences in how live-in care is legally regulated in the three countries.

Formalised Informality in Live-in Care in Germany: "Posted" Workers

With the introduction of statutory long-term care insurance in the German social security system in 1995, it was accepted for the first time that the care of seniors should no longer be provided entirely privately and that the state has a role in offering financial support (financed by mandatory taxation).[4] While the aim was to relieve more women of domestic care responsibilities, this occurred only to a limited extent. In private households the provision of care continued to be provided mostly by women (spouses/ partners, daughters-in-law, granddaughters, sisters, cousins and friends) (Backes et al. 2008). However, the increasing labour force participation of women makes it more difficult for them to manage familial caregiving activities. Since the care allowance does not generally cover nursing home care, the emergence of an (informal) live-in care sector was ultimately encouraged, although low benefit rates means that people must bear part of the costs themselves (Dammert 2009: 44; Benazha 2021: 25).

The early 2000s saw the emergence of agencies brokering care for seniors by migrants from post-socialist countries. The placement of migrant live-in-caregivers is now essentially based on the "posting model" whereby an agency in Germany collaborates with one or more agencies from the sending countries. The 1996 EU Posting of Workers Directive (RL96/71/EC) regulates the free movement of persons and goods, as well as services, between EU member states (Benazha 2021: 55–9). According to this directive, "posted workers" and "posting agencies" are exempted from the obligation to abide by the labour laws of the state where they are posted for a period of 12 to 18 months (ibid.). This is advantageous for German agencies who comply by meeting the lower ancillary wage costs in the sending ("posting") countries. There are an estimated 800 agencies in Germany offering 24-hour carers for seniors.[5]

In her analysis of the effects of the posting model, Aranka Benazha emphasises that compliance with regular working hours and rest periods is generally not monitored and overtime is not paid (2021: 58). There is no entitlement to leave, and the costs of medical care are not covered in the event of illness. Client expectations that live-ins are indeed available for full-time service are encouraged by advertisements on the websites of German agencies with taglines such as: "Our care staff are available for care 24 hours a day, seven days a week" (ibid.: 54). According to the assessment of jurist Barbara Bucher (2018: 350), such an arrangement undermines the limits set by legal norms. The issue is complicated by the fact that, as a rule, a German agency works with an agency in the caregiver's country of origin. While the former acquires the German clients and maintains contact with them and/or their relatives, the latter takes care of transportation to the client household and supports posted migrants via a hotline. The sending agencies in Poland, Romania, Slovakia, Hungary, Estonia, Moldova, Croatia and Bulgaria are obliged to pay monthly social contributions for their employees, but this is not done regularly.[6] In Poland, which is the main sending country of caregivers to Germany, the posting contracts are often referred to as "garbage contracts" for this reason.

Overall, in the German posting model a legal grey area of "formalised informality" (Benazha and Lutz 2019: 949) has developed in which the de facto suspension of labour protection regulations is tolerated and indirectly financed by the state. Despite the existence of support services for caregivers in large German cities, such as the trade union-affiliated association Fair Mobility, assistance can be provided in a very limited number of cases. Even a landmark ruling in the Federal Labour Court in 2021 – in which a Bulgarian caregiver received €38,000 in backpay because she had been caring for her client for 21 hours a day rather than 30 hours a week (see Janisch and Stadler 2021) – has not led to greater public scrutiny of the activities of placement agencies and employer households.

The Federal Association for Home Care and Nursing (VHBP) is a powerful actor in the care economy and a loud voice in public discourses about live-in caregiving. According to its own information, it represents 45 agencies and seeks to establish live-in care in health legislation as a third pillar of care for the elderly and sick, alongside outpatient and nursing home care (VHBP 2023). In its lobbying, the association advocates for the self-employment model that prevails in Austria (see below). In such a model, the responsibility for issues such as working hours and overtime falls on the migrant caregivers. Trade unions denounce these proposals as "questionable bogus self-employment" (Deutscher Gewerkschaftsbund 2022) and call for a solution that conforms to labour law, with clear limits on working and on-call hours. In its 2021–5 coalition agreement, the German federal government pledged to create a "legally secure basis for 24-hour care," without giving any indication what form this may take (SPD et al. 2021: 64). The formalisation of live-in care in Germany thus remains contested, and will likely remain so for a long time.

The Self-Employment Model in Austria: From Formalisation to Normalisation

The broad acceptance of informal care work in Austria was hastened by the introduction in 1993 of care allowances, provided by the state as an income-independent and freely disposable cash-for-care benefit (Appelt and Fleischer 2014). After a series of scandals involving public figures who had illegally employed migrant caregivers, the Home Care Act came into force in 2007 aimed at regulating the employment of caregivers in private households. To this end, it established a new trade, that of "self-employed personal care", disregarding critiques that such forms of self-employment are spurious. In order to cover the social security costs of live-in workers required under the legalisation, a state subsidy of a maximum of €550 per month was introduced allowing live-in employment to grow exponentially and become a taken-for-granted and common service (Bachinger 2009: 216; Weicht and Österle 2016). This form of senior care became a "route of quasi-familial care, accepted by the welfare state" (Aulenbacher et al. 2018: 54). Indeed, since caregivers are presented as quasi-family members on the websites of placement agencies, live-in caregiving reproduces the discursive construction of an ideal of home-based family care where women family members are replaced by women migrant workers (Weicht 2010).

Like the work of all self-employed persons, live-in caregiving differs from salaried work in many respects and caregivers do not have the same rights as employed workers in Austria. Although they are largely covered by social security, stipulations with regard to maximum working hours, rest periods and minimum wages do not apply to them, and they are not entitled to sick leave or paid holidays (Haidinger 2013). While the Home Care Act was intended as a transition from irregular status to a more regulated one (Bachinger 2010: 409), this model is now accepted by a large part of the population not least because it appears to be the only affordable solution for families, particularly when someone is in sudden and urgent need of care. In theory, caregivers could offer their services directly by making contact and introducing them-selves to the persons in need of care (or to their relatives), and so

could function as direct contracting partners. Such a direct negotiation would include offering of services, negotiating fees and
working hours (including availability, breaks and length of their
stay, board and lodging), as well as a procedure for organising
replacements in case of sickness or holidays (Österle and Bauer
2016). The reality, however, is that the majority of care workers in
Austria find work through placement agencies established in the
wake of the introduction of the Home Care Act, which set the stage
for quickly establishing a new business model and ultimately a new
market.[7] More than a decade after the legalisation was passed, this
model has become an "essential transnational pillar of the care
regime" (Österle 2016: 266), and Austria is now seen as a pioneer
in the institutionalised marketisation of care (Shire 2015).

Agencies in Austria are dependent on the recruitment of organisations and agencies in the Central and East European countries of
origin. While the agencies advertise the legality of their services, it
is the caregivers, as self-employed persons, who carry the responsibility for the actual care and support they provide (Steiner et al.
2019: 26). The formalisation of the industry in its current form
was cemented by the 2019 introduction of the Austrian Quality
Certificate for Placement Agencies in 24-Hour Care, for which
the Ministry of Social Affairs has issued guidelines. As Benazha
and colleagues note, however, "whereas exploitative and unprofes-
sional practices of agencies are repeatedly criticised in the media,
the undercutting of practices in other areas of care work is legitimised by the legality of the self-employment model" (Benazha et
al. 2021: 33). The Austrian scheme now functions as a standard
and model for other countries; in its development from formalisation to normalisation, it has created an ideal type of welfare-state
discourse.

*The Employee Model in Switzerland: Formalisation and
Contestation*

Switzerland has neither a long-term care insurance system as in
Germany nor a rudimentary one as in Austria. It was not until 2011
that Swiss migration policy changed extending the free movement
of persons to those from post-socialist countries, thereby allowing
for the employment of migrant caregivers from Central and

Eastern Europe. Since then, in a way that is comparable with practices in Germany and Austria, a commuting system has developed whereby a migrant worker lives in the household of a senior citizen for a period of one to three months, after which they are replaced by another.

In contrast to Austria and Germany, the Swiss care regime draws a technical distinction between nursing and care, whereby only the former is supported by state-financed health insurance which is limited to "medically indicated plans". Non-medical care services must therefore be paid for privately. In its Strategy for a Swiss Ageing Policy (Federal Swiss Council 2017), the Swiss government explicitly emphasises the priority of outpatient care over inpatient care, and an extensive sector of personal home-based caregivers has indeed developed over the last decade. Unlike in Austria, self-employment in personal care is considered to be spurious self-employment and is prohibited. The posting of workers to private households, widespread in Germany, is similarly not permitted. Notwithstanding this, there are companies that operate in this way in order to achieve savings in social security contributions, since in the posting model social security obligations are shifted to the country of origin (Benazha et al. 2021: 34).

As a rule, caregivers in Switzerland must be treated as employees of a Swiss-based agency or household (Medici 2015).[8] Nevertheless, they are excluded from key protections that employees in other fields of work are afforded, including regulations regarding maximum working hours, night work, the continuity of rest periods and paid holidays. This is because private households have been explicitly excluded from the scope of the Swiss Labour Law (Art. 2, para. 1, lit. g, ArG). When the law was enacted in 1960, the Swiss Federal Council explained with regard to domestic workers: "There is no need, according to general and undisputed opinion, for their subordination to the Labour Act, quite apart from the fact that, for obvious reasons, such regulations could hardly be enforced" (Bundesrat 1960, 945, cited in Steiner 2020: 286). Just as in Austria and Germany, private households are subject to special protection by the state making it difficult to detect or sanction labour violations. However, the indisputability of this regulation has been contested in Switzerland for some time, and over the last decade a series of state interventions has been directed towards the improvement of live-in care working conditions. In particular, groups of self-organised caregivers, trade unions and parliamentarians have drawn attention to the exploitative working conditions of live-in care and demanded action (Schilliger and Schilling 2017).

The Federal Council intervened for the first time in 2011 in the face of this mounting pressure. In light of the recognised risk of exploitation of Central and East European caregivers, the council enacted "flanking measures" against wage dumping, and introduced a minimum wage for all employees in the domestic sector, including live-in caregivers. A collective labour agreement was reached in 2012 that initially applied to large agencies before the Federal Council extended its scope to all care agencies (see Lutz and Schwiter 2024). The collective agreement provides for slightly higher minimum wages, maximum working hours and provisions on night work (Steiner 2020). It transpired, however, that these measures could be circumvented relatively easily: agencies reacted by reducing the hours worked under the terms of the contract and increasing the unpaid or barely paid hours on call with the result that live-in workers did not receive better wages (Steiner 2020: 288).

Responding to repeated parliamentary requests to examine the employment conditions of live-in care workers, the Federal Council came to the conclusion in 2015 that:

> There is a lack of clear legal guidelines for this employment group in various central issues such as limitation of working hours, excessive responsibility, regulation of the precarious employment contract situation, lack of privacy. From this, it can be deduced that there is a need to better regulate the working conditions of geriatric caregivers. This is in order to ensure the protection of female workers and to give legal certainty to private households (Bundesrat 2015: 21).

An examination of the regulatory proposals indicated that extending the scope of the Labour Code to private households, or at least to live-in caregivers, was possible (Bundesrat 2015: 23). This directive led to a regulatory impact assessment report which noted that if these changes were introduced, the costs of live-in care would radically increase (BSS 2016). The Federal Council thus decided in 2017 to refrain from further binding regulation of the industry for the time being (Steiner 2020: 291). The Union of Public Service Employees (vpod) objected, and finally achieved a landmark decision in the highest Swiss court in 2021 in which it was stated that with regard to agency-based care, "the work of the caregiver [...] serves not only to meet the private needs of the person being cared for, but also the commercial purpose of the care organisation" (BGE 2C_470/2020 of 22.12.2021, E. 4.6). This means that where the Labour Code applies, it limits the on-call duty of a worker to a maximum of seven days (exceptionally 14 days) per month. In addition, a daily rest period of at least eleven consecutive hours must be granted, during which the worker does not perform any on-call duties (SECO 2022: 4). If this were enforced, it would mean that the agency-based care of an elderly person by a single worker would no longer be possible in Switzerland, while the employment of workers directly by households would remain permissible. The agencies have responded with heavy lobbying to negotiate an exemption that would allow agency-based round-the-clock care to be provided by one person (see Lutz and Schwiter 2024). Whether the commitment of activists and trade unions – who have consistently publicly problematised the working conditions of live-in care and initiated a series of regulatory efforts to improve them – will lead to tangible change remains uncertain. Nevertheless, it is not least due to their interventions that live-in care in Switzerland has been less widespread or normalised than in Germany or Austria.

Commonalities and Differences

A transnational service market of home-based long-term care has developed in Germany, Switzerland and Austria, each one organised somewhat differently. Although the issue of caregiver exploitation has been put on the table in Switzerland by trade unions and politically committed individuals, caregivers face problematic working conditions that are consistent with those of the other two German-speaking countries. Switzerland is the only country where migrant caregivers work as employees of placement agencies and can accordingly assert their rights as workers. In all three countries, the network Respect[9] is committed to improving the working conditions of care workers, but its activities have much less impact than those of the associations representing placement agencies who are active in asserting their interests in political decision making. Trade union membership of migrant care workers is generally low, and in Germany for example networks like the trade union-affiliated Fair Mobility[10] are supportive, but have not been able to achieve any long-term successes.

Social associations and (Christian) welfare organisations such as Caritas,[11] FairCare[12] and Diaconal Work[13] offer placement services for caregivers from Central and Eastern Europe in Germany, Austria and Switzerland. Although they present themselves as a fair alternative to private-sector services and are generally responsive when problems arise in households, they work with the same model of rotational live-in care which is prone to exploitation. Little known and with a small share in overall placement activity, they have not had much success in preventing the emergence of a private market, but they do in principle offer an alternative to the market of agencies.

The German-speaking countries' organisation of long-term care is characterised by an increasing commodification of care work, whereby the organising principle is individualised responsibility for care rather than societal responsibility (see Aulenbacher 2020). This commodification is closely connected to a progressive formalisation of care work, which promises good care without guaranteeing good working conditions (Aulenbacher et al. 2021a). Here, legal formalisations are instrumental in legitimising and normalising a new model of care. As a result of the Home Care Act in Austria, live-in care is now unquestioned by large segments of the population. In Germany, too, the introduction of a care allowance and the use of the Posting of Workers Directive have led to an informal market in which working conditions are not reviewed and the state does not intervene to ensure adequate protection for care workers. The prevailing view in both countries is that there is no feasible alternative to such arrangements or the role of agencies. The German agency associations are seeking to introduce the Austrian Self-Employment Model, which they present as a "third pillar" alongside inpatient and outpatient care in Germany's long-term care sector.

In Switzerland, on the other hand, the spread and normalisation of exploitative labour relations has been repeatedly contested. As a result, regulatory interventions (for example, minimum wages and collective labour agreements) have helped to problematise and partially de-legitimise this care model. There has been no major breakthrough, however, and the situation is tenuous. This is regrettable not least because hopes for the improvement of the situation of migrant domestic workers were high when the Domestic Workers Convention was adopted by the International Labour Organisation (ILO) in 2011 after years of global activist struggles. The convention stipulates that domestic workers be treated like other workers with regard to working and living conditions, wages, social security, health, rest and vacation periods. It has been signed by fewer than 40 countries worldwide; Germany and Switzerland are among them, while Austria and many other European countries are not.[14] Germany was one of the early signatories but it excluded persons who "live in domestic community with the persons entrusted to them and who raise, care for or look after them on their own responsibility", meaning that the protection of the Working Hours Act was withheld from live-in caregivers.

In summary, the marketisation of care work in the private households of senior citizens is intimately tied up with the transnationalisation of labour policies, the absence of control of working conditions in private homes, and new forms of governance and social statehood.

2

On the Road: The Supply Chain of Care Workers Between Germany and Central and East European Countries

The Caravan of Caregivers,[1] a documentary by Ingo Dell (2017) about Polish women shuttling back and forth between their home country and their workplaces in Germany, respectfully highlights their precarious working and living situations and the consequences of their employment for family members left behind. Films of this kind have recently appeared more frequently on German television (albeit usually late at night), which can be considered an indication of increased interest in care migration among a broad audience. The documentaries repeatedly illustrate that the employment of female caregivers, usually labelled as "domestic or nursing help",[2] has become a widely culturally accepted solution for the care of elderly people in German private households. As in many other affluent countries of the Western world, a large proportion of the elderly population prefers to remain in their own homes and living environments rather than being placed in nursing homes (Aulenbacher et al. 2024; Aulenbacher et al. 2021a, 2021b; Leiber et al. 2020; Pfau-Effinger 2005: 13). Moving to a care home is generally considered a last resort for emergency situations or cases in which relatives are unable to provide care because the person's disability is too severe for example. Otherwise, the living conditions of senior and care homes for the elderly are widely considered to be unacceptable, even inhumane (see Fussek and Schober 2013).[3] The "familialist" orientation of the care regime reinforces this situation by holding onto an intergenerational (moral) contract that stipulates that children are responsible for their parents and that care provided by family members is not only a duty but also an expression of affection and love. Statistics on the ageing process show that by 2027, six million elderly people out of 82 million inhabitants of Germany will be in need of care,[4] and it is expected that the majority will be cared for in their own homes by female family members (see Kuhlmey and Budnick 2023; Backes et al. 2008).

This chapter will outline multiple contradictions in the field of migrant care work. In order to understand why so many Central and East European women (and some men) rely on these employment opportunities and accept the associated circular labour migration as a way of life, it is important to take into account post-socialist living conditions. I will point out dilemmas and pose questions that are absent from most current representations of care migration.

I will start by taking a closer look at the care regimes of two East European sending states that are important for the migration to German-speaking countries: Poland and Ukraine. Whereas in many receiving countries in the Global North, as well as in many Asian and Arab states, the "racialisation" of care workers is an important feature of care migration, the situation in Europe deviates from this pattern: "white" workers are hired by "white" employers and ostensibly racism does not feature. A consideration of the history of the German Empire and Nazi dictatorship will show that this understanding must be revised.

Finally, I will discuss three currently important theoretical frameworks used to analyse the phenomenon of care migration. First, the Global Care Chain Concept (GCCC) will be presented, followed by the concept of Care Circulation (CCC) and the concept of Transnational Social Inequality (TSI), which is still under development.

TRANSNATIONAL CONNECTIONS – THE CARE REGIMES OF POLAND AND UKRAINE

Poland – A Sending and Receiving state

Of all East European sending countries, the most important home country for care migrants commuting to Germany is Poland. The country's post-socialist care regime is the result of the decentralisation and privatisation of social systems since the early 1990s (Österle 2014: 369). It is described as "explicitly familialist" (Krzyzkowski and Mucha 2012), meaning that the Polish state is only involved to a very limited extent in the provision of care and support services for children and those in need of care; instead, it makes families, mothers in particular, responsible for their children's well-being and care. Although the "family care" model (Anntonen and Sipilä 1996) already existed in the socialist system with regard to the care of the elderly and sick, in the post-socialist period the state emphatically reduced its involvement (Golinowska 2010). In 2010, expenditure on care amounted to just 0.37 percent of GDP (Österle 2014: 366; see also Sawulski 2017[5]), which is significantly lower than expenditure in western, northern and, in some cases, southern Europe. A particular burden for Polish families arises from the fact that there has been a break with the pre-1989 era in many areas of care: in order to promote female employment under socialism, comprehensive infrastructure facilities (crèches and kindergartens, all-day schools, school canteens, retirement homes, etc.) were established; many of these no longer exist or have been privatised. At the beginning of the 1980s, almost 70 percent of all married Polish women were employed (Sikorska 2009: 92), while in many other Central and East European countries, the proportion was much higher. However, neither in Poland nor in other socialist countries did the high labour force participation of women lead to a gender-balanced division of household chores and care work. Instead, reconciling work and family life continued to be considered a women's issue. For women to manage full-time work, their mothers or mothers-in-law often took on family care tasks on reaching retirement (Saxonberg and Szelewa 2007: 356). The trend towards the refamiliarisation of care policy is not limited to Poland, but can be seen to different extents in all post-socialist countries in the region. Éva Fodor describes this trend as a "return to domesticity" (2011: 3). Due to massive cuts in family benefits and the rapid loss of jobs in female-dominated fields of employment (Kałwa 2007: 208; van Klaveren et al. 2010), many Polish women were forced to leave the labour market after 1989.[6] This corresponded to the increasingly prominent conservative ideology of new motherhood (Szelewa and Polakowski 2008: 117).

As a result of the so-called "turnaround" of 1989, the incomes of 60 percent of the Polish population fell below subsistence level (Tarkowska 2007); even women who had jobs could not live on their wages and became "managers of poverty" (ibid.). In many municipalities, public kindergartens were closed and private institutions were established which are not affordable for the majority (Keryk 2010: 433–4); state-run old people's homes were also closed and replaced by private institutions. Moreover, the welfare state reforms implemented since the mid-1990s have increased the risks to women's social security. The partial privatisation of old-age provision has created a gender-specific pension gap due to the failure to sufficiently take into account the interruptions in women's employment biographies for childrearing and care. As Christina Klenner and Simone Leiber elucidate, "in the pension reform processes – supported by corresponding policy recommendations from the World Bank – the focus was primarily on questions of financial consolidation of the pension systems, and there was a failure to take the gender perspective into account in the sometimes fundamental changes" (Klenner and Leiber 2009: 25). Here, one way out of the feminisation of poverty is migration to western, southern and northern European countries.

Overall, the post-socialist transformation process led to paradoxical changes with regard to family and gender orders: on the one hand re-familiarisation representing a return to the traditional model received ideological, cultural and political (church-based) support, and on the other hand the dual-earner model became a financial necessity more than ever for survival (Giza-Poleszczuk 2007: 309).

Migration pressure has eased over the past 30 years, particularly in the now prosperous urban regions. The employment rate was 60 percent in 2013, significantly higher than ten years earlier at the time of EU accession when it stood at 51 percent. However, the average monthly gross salary in 2015 ($780) was notably lower than in other EU member states, such as Germany (€3,597) or the UK (£2,800) (see Kindler et al. 2016: 4). According to 2023 data,[7] the female work force in Poland makes up 45.5 percent of the total, which places the country at number 83 in the world; in comparison Germany is ranked at number 67, with 46.71 percent female labour market participation.[8]

Migration from rural regions and depleted industrial areas to the booming cities and, above all abroad, has therefore continued, with women continuing to make up the majority. In 2011, a total of 3.5 million out of 38.3 million inhabitants were temporarily abroad (for between 3 and 12 months) and 190,000 people deregistered their residence in Poland between 2004 and 2011. The proportion of women among migrants has risen steadily since 2004 and amounted to 52 percent in 2011 (see Slany and Ślusarczyk 2013; Anacka et al. 2014: 26).[9] Although emigration figures to the UK have fallen as a result of Brexit, they have remained relatively stable in Germany since 2017 (880,780 in 2022)[10] which continues to be the most important destination country for migrant care workers from Poland. However, these figures do not for the most part include the migrant women who are the subject of this book, because they commute transnationally at intervals of between four weeks and three months, a way of life which is largely undocumented and not considered in the statistics.

Transnational Care Migrants from Ukraine

Paradoxically, Poland has not only become a country of emigration, but also one of immigration, particularly for migrants from Western Ukraine. This was already the case before the Russian invasion of Ukraine in February 2022, and has intensified since then. Although Poland, since joining the EU in 2004 has had to strictly control the EU's external border, leading to the enforced introduction of visa controls, the border has remained permeable for Ukrainian migrants. Initially, it was mainly women who were in demand to carry out domestic work and childcare in the urban households of the newly emerging middle class, but as the birth rate fell and the number of elderly people in need of care increased, so too did the demand for migrant women to provide elderly care at home.

The migration from Ukraine that followed the declaration of independence in 1991 is referred to by Ukrainian researchers as the fourth wave (Fedyuk and Kindler 2016: 2). The migration history between Ukraine and Poland dates back to the period after WWI, when the rest of Ukraine was part of the USSR, and Western Ukraine was part of the Republic of Poland.

After the fall of the Soviet Union and the establishment of the new state of Ukraine, the population was hit even harder than that of Poland by the collapse of the economic system. The incorporation of the country into the world market was driven forward with the help of fiscal consolidation through the abolition of state subsidies, drastic reductions in public services, privatisation and the deregulation of markets. In this period, "mass privatisations and cutbacks were carried out in the formerly state-owned companies, which led to enormous cuts in social benefits for employees" (Haidinger 2013: 87). This desolate situation led to corruption, dramatic job losses, increasing instability and growing social inequality among the population. Several state-owned companies could not or would not pay wages during the transition period and many people were only able to secure their lives through subsistence farming (Zhurzhenko 2001: 37) and the help of remittances from family members working abroad. As recently as 2002, the proportion of people earning less than the minimum subsistence level was 83.3 percent.[11] Between 2002 and 2021 the average income went up from $60 to $641 in 2021, but dropped to $521 in 2022 as a result of the war.[12]

Bettina Haidinger describes Ukrainian social policy established after 1991 as the contradictory restructuring of a welfare system:

On the one hand, tendencies in favour of a liberal, Anglo-Saxon system are becoming stronger, as can be seen in the introduction of the three-pillar pension system or the introduction of means-tested social support; on the other hand, proposals that insist on a drastic increase in general minimum standards are also gaining ground. (2013: 90)

The system transition has so far had drastic consequences for the situation of women. Despite legal provisions for equal rights and better educational levels than men, wages fell to 70 percent compared to men's incomes (ibid.: 91). Before the economic transition, over 90 percent of women of working age were in full-time employment; in the 1970s, the proportion of women in employment was even higher than that of men. This has fundamentally changed: "Since 1995, however, female employment has been falling steadily and stood at 58.1 percent in 2009" (ibid.: 92).

As in Poland, there are measures to reduce government expenditure, manifested in the deterioration of medical care, the privatisation of (university) education, and the reduction of benefits in kind and infrastructural services (Zhurzhenko 2004). For example, the Ukrainian statistics office documented a dramatic decline in the number of kindergartens from 2,300 in 1991 to 1,100 in 2010. For the Ukrainian population, which has been shrinking dramatically since 1991 – from 51 million in 1991 to 38 million in 2022[13] – emigration and transnational circular migration offer a (temporary) solution that may be able to provide social cushioning and poverty reduction. According to data from the UNHCR,[14] approximately 6,752,000 people have left Ukraine since February 2022, which corresponds to around 13 percent of the country's population; two million have now returned. According to the World Bank, before the war an estimated 6.2 million migrants transferred remittances of 5.8 million dollars in 2008 (World Bank 2010); their contribution to the gross national product (GNP) was estimated at 4 percent (ibid.).[15] As the World Bank data does not include informal remittances, however, researchers estimate the real share at 20 percent of GNP (Ambrosetti et al. 2014: 147; Gropas et al. 2015: 36). In 2021 the remittance flows were estimated to have been higher: 14 billion dollars were mobilised, amounting to 7 percent of GNP.[16]

Like Polish migration, Ukrainian migration can be characterised as feminised. Destination countries for female care migrants are Poland and Italy (Cvajner 2019), as well as Germany and Austria (Haidinger 2013; Safuta et al. 2016; Kindler et al. 2016; Fedyuk and Kindler 2016; Solari 2017). However, Ukraine is still not a member state of the EU but a so-called third country and so access to the EU labour market is legally restricted or prohibited, meaning that the majority of Ukrainian care migrants in the EU are employed in the informal sector.[17] Those working in Germany were mostly brokered by Polish placement agencies, but they were not eligible for work permits. Paradoxically, as a result of the Russian attack the situation has somewhat improved as those who fled to Germany received a residence permit with the associated right to work. To date, there is no reliable data on the number of women working as caregivers in Germany or elsewhere.

"EASTERN EUROPE" – AT THE EDGES OF EUROPE

What explains the apparent preference for Polish/East European women as caregivers in German households? The simplest and often-heard answer is that Polish women are an affordable alternative for the relatives of German care recipients given that German outpatient care services charge three to five times higher rates. The affordability argument might be supplemented by the statement that the migrant women are hardly in a position to generate an even remotely comparable income in Poland; overall, this creates a win-win situation that is advantageous for all sides.[18] Apart from the financial aspect, there are also repeated references to the cultural proximity to East European women, which is said to make it easier to live together in the household. This includes belonging to the Christian religion, as well as appreciation for the family or the emotional devotion of the caregivers to their charges. The latter is not only a topic of reports in the German press and in popular descriptions of experiences with the "care crisis", for example in the book *Wohin mit Vater?* (Anonymous 2007), in which the Polish carer is praised for her warm-heartedness and reliability. The (self-)marketing of migrant women on internet portals also goes in this direction.

Notwithstanding these claims of cultural proximity, migrant women mention (both in the interviews that we conducted, as well in the documentary films) that the children of frail care receivers, who usually take on the role of employers, have no knowledge of and little interest in their countries and their families of origin. They also mention that the care receivers sometimes insult them as "Polacks". This can be seen as a sign that among the current generation of care recipients there are elderly people whose child-hood, youth and productive years fell in the Nazi era. They would have been active either as henchmen of the Hitler regime, as soldiers in WWII (on the "Eastern Front"), in the Nazi women's movement, in the labour service, the Hitler Youth or the League of German Girls, and would have been influenced by the pedagogy of fascism during their school years. The designation "Polack" has its roots in National Socialist racial doctrines, which took up and expanded the ideology of the inferior "Slavic race" that was already widespread in the Wilhelmine Empire and Weimar Republic. In particular, hostility towards Poland and Polish people was a core component of the growing nationalism in the German Empire, which was in vogue not only among right-wing conservatives, but also liberal-bourgeois circles. One notable example of this can be found in the inaugural lecture of the German Ostmark Association[19] given by the sociologist Max Weber in which he stated:

> The Polish peasant is gaining ground because he eats the grass from the ground, so to speak, not despite but because of his low standing physical and mental habits. ... And it is not only the interest in stopping the Slavic tide that calls for the transfer of significant parts of the eastern land into the hands of the state. (Weber 1895: 10–11, 14)[20]

Adolf Hitler's chief ideologue Alfred Rosenberg elaborated this doctrine of the "inferior race", which was to be subjugated, Germanised and de-culturalised in the course of the conquest for "living space in the East". According to the philosopher and historian Hans-Christian Harten (1996), the racial policy of fascism in Poland was by no means aimed at assimilation, but rather at a radical separation and segregation of "master" (Germanic) and "working" races (Slavic). In the National Socialists' racist ideology, Jews, Sinti and Roma, along with population groups classified as "unworthy" such as physically and mentally disabled people, were no longer envisaged as citizens with equal rights in a Greater Germanic Empire. In this context, Polish women, along with the Slavic races in general, were destined for a "colonial status" as "future labour slaves" (Harten 1996: 9). Therefore, after the invasion of Poland by German troops in 1939, the Polish elite was killed first,[21] and Polish and German citizens were placed under different legal systems; in the Polish Government General, Poles had to show their humility to every German person by making way on the sidewalks, taking off their hats and saluting. Visiting cinemas, concerts, exhibitions, libraries, museums and theatres was forbidden, and the possession of bicycles, cameras and radios was prohibited (Zimmerer 2004: 121). In his essay "From Windhoek to Warsaw", historian Jürgen Zimmerer substantiates the thesis that the racial cleansing policy first tested on the Herero and Nama peoples in the colony of German South-West Africa at the beginning of the twentieth century,[22] was reactivated in the occupied Central and East European countries during the Nazi era. The aim of the fascist "conquest of the East," also a colonial project, was the establishment of a privileged Germanic race. The fascist construction of a "Slavic working race" also generated the legitimacy for the deportation of half a million women and girls between the ages of 15 and 35 from the occupied Eastern territories (especially Poland and Ukraine) by the German army. These children and young women were obliged to perform forced labour as so-called Eastern workers; an estimated 100,000 of them performed "forced labour in the nursery" (Mendel 1993; Winkler 2000) in German households where they had to work as maids for families regarded as staunch National Socialists, who had many children.

This past is barely present in the German culture of remembrance, while in Poland and Ukraine it is part of family histories and engraved in the collective memory. The fact that these historical contexts have largely disappeared from view in Germany and do not play a role in the debate on care workers from Eastern Europe today is probably not only due to Germany's economic strength, but above all to the political and cultural discourses on "Eastern Europe" and East European societies. Manuela Boatcă, for example, argues that these societies are (still) seen as the gateway to the East: "Eastern-ness in the European imaginary" (Boatcă 2008: 2231) functions in the Western imagination as both a buffer and bridge between the Occident and Orient (or between Christianity and Islam), as a space in intermediate stages that is "always in the process of catching up with the West" (ibid.: 2232). In Boatcă's view, the societies of Eastern Europe remain trapped in an intermediate space which she calls the "hem of the velvet curtain" whereby "the coveted stakes – access to Western markets, employment opportunities and financial aid – require the subjugation – or at least the downplaying – of their 'Eastern-ness' and the declaration of an intention to Westernise" (ibid.: 2236). Eastern Europe does not represent the "other" of the Western European self; this discursive function is reserved for the "Orient/Islam", argues historian Maria Todorova (1997). Rather, it fulfils the function of the incomplete self, which is white, Christian and European but at the same time backward, traditional and agrarian (Todorova 1997: 18).

In contemporary debates about Whiteness, it is argued that Whiteness as an unmarked position functions as a normalising standard that entails privilege, but is ultimately attainable for a minority, because it is cut through by intersections of class, gender, sexuality etc. In other words, the stratification of Whiteness is a core dimension of the discourse about Eastern Europeans (Hartigan 1999). In her article "Fifty shades of White", Anna Safuta locates migrant care workers from Central and Eastern Europe within the stratum of "peripheral Whiteness" and writes that "the concept of 'periphery' and 'semi-periphery' encompass a broad spectrum of countries located both south and east of Western Europe" (2018: 219). She elucidates that "the West" remains the normalised yardstick and the inferior shades of white are white workers from the Central and Eastern European states of the European periphery: "Peripheral Whiteness is a subject position characterised simultaneously by privilege (compared with the social position of non-white migrants) and subordination (when compared with white Westerners)."(ibid.: 227) This means that, on the one hand, these workers enjoy the privilege of being racialised as white, but on the other hand this privilege is inextricable from the subalternity of their status. I would add that over such a status hovers the danger that this privilege can be withdrawn, as seen for example in the pressure on large numbers of Polish migrants to leave the UK after the country left the EU and implemented Brexit. Another example of the "scaling of Whiteness" (ibid.) is the downgrading of Ukrainian care workers by their Polish employers.

These voices of post-colonial debates seem to me enormously important for the understanding of racialised relations between East and West Europeans. Through an ideological framing of living together in a private household, in which closeness and distance and thus one's own identity is negotiated on a daily basis via self-perception and the perception of others (see Lutz and Benazha 2024), migrant care workers are assigned a subordinate place in the household. Both in terms of daily routines, and in caring or catering activities, they must adapt to the instructions of the care receivers (or their family members). Care brokering agencies emphasise to their employees that they are working in someone else's household, which they must not confuse with their own, and tell them to follow the instructions of their employers (see Chapter Three and scenes in the documentary *Family Business* by Christiane Büchner, 2016).

It can be assumed that the care work of East European migrant women functions so silently precisely because the relationship of dominance between employers and migrant women is ideologically and practically codified. As Regina Becker-Schmidt puts it, "What 'at home' means for wealthy white women is something different for their domestic employees, namely social alienation and a place of exploitation" (1992: 221). This is a very apt way to describe relationships of dominance in the private household which have survived the colonial era and the bourgeois class society of the nineteenth and twentieth centuries, and now manifest themselves in new forms of racialisation in the neoliberal economy of the twenty-first century.

In the remainder of this chapter, I attempt to theoretically situate care work migration with the help of three concepts. These should help to sharpen the analytical view of the case studies presented in the following chapters, which focus on the working and living conditions of migrant care workers and their families.

THE GLOBAL CARE CHAIN CONCEPT

The global care chain concept (GCCC), a term coined by sociologists Arlie Hochschild (2000) and Rhacel Parreñas (2001), describes the chains of relationships that have emerged on a global scale in relation to paid or unpaid care work. It is used to describe and link the interaction of different phenomena such as globalisation, the feminisation of migration, gender relations, and care and emotional labour in neoliberal capitalism's employment relationships. Hochschild and Parreñas are concerned with the commercialisation of care work in countries of the Global North, in which care and family work is passed onto migrant women, who in turn spend part of their income on providing for their own families. This exchange relationship causes a gain in care in the receiving country and a loss in care in the sending country and promotes the perpetuation of social inequality on a global scale (Hochschild 2003: 186f). Families at the upper end of the GCCC purchase care work and also benefit from "emotional added value" (Hochschild 2010), while at the lower end of the supply chain the partners, children and elderly family members in need of care in the sending countries pay the social and emotional price for the care deficit. This critical feminist approach rejects a viewpoint held by influential economists, according to which global care migration promotes the upward economic mobility of migrant women and their families. For example, the World Bank describes migrant remittances, which are the main source of income in many sending countries' national budgets, as a driver of development (see Dayton-Johnson et al. 2007). This view, often referred to as the "triple bottom line", assumes that these migrants reduce the supply deficit in the destination countries, that their income is also profitable for the families in the countries of origin, and that it ultimately improves the economy of the countries of origin (for critiques, see Yeates and Pillinger 2013; van Haer and Sørensen 2003).

In GCCC analysis, transnational motherhood is a core aspect of the discussion. The evaluation of the situation of children left behind continues to lead to considerable differences in the assessment of the consequences of care migration (Lutz and Palenga-Möllenbeck 2012). In "24-hour care", it is often legally impossible and practically infeasible for mothers and children to live together outside the care recipients' household because the payment is not sufficient for this, while the presence of children in a care household would prevent the care recipients from receiving undivided attention. Accordingly, a family model in which children, parents and partners stay behind in the country of origin dominates in East European commuter migration. The studies available to date on children who stay behind do not paint a clear picture. While some view high educational achievements as a positive consequence of the financial support provided by their mothers (Nicholas 2008), others emphasise the negative effects of the absence of mothers on their underage children in particular (Parreñas 2005; Gamburd 2000; Cortés 2007; Coronel and Unterreiner 2007). It is clear from the case studies presented in the following three chapters that it is not useful to characterise transnational motherhood as exclusively negative or positive. Rather, assessments need to take into account a range of place-dependent and case-dependent factors, such as the organisation of childcare locally, the impact of these arrangements on children of different ages, and gender relations in childcare in terms of the re-distribution of care responsibilities within and outside the family (see Hondagneu-Sotelo and Avila 1997; Parreñas 2005; Madianou and Miller 2011).

Virulent public debates on transnational parenthood in many Central and East European states focus on the absence of mothers, but rarely include absent fathers. In general, it is noticeable that the absence for months or years of male seamen, lorry drivers, soldiers or managers has rarely strained their paternity imago. In contrast, the (temporary) absence of mothers has triggered national debates and a sense of crisis (see Chapter Four) in which the presence of mothers is regarded as indispensable for the well-being of their children, and their absence is seen as a trigger for psychological and physical distress.

In summary, these studies show that as a result of female migration, in many sending states gender orders are under pressure. It is necessary to take into account the differences in gender regimes: the key elements for understanding transnational motherhood and fatherhood are culturally encoded gender norms, such as the gendered division of labour, and the coping practices of those affected (see also Chapter Five).

THE CARE CIRCULATION CONCEPT

For some time now, the GCCC concept has been criticised as rigid and one-sided. According to the critics, many research papers are dominated by the dichotomous idea that migrants migrate in one direction to earn money in the Global North and then send their earnings back in the opposite direction, to their countries of origin in the Global South,[23] where the relationship between the two poles remains generally static. Critics emphasise that this image concentrates one-sidedly on the bilateral care relationship between mothers as givers and family members as receivers (see Kofman 2012), arguing that the metaphor of a supply chain does not sufficiently take into account the various network members participating in the care exchange. Loretta Baldassar and Laura Merla, for example, comment:

> We argue that the idea of a *chain* is not the most suitable way of portraying the mobilities of care from a family perspective. The *chain* metaphor tends to limit these mobilities to back and forth movements between two nodes of a chain, where migrant and non-migrant exchange various types of support, thus reinforcing the distinction between the two sets of actors. (2013: 29)

Baldassar and Merla further criticise the way that care is embodied in the GCCC framework by the person of the migrant woman, which creates the impression that care is the incorporated capital of female migrants. They argue that this is only true if the focus is reduced to the labour market perspective, which creates a physical separation between family members; by contrast, the inclusion of the concept of the moral economy of families enables a different perspective, which makes the bilateral flow of virtual forms of care visible (ibid.). Baldassar and Merla therefore propose to speak of "care circulation", since this term is able to capture the mobility of care as multidirectional, simultaneous and diachronic, and does not limit the exchange of care to that between the migrant on one side and family members who remain behind on the other. Instead, it recognises any form of exchange as part of an extensive network of care flows.

These authors also emphasise that care movements are by no means symmetrical, but rather asymmetrically reciprocal, and that care, as a resource, is distributed unequally within and between families (ibid.: 30–1). Their concept of care circulation (CCC) thus takes up and expands the debates on transmigration, i.e. migration movements in multiple directions.

What is compelling about the CCC critique is the indication that network relationships are significantly more complex than an exchange between two ends. The point that social relationships in migration should not be reduced to the labour market perspective is also well taken. It is rightly emphasised by proponents of the CCC framework that the transformative potential of migration can only be considered if the moral family economy is taken into account, which means that the moral obligations of family members to each other must be included as part of a family economy: "If we move from a labour market focus to a focus on the moral economies of the family, we can see that not only do embodied and commodified forms of care travel along the chain, but also other 'virtual' forms of care travel in both directions" (ibid.: 29).

Convincing as this may appear at first, Baldassar and Merla overlook the ways in which asymmetrical relationships between caregivers and recipients make reciprocity difficult or impossible. Neither the poor working conditions nor the lack of rights of many migrant care workers (especially the absence of the right to live together with their loved ones) is addressed in the CCC framework. This framework is also based on the assumption that there is ubiquitous access to new technologies that enable virtual "co-presence"; however, this is by no means the case everywhere. The limitations of technology are overlooked, because although they facilitate the exchange of emotional attachment, they do not substitute for hands-on care, i.e. the direct, physical care and support of children, spouses and friends. This should not detract from the point underlying the concept of care circulation that the characterisation of transnational families as a deviation from the sedentary family, which is considered "natural", is outdated in the twenty-first century (see Amelina and Lutz 2019; Chapter Three).

In a way that is comparable to the debate on the circulation of educational capital (brain circulation), which sees itself as a counter-model to the dichotomous "brain drain and brain gain" idea, the CCC framework neglects the social costs of migration, which become virulent as "emotional inequalities" (Yeates 2009), and so runs the risk of ignoring neoliberal social inequality and exploitation globally. As a result, there is a danger of losing sight of the question of how social inequalities are recalibrated on a global scale.

TRANSNATIONAL SOCIAL INEQUALITY

The transnational social inequality framework (TSI) begins from a critique of the way that most definitions of social inequality use the nation–state as a "natural" reference category. Monika Büscher, John Urry and Katian Wichtger (2011) refer to this basic assumption as "sedentarist", as it treats sedentarism or geographical immobility and lifelong affiliation of people to one nation–state as the standard of analysis and regards mobile lifestyles, such as those of migrants, as deviating practices from a sedentary "normality". Andreas Wimmer and Nina Glick Schiller (2003) have also rightly criticised this approach as "methodological nationalism." It nevertheless remains dominant in much social science research whereby mobile lifestyles are associated with non-sedentariness – and often assumed to be a deficit – with such assumptions implicitly informing research designs. Büscher and Urry argue that both mobility and immobility, as well as their mutual conditionality, must be taken into consideration in order to grasp the "grammar of mobility". This requires not only the application of the method of "mobile ethnography" as developed by Büscher and Urry, but also an attention to the significance of borders and the drawing of boundaries in the analysis of "simultaneously unequal life chances" (see Beck 2007). To overcome methodological nationalism, Floya Anthias (2012) has proposed theorising social inequality transnationally, as "multilocal hierarchies," while Parreñas (2001) speaks of "contradictory social mobility." Meanwhile, Boris Nieswand (2011) uses the metaphor of the "status paradox of migration" in order to describe the simultaneity of downward and upward social mobility, which leads to migrants being positioned differently in the social class hierarchies of sending and destination countries (see also Amelina 2017a: 33).

In the case of care migration, this status paradox can be illustrated, for example, by the fact that many migrant women, due to their formal level of education in their country of origin, belong to the (educated) middle class and they strive to maintain their status by generating income and sending remittances from abroad, while at the same time they are at the bottom of the social hierarchy in the destination countries. Relationality and reflexivity are key components in dealing with such status differences. Philip Kelly and Tom Lusis (2006: 836) argue that the development of a relational, transnational habitus, in which cross-border mobility functions as capital, enables migrants to transfer from one type of capital to another, depending on what is expected of them. Researching transnational inequality therefore means establishing a relational multilocal setting that includes localities in the sending and receiving countries in which these specific status differences are co-produced (Amelina 2017a).

I will briefly distinguish three aspects of the TSI approach that are relevant to my research. First, for migrant women, care work has a double meaning: on the one hand, it is closely linked to the social construction of femininity, which generates a gendered form of social capital relevant to employment, while on the other hand, care work is part of their gendered obligation, which is under pressure based on hegemonic notions of motherhood and the familial responsibility of the moral kinship economy. The provision of unpaid "emotional labour" (Hochschild 2001) is not only a family obligation, but also a core task of care work. The availability of care thus becomes a special target value that is desired at both ends of the care nexus and can be seen as a decisive factor in terms of quality of life. Amelina (2017b) therefore identifies transnational inequalities as a "'doing' of socio-spatial inequality." This "doing", however, is subject to structural limitations, because presence in one setting implies (physical) absence in the other. Emotional inequality becomes an implicit component of transnational care chains, because as long as the care migrant is occupied with the daily care of clients in the destination country, contact with the family members who remain behind is limited to digital connectivity and temporary visits.

A second aspect of TSI is the question of social security protection, which is not exclusive to care migration. As Johanna Avato et al. (2010) point out, there are hardly any bilateral agreements between sending and receiving countries that stipulate the portability of social security rights and payments. Although these authors emphasise that EU member states have introduced portability agreements that in theory guarantee access to social benefits, there are several ways that national labour law requirements can be circumvented in the service sector. In the EU, so far only Austria has established an official recruitment policy for care workers, which also defines the level of social security payments (see Österle and Bauer 2016). In many other countries, migrants from Eastern Europe provide services as self-employed entrepreneurs or as posted workers (see Chapter One). As described above, transnational social security systems are not monitored and encourage exploitative practices.

A third aspect of TSI relates to the racism–migration nexus (Erel et al. 2016). Umut Erel and her co-authors emphasise that the EU's migration policy, like that of the US, is characterised by institutional racism, which creates and reinforces class-specific and racialised career paths (ibid.: 1344). Since the concept of racism tends to be ignored and avoided in many European destination countries, there are almost no studies on migrant care workers' experiences of racism. We are by no means living in post-racist European migration societies in which the social construction of race and forms of racism have become obsolete (ibid.: 1352); to the contrary. The fact that the racism–migration nexus has hardly been studied in relation to care migration from Eastern Europe is certainly related to the fact that the inclusion of these migrants is based on cultural similarities in terms of religion (Christianity) and skin colour (whiteness), but as discussed above, discourses that contain elements of the fascist understanding of race, for example the "Slavic working race", repeatedly emerge. Further research is no doubt required.

I suggest that the three concepts – the GCCC, the CCC and the TSI – are not only complementary but equally relevant for the analysis of care migration. The Global Care Chain Concept (GCCC) paved the way for understanding asymmetric dimensions of the global commercialisation of care. It emphasises the transformation process of care into a fictitious commodity[24] that emerges as a consequence of neoliberal marketing logic. However, the concept neglects the transformative potential of migration, which opens up new opportunities for migrant women to improve their income and life chances. In contrast, the Care Circulation Concept (CCC) insists that care chains should not be reduced to unilateral relationships between migrant women and their employers etc., but that "care" circulates in various forms in family networks across the globe. This concept emphasises the transnational dimension of (material and emotional) care within the kinship economy, but neglects the analysis of precarious working conditions in the care economy and the asymmetrical differentials between countries of origin and destination. The concept of Transnational Social Inequality (TSI) sheds light on the emergence and co-production of social inequalities in and through transnational spaces and focuses on the status paradox of cross-border mobility. I will use the heuristics provided by these frameworks in the following chapters to show how migrant care work is shaped in the context of norms and power structures (religion, politics, economy, culture, etc.) in discourses, practices and institutions.

3

Distance and Proximity: Transnational Mothering and Emotional Inequality

Migration processes result in the constitution of multilocal families whose members are connected via a network of relationships spanning countries, places and households. In this chapter, I will look at how migrant care workers deal with being absent from their families and how their (repeated temporary) absences affect the family members at home. Migration researcher Thomas Faist (2000) identifies reciprocity and focused solidarity among the members of a family network as the central reproduction mechanism of transnational families. These networks link migrants physically engaged in cross-border mobility with those left behind in their hometowns and countries through reciprocal relationships of exchange (see also Baldassar and Merla 2013). I will explore how "doing family" (Schier and Jurcyk 2007) is practised in families in which mothers, in particular, engage in migration. As already said, the transnational migration of women is a relatively new phenomenon in the Central and East European sending countries. Earlier migration flows between the states of the former Eastern bloc involved men for the most part, and their departure was not generally linked to any fear of family fragmentation. In contrast, the migration of mothers has become associated with a care crisis and moral panics. The 24-hour care sector is a predominantly female arena: both the caregivers and the employees of the agencies that place them in private households are women, but this is not necessarily true of the agencies' owners.

How exactly do reciprocity and solidarity develop in families in which mothers migrate? Who performs the maternal care work in their place? How is the "backstage" of care migration organised?

How do migrant mothers experience transnational motherhood, and how do they deal with experiences of emotional loss? How, in practice, do they "do" mothering from a distance? I present the findings from a comprehensive evaluation of the replacement care arrangements carried out with Ewa Palenga-Möllenbeck (for full details, see Lutz and Palenga-Möllenbeck 2011a). For this analysis I have selected two particularly typical cases of two Polish mothers who are single parents from our extensive empirical material concerning shuttle migration. Their narratives are contrasted with that of a rather unusual case of a young man who is a father and works as a care worker in Germany.[1] Reflecting on mothering practices of female migrants in the context of motherhood ideals – maternalism – I will suggest that the separation of mothers from their children is an important dimension of transnational inequality.

DILEMMAS OF TRANSNATIONAL MOTHERHOOD

Halina

Halina begins her narrative with a legitimisation of her decision to migrate and a reference to her precarious financial predicament.[2] When she travelled to work as a caregiver for the first time in 2003, she was already 42 years old.

> My parents supported me all their lives, so that's why I say to myself that now it's my turn to support my children. That's why I'm here [Germany], because I know I can earn more here, then I can give this money to my children. I mean, if I were to earn 1,000 zloty in Poland, I would have to pay 500 zloty in rent and the rest for my telephone, and then I can think about whether I pay for the apartment [needs] or buy food for my children. And that's just it, it's our situation in life that forces us to be here. Because I don't think there's anyone who feels called to come here, to Germany.

Halina's decision to go to Germany to care for an elderly woman in a private household was a difficult one. Her resistance to working in Germany was not only about her limited command of the German language but was also rooted in her family biography.

As a child, Halina's father, along with his siblings, were transported by the German army to Auschwitz; only he and one sister survived the concentration camp. He tried for years to deter his daughter from migrating to Germany. Halina initially followed her father's advice and planned to go to the Netherlands, but caught in a financial predicament and unable to secure a job there quickly enough, she decided to go despite her father's misgivings. Born in 1961, she grew up with seven brothers and sisters in a village in Lower Silesia, where she took her baccalaureate in 1978. Having missed an application deadline for a law degree, she started work as a trainee accountant in a cooperative business that sold agricultural products. A year later she left her parents' home, moved to Upper Silesia and worked as an accountant in a famous porcelain factory, the largest employer in the region. There she met her future husband, who was working in production (on the assembly line), and they married in 1981: "We were a very happy couple; my husband was very good to me [laughs]. All my girlfriends envied me. There was no household chore he couldn't do – he even sewed my wedding dress."

In 1982 she had her first child, a daughter, four years later she had a son, and in 1997, her youngest child, a daughter named Iga was born. Throughout this period, Halina worked in human resources management in different companies. She had wanted to continue studying, which was permitted even in parallel with employment in Poland at the time. However, this was obstructed by her husband, who had no educational aspirations – according to Halina, out of jealousy and fear that she might meet other men and grow apart from him as a result of her studies. But equally, she herself was not inclined or in any position to leave him and realise her dream of studying. After the system transformation at the start of the 1990s her husband and a friend opened a bar, for which Halina took out a loan, and at his request she gave up her job. To begin with, the business they owned did very well, but following financial disputes it was necessary to file for bankruptcy. Her husband "fled" abroad to escape his creditors and worked on construction sites in Germany and Austria. When he was killed in a car accident in 1996, Halina was already pregnant with Iga. She returned to her former job at the porcelain factory. She then found out that her husband had not paid insurance contributions for the family, and that she had to settle the debts he had left behind; this presented her with massive financial difficulties. Nevertheless, as if she had been waiting for this moment of freedom, soon after her husband's death Halina enrolled for a degree by distance learning in the subject that came closest to her dream, European Administrative Law. She continued to study even after Iga's birth, and her employer granted her leave to attend the face-to-face phases of her distance learning degree. Her financial situation was dire: she had to sell her jewellery and the flat she owned, while her sick parents helped her to maintain a minimal standard of living for herself and the children. Yet she persisted with her studies, earning a Master's degree in 2000. This qualification did not help her find a better paid job, however, and she remained at the factory until it declared insolvency and closed its gates in 2002. By then her eldest daughter was 20 years old and had already graduated from high school with a very good baccalaureate, but refused to succumb to her mother's pressure to go to university. Instead, she found work in the service sector, in Poland first and later in the Netherlands. Halina was not happy about this, but it meant that her daughter had her own income and therefore needed no further help financially.

When Halina travelled to her first job in Germany, her son, who had major learning difficulties, was 16 years old. As a schoolchild, Patryk sought psychological counselling, and Halina had tried for a long time to compensate for his learning difficulties with familial and paid tutoring. He finished school without qualifications and started working, became unstable, took drugs and had regular spells of unemployment. During these periods he moved back in with his mother, where he did not take on any domestic tasks, neither in terms of caring for his little sister nor doing household chores: "Patryk is used to doing nothing because Mum always does it for him....He was always a mother's boy, I always took care of everything for him. I even tied his shoelaces when he went to school."

He threw parties in his mother's apartment while she was out, and even when he stole from her, Halina found excuses for him: "He's so naive, he lets people exploit him." The first time she travelled to Germany, her youngest daughter Iga, who was five years old, was initially cared for by the elder daughter, Alicja, before she moved to the Netherlands. After her departure, Halina found new, rotating solutions: various female friends moved into Halina's flat and took care of Iga, receiving symbolic payment in the form of gifts. There were problems with the continuity of care, and Iga periodically ended up staying with Halina's sister. Halina reported that Iga and her friend Lucyna who was caring for her at the time of the interview had a poor relationship:

Iga is certainly defiant and argues with her all the time. And Lucyna says: "Your Iga is so defiant, she won't listen to me." Recently Iga said to me: "Mum, my room is clean and tidy but she still comes in and vacuums the floor." …Iga simply didn't have enough privacy staying with her, right.

Halina was proud of being able to provide her child with "privacy":

She has her room, I have my room, right. They may be small but they're better than nothing, and each has her own space. She says she doesn't want to talk to her aunt [meaning Lucyna] all day because she can't see the sense in it, right. I say: "Iga, watch that series [meaning a soap opera] with her. After that, do your homework, and that's when you both turn the television off, that's the deal." And I also say to her: "There aren't any new treats: that's your lot, that's your lot!" Iga always phones me and complains.

Evidently Iga, ten years old at the time of the interview, had clear preferences and detested the soap operas that her caregiver watched. When she had her own computer, she could – with her older brother's help – download films that she enjoyed watching. Iga and her mother were in daily telephone contact, and Halina described her relationship with her daughter as very close.

Between 2003 and 2007, Halina worked as a 24-hour carer for seniors and invalids on a two-to-three-month cycle in German households, initially as an undocumented worker, from 2005 via an agency, and from 2006 as a so-called self-employed carer. Over the four years she had to change households seven times because her care clients were gravely ill (cancer, Alzheimer's) and died or their relatives decided to transfer them to care homes. In some cases, Halina took work that included end-of-life care, although she did not have the relevant training and her German language skills were weak. She made several attempts to take Iga to Germany with her, but this was always vetoed by her employers. Halina's leisure time was limited to five hours twice a week, and her monthly pay was just over €1,000. When she was a self-employed worker she received €1300 but had to pay her social security contributions. In four years, Halina never tried to negotiate a pay rise with her employers. She not only lacked the necessary language skills but also any awareness of the way that her clients' dependence on her might have strengthened her negotiating position. In the interview, she spoke about how her Christian faith helped her to develop a humanitarian attitude. Ultimately, she never complained about her working conditions. In August 2007, Halina quit her job, returned to Poland and started work as a bookkeeper and manager of a Polish care agency.

Not only was Halina a single mother, but she also had little family capital to draw upon. Her parents and in-laws had either died or were too sick to be able to care for her children, and while Halina's elder daughter took responsibility for her younger sister for a time, she then migrated herself to lead her own life. The son was unwilling or unable to take care of his little sister, and in any case his mother did not expect him to. In contrast to many other interviewees, Halina's care-replacement network at home was not stable; she could not depend on it and had to anticipate that problems might arise at any moment that she would not always be able to solve satisfactorily from a distance. Her eldest daughter showed solidarity while she was there, but this bond of reciprocity bore no comparison to the relationships with the women friends who cared for Iga. Likewise, the relationship with her sister, who had Iga to stay when other care arrangements broke down, was not strong enough to be the basis for establishing a long-term solution. Halina emphasised that apart from the necessity to repay the debts her husband left behind, the most important stimulus for her migration was her hope of improving the circumstances of her children's lives. Halina found it extraordinarily hard being separated from her children, and most of all from Iga:

> In the evenings, when I go to my room, when I have free time, these terrible thoughts go through my head. What am I doing here? Why is it like this? I try to find an explanation for it. Could I not have managed my life differently? Could I have done this or that? Those are the thoughts that go through my head.

Halina regrets that every time she said goodbye to Iga, she told her she would not go away any more, but then kept breaking that promise:

> I said: "You know how hard it is, look how much people earn in our country, how hard life is, how poor the people are." And that's how I went about it, yes, that was bribery. The other two are already grown up, they, they were already big, that's why they didn't cry so much, right.

Halina's narrative makes it clear that compensating for her absence with consumer goods, which she calls "bribery", conflicted with her ideals of motherhood. In the phases she spent back home, she would arrange to see Iga's teachers, just as she had previously done for Patryk, and she would try to find him a job. She was always afraid that the geographical separation from her children would turn into emotional distance in the long run. Partly because of the difficult working conditions but also because of Iga, Halina decided to stop working in Germany and return to Poland in 2007.

Kasia

The second interview with a single mother that I am presenting here was conducted ten years later, in 2018. In the intervening time, the 24-hour care sector had established itself as a thriving new market, not only in Germany, but also in several other European countries (Aulenbacher et al. 2024). Although there are still no precise figures on how many migrant women work as carers in German households, estimates put the figure at 700,000–800,000.[3]

Kasia, a single mother, aged 56 at the time of the interview, had been working for a decade in the homes of dementia patients in Germany.[4] She had previously worked in Poland as a trained laboratory technician in a hospital. When this was privatised in the context of the privatisation of the public healthcare system, her working conditions changed, and she fell ill for a long time before she lost her job, leaving her with a very small pension on which to survive. As a mother who received no alimony from her child's father, she tried to support herself and her son, Szymon, for years by cleaning in private Polish middle- and upper-class households and by repeatedly taking on short-term employment. In 2008, at the age of 46, she decided to start working as a 24-hour carer in Germany. Her parents desperately tried to dissuade her from going, pointing to the racism and the crimes committed by the German army during the occupation of Poland (1939–45). Nevertheless, Kasia decided to travel to Germany through a Polish agency to take on the care of a man with dementia during the Christmas period.[5]

As it was my first job, the agency didn't assign me a difficult case, it was just like here.[6] You just had to keep an eye on things, prepare meals and provide care, or do work that had to do with the household or go for a walk. Care that, as they say, doesn't require as much knowledge as, for example, caring for bedridden people. I acquired this knowledge over time because I was also involved in such cases. So, the first time I was only there for a short time, three weeks in total, over the holidays and it was difficult for us, for me and my son, but... It was a kind of lifeboat for me at the time.

As neither the child's father nor her parents or other family members were willing to engage in caring for her 16-year-old son, Kasia asked her neighbour to look after him and to cook him lunch from time to time. Looking back at these experiences ten years later, she reflected:

It wasn't easy... He was aged 16, then 17 to 18. Those are, as they say, the difficult years: "I am already an adult, I can do anything, I can do it!" And I was here worrying that he was... looking for the wrong company as a substitute for being alone, without a mother.

Fortunately, her fears turned out to be unfounded. Now, she was proud that her son had developed well and avoided contact with "false friends": "We did it on our own. It went well, thank God!" Proudly, she described her son's development as a learning process that she initiated:

So, he realised then that he had to look after himself.... He realised that he had to clean because there was no one to take the rubbish downstairs, because no one was doing the dishes. Yes, he realised a bit that the parent does something at home, doesn't just go to work. Home is also work. Yes, he has to do the shopping for himself, has to go to school, in between, as I said: shopping, organising the food, yes... I wasn't one of those mothers... who did everything around him, was I? Serving breakfast, making tea, "Here for you, my son, lunch." No! For example, "If you want a cup of tea, make it yourself!"

Interestingly, here Kasia referred to herself as "the parent", drawing attention to the complete absence of the father and the associated difficulties in raising her son.

When I was in Germany, I was worried about what he was doing at home. Whether he wasn't getting into the wrong circles.... Luckily there was a neighbour – she was a bit older than me, by about ten years. We knew each other from the hospital, she was a nurse.... I could ask her, for example: "Listen, I phoned Szymon at around 11 pm. He's not answering. Can you knock on his door and see what's going on?" That was literally across the corridor – she didn't even have to go out because we lived on the same landing. She went to him and told me, "He's not there, it's quiet." So, a call to the [his] mobile phone.

The fact that she was not at home and could not look after him "robbed me of my peace of mind." She related that soon after she started working as a care migrant, Polish schools introduced new rules for the protection of children: if a pupil was absent for three days without a written excuse from the parents, the family would be checked on. There was also a threat that the police and a guardian could be called in.

> Fortunately, I had a good relationship with the teacher, so I could rest assured that if he didn't turn up at school, there would be a phone call or text message straightaway.... We communicated via text message and I was able to text my son immediately: "Get in touch!" Of course, we had to agree on what time we wanted to call because of the call costs, which were very high then. So that was also an obstacle to contacting him. And then there was a conversation: "Why weren't you at school?" He said he had overslept or ... We often had to write apologies. He had to sign them with my signature, but the class teacher knew that.

The three years before her son finished school were particularly hard for her:

> I often called when he wasn't home at night. I was anxious about where he was going. In some cities, there were measures in place, so that if he was found on the street after 10 pm by the police... they ended up taking the young person home and checking whether their parents were there. If they were not, and in our case, I was a single parent, and if it had turned out – he was still a minor – that I had left him alone because of work, then there would have been a heavy fine. Back then it was 5,000 [zloty]. I was afraid of that. There were always conversations with my son: "Don't go out late! Or, try to come back on time! Always take your ID with you to avoid problems, so it doesn't end with a check like that!" Those were my worries. But on the other hand, I was also reassured because my son, how can I put this... He had many hobbies and was interested in graphic design. He could spend hours on it.

In the course of the interview, she finally talked about her major preoccupation in relation to her son; she suspected that his homosexuality arose during and because of her long absences:

The first signs were during secondary school, but he never wanted to say what was going on. He couldn't keep up in sport lessons. The others would bother him. But I never thought that something like *that* could start here, partly because he was a footballer, for example. And that... But well... But that was... maybe the fact that I wasn't at home and he was alone. And maybe he was looking for support from his peers or older people... Maybe my work also had an influence on that. These are just the consequences. There are advantages and disadvantages to something like this happening, for example in my case. I've heard various examples. I'm not going to talk about them here, because I'm sure there will also be statements from other people[7] that this work across the border, not just as a caregiver, but across the borders of our country, or at a great distance – if I had worked in another city, for example – that this provokes situations that might have gone very differently, if I had been at home all the time. Although, you don't know that either.

The interruptions in this quote indicate that Szymon's sexuality continued to be a significant problem for Kasia. She was tormented by the question of whether she could have prevented her son's homosexuality. More than once in the interview she underlined that she was aware of her son's needs and tried to support him accordingly:

And, coming back to the subject of the Abitur,[8] I had to put the brakes on here and stay at home. To do the simple things: going shopping, cleaning, to take the pressure off him. He had already been through a lot in those two years anyway. He had no time to study, but had to take care of the everyday things. The "prosaic stuff", as he calls it. So yes, I was at home. I only travelled for short stays, as they say, so that we could survive this time. There were also the expenses, the graduation ball and the clothes for the graduation. He didn't go to the ball because of our financial situation. I said to him, "Go! It's only one time in your life. You'll regret it!" and he said, "No, I'm not going!" That's how it was. But he passed his A-levels without any problems.

Her son then passed the university entrance exam:

I was also at home then so that he could prepare for university in peace. He passed and was accepted…. We were lucky that everything turned out so well for us. Me too… even as an adult you can get into bad circles. It could have affected me too and ended badly for me. But I'm not in any danger now, and he's not really in any danger either. Although…he's just…I don't know…. Because of his psyche, his nature, I still have to look after him. I still have to call him… Although there are no more problems now. There is the internet, different apps, you can call for free. I also look for places where … we can talk at any time, stay in touch. I can give him advice… He also has health problems.

She thought that her son's gluten allergy may have developed through eating the wrong food (pizza and other fast food) which he favoured during her absences.

He is now having tests, which are quite expensive because everything has to be paid for privately. The good thing is that we are both earners now. But it's been four years and we still don't know what it is. Some doctors say it's all in his head, that he's imagining it.

After a decade of care work in the homes of dementia patients, where she often had to be available around the clock, Kasia did not earn more than €1500 per month. She explained this by saying that her German language skills were weak, although she was able to communicate very well, especially with digital language aids. Her summary of the last ten years was therefore ambivalent: she was happy that she had found her way out of poverty in Poland, but also unhappy about the way she was treated by some clients, especially their families.

But to summarise, if I may say so, I don't regret taking this step. My son… I'm debt free. I'm in a completely different frame of mind. The work makes me feel valued somehow. And it means a lot to me. It boosts my self-confidence that I'm needed. I had to earn the money and I thought to myself that if I help someone, I might also have a better paid job at the same time. That helps me in my life, in my specific situation. And it has helped. And I don't regret taking this step. I have cried. There were such places here in Germany that I wanted to give up! Ah, I can't take it anymore! I'm going back home! I've had enough! I was fed up with the Germans... Maybe that also had a big influence on me, because I thought, I'm fed up with the Germans! Because it was also my parents' past when they were still children. These historical aspects also influenced my way of thinking, didn't they...?

Feelings of Guilt

Halina and Kasia's biographical interviews reflect the dilemmas of single mothers who are the breadwinners of their families. Although maintaining contact with children has become easier as digital communication options have expanded and improved, the constant worry and fear that their absence will lead to undesirable developments remain. They feel guilty that they are not able to fulfil their maternal duties, that they will be judged both by their children and society. Added to this is the mother-blaming discourse (see Chapter Four), which reinforces doubts as to whether they can fulfil society's expectations of good motherhood.

Like all other interviewees, Halina and Kasia emphasise the role played by the precarious economic conditions in the post-socialist period in leading them to take a step they had not envisaged in their life plans. The women accept without question that motherhood should be combined with employment; these duties or civic obligations had been fulfilled by their own mothers before them, an arrangement that had been supported by state institutions under state socialism. The compatibility of these responsibilities – motherhood and employment – becomes even more complex in the context of migration: when the home and workplace are separated by hundreds of miles, when national and linguistic borders are crossed, and when the physical distance gives rise to new requirements that did not previously exist, mothers leave behind a care gap that has to be filled with care-replacement arrangements back home.

In their narratives, the care workers place great value on presenting themselves as good mothers, which suggests that both their own and society's conceptions of motherhood are under pressure. The so-called Euro-orphans debate (see Chapter Four), which catapulted the absence of mothers to national attention as a social problem, was virulent in Poland (and other East European sending states) during the data collection period and continues to this day. Its traces can be seen in the narratives of the interviewees who are mothers. Besides vulnerability and problematic working conditions, other commonalities are the mothers' suffering and sense of guilt due to the geographical distance from their children, which will be discussed in more detail in the final section of this chapter. Differences between the cases relate primarily to the stability or instability of the family networks – which are a form of social capital – and it is the state of the family network that appears to decisively influence someone's interpretation of her own migration as a failure or a success. Before I go into this in more detail, I would like to briefly present an interview with a young man. As already mentioned, there are very few men working as caregivers in German homes; the narrative of a male caregiver serves here to provide an elucidating contrasting comparison with the narratives of the mothers.

Mateusz

Mateusz, a Polish man, had been working as a caregiver in private German households for four years and was 29 years old at the time of the interview.[9] After finishing school, he had worked in various jobs: "From sweeping the streets to... I don't know... working in the kitchen." Shortly after the birth of his daughter he and his wife separated. Mateusz justified his work as caregiver with the fact that he had accumulated debts in Poland during his younger years, and in addition he now had to pay alimony for his daughter. He could not have afforded to cover his debts and the alimony on his Polish salary. Both his mother and sister lived and worked in Germany. Mateusz preferred long employment periods (up to six months), explaining this by saying that he no longer had a family in Poland to return to. Mateusz explained that he visited his daughter, four years old at the time of the interview, once a year for her birthday.

His mother was his role model; she had already worked as a caregiver – first in Poland, then in Germany – and he himself had completed an internship in a retirement home. After the separation from his wife, he decided to look for work as a 24-hour caregiver in Germany.

> When my mum went to Germany, I had just got divorced... actually it was before the divorce, but already after the separation from my wife. So, if my mother, an older woman – well... older... she wasn't even 50 years old at the time – manages this work...then I can do it too, yes?

Mateusz found all his clients through the placement of a Polish agency.

> I have to say that there are also critical opinions about my agency. But almost every Polish and non-Polish company... is dirty.... Very rarely is there an employment contract between the agency and the carer. Although I think there should be an employment contract. Because in reality, what we do here and what is written in the service contract looks more like an employment contract.... An employment contract would be much better for us, but not for the agency.... It's all about the money.... For example, the family pays the agency quite a lot of money for me being here...and I get maybe half of it.

The only advantage he saw in working through a placement agency was that the agency paid his social contributions. When asked to give more detail on this, he responded: "I have no idea. I am not interested. It is important that they are discharged." Interestingly, he then fetched his service contract and read passages from it. In principle, 24-hour carers are instructed not to talk to anyone about whether or not they have a contract or their salary. He emphasised a passage containing regulations on refraining from consuming alcohol, and reported that he had problems with violating this ban on drinking alcohol at work "because if you're treated like a family member – at least I meet families like that, where I'm treated like a family member – there are various invitations to parties or family gatherings." These parties apparently included a lot of alcohol consumption, and he found it difficult to be a spoilsport. "Now soon, in a fortnight I think, the granddaughter will have her fortieth birthday. And I've been invited again." Interestingly, Mateusz was the only person among all our interviewees who talked about invitations and parties.

Mateusz underlined that he did cook for his client, but that he was not a cleaner.

> The company sends you to one of these positions and you have to organise everything yourself. From A to Z. Basically, you only have a place to sleep, but you organise the rest yourself. What you cook for your client, how you spend your breaks, what you.... basically everything. From A to Z. Here, for example, I don't cook in the Polish way, but more in the German way. The client is... he can't stand Polish cuisine.

Asked to describe his activities on a typical day, he said: "It starts at about 7:45 am and ends at 10 pm. It's like that here, but I make sure I don't exceed six hours a day…working hours… I don't exceed them… I simply take the opportunity when Grandad sleeps from 1:30 to 4:30 pm. I start the preparations at 4 pm, so from 1:30 pm to 4 pm I have time for myself."

He went on to emphasise once again that he has a right to free time: "Many carers don't really know what rights they have. They don't know exactly how much.... In the beginning, I didn't know exactly how much free time I was entitled to. That's one of the things that isn't regulated enough legally…but I do what I want." Asked by the interviewer if this meant that there was someone who looked after his client during this time, Mateusz replied, "It varies…either the daughter is on the phone or the granddaughter is upstairs. I just either say that I'm away…or if I'm at home, that I'm not available for him at that time." This statement is very interesting, not only because no similar sentiments were articulated by the female interviewees, but also because Mateusz was implying that he could switch off during his breaks, in other words that the mental load did not weigh him down. He thus appeared to be able to escape the constant worry about the clients that characterised the narratives of almost all other interviewees who were the only person usually present in the care receiver's home.

When the interviewer asked: "And do you ever have to get up at night?" Mateusz answered: "No… not here. In state X,[10] when my client was dying, I already knew that I could be called at night, so I was prepared for that. He actually died around midnight."

When asked to say something about his daughter, Mateusz said that he Skyped with her from time to time, adding:

I tell myself that because she's still so little, she doesn't miss me that much yet. I don't know if I am compensating her when I give her something in addition to the maintenance money, or when I send her a parcel from Germany to Poland… But I tell myself that she's still small and doesn't miss me…. Maybe she'll need me more when she gets older…. My wife is in a new relationship, so I'm aware that there's a new man… I don't know how to say this… maybe my daughter calls him "Dad" too. I'm aware of that, I was in a situation like that too. My mum didn't remarry, but she was in a new relationship, so even though I had a biological father, I call my stepfather "Dad".

The narrative and work situation of Mateusz, a divorced single father, differs in many respects from that of the single mothers Kasia and Halina: he appeared not to be mentally burdened with the constant worry about the situation of the child left behind. Furthermore, he seemed to be able to implement his ideas of regular working hours unproblematically, and – compared to the female interviewees – he could better communicate his boundaries with respect to the family members of the care recipients.

The interviews reveal classic patterns of caregiving: despite decades of debate on overcoming gender-specific responsibility, mothers generally continue to feel primarily responsible for caregiving. In her study on the fatherhood experiences of Polish male migrants working as handymen in private households in Germany, Palenga-Möllenbeck (2016) has rightly pointed out that their work situation is similarly precarious and that separation from their families is also a significant problem for them. However, unlike migrant mothers, they do not need to justify leaving their families behind in Poland. Neither are they expected to take on care responsibilities during their absence from home; their paternal task is to generate an income. This implies that fathers face great pressures of expectations too, but they are not subjected to the same societal demands as mothers. This debate is moving slowly, and by no means necessarily in the direction of shared parenthood in terms of time, rights and finances: one indication of this situation is the discourse about so-called Euro-orphans apparently abandoned by their mothers to work abroad (see Chapter Four).

MOTHERING PRACTICES FROM A DISTANCE

As we have seen in the narratives of Halina and Kasia, mothering from a distance entails highly complex management of time and emotions that depends on maintaining good relationships with family and friends who act as "surrogate mothers". Contrary to what might be expected, the circular migration of mothers does not usually result in any redistribution of familial care obligations onto the children's fathers. Such redistribution occurs not between genders but between female members of the family network, which means that the feminine gender coding of care work remains intact. Incidentally, the interviews gave no empirical confirmation of transnational mothers arranging a care-replacement solution described by Hochschild (2000) and Parreñas (2001) in which a female migrant from an economically weaker country is recruited to mind the children and care for relatives. This finding is corroborated by other studies about care migration in Poland and Ukraine (see Kindler et al. 2016: 6; Safuta et al. 2016). In the following, I will present an overall evaluation of the range of mothering practices drawing from our interviews and analysis (see Lutz and Palenga-Möllenbeck 2011a).

Care Replacement

Transnational mothers from Eastern Europe prefer a rotation system on a four-weekly to three-monthly cycle which enables them to return to their families on a regular basis (Lutz 2007a). The majority of the migrating mothers in our samples organised their work and family lives in line with this model, representing an attempt to establish a balance between the frequency and quality of their presence with the family and the replacement organised, usually by the mothers themselves, to cover their absence. Three replacement models were identified:

1. The dominant model of childcare, confirmed in several other studies (Haidinger 2013; Solari 2017; Kindler et al. 2016; Safuta et al. 2016; Wirz 2021), is characterised by the redistribution of care work to grandmothers. Migrant women describe grandmothers (both their own mothers and their mothers-in-law) as devoted caregivers who can be relied upon. The grandmothers confirm that they gladly expend this effort for their grandchildren but often feel overtaxed by the role. Difficulties arise when there are problems at school that need to be resolved, when conflicts with adolescents flare up, and when the grandmothers feel unable to properly supervise everyday activities, such as computer games and time spent on online platforms, due to the digital divide. In addition to caring for their grandchildren, they often take charge of overseeing or instructing the stay-behind fathers in the management of household chores. As grandmothers age, however, alternatives to this care arrangement must be found.

2. Less commonplace but still found, as in the cases of Halina and Kasia, is temporary childcare performed by women friends and neighbours, who also occasionally take on paid or unpaid help with children's homework and care for older relatives. Mothers tend to describe these arrangements as unstable while the replacement caregivers – and often the grandmothers, too – report recognition problems: they feel overtaxed when they have to assume parental responsibilities. Similar problems are reported by female relatives, including aunts and older children, particularly girls when they have taken charge of caring for younger siblings.

3. In very few cases, fathers fully take on the responsibility for the care and upbringing of their children (see Chapter Five on fatherhood and masculinity). As a rule, fathers remain in employment themselves during their wives' absence and limit their involvement in care and domestic work to a few hours in the evening or at weekends. In some cases, they do not come home at all for the entire period that their wives are working abroad and stay instead

with friends or other family members, a pattern more common among businessmen.

Another model of transnational female care migration applies to women aged fifty plus who lost their jobs in the course of the system transformation and were forced to retire early (see also Satola 2015; Lutz and Palenga-Möllenbeck 2011b). This pattern of migration affects the viability of the most common care-replacement model of relying on grandmothers. These women normally cannot live on their pensions and are reliant on additional earnings. Apart from that, they want to contribute to the income and well-being of their families, perhaps to purchase consumer goods or an apartment for their children or to support their grandchildren's education at private schools and universities (see in particular Solari 2017 on Ukraine; Satola 2015 on Poland). This phenomenon also indicates that grandmothers see themselves as part of a moral economic family network and maintain very close relationships with their children and grandchildren, in part with the expectation that they will be provided with care in return when their health deteriorates.

Managing Emotions

An important component of migrant motherhood is sensitive management of emotions to maintain a balance between proximity and absence. During the 1990s and early 2000s, migrants from Eastern Europe had to limit communication with family members back home to a few telephone calls a week due to the high costs. Now, as information technologies have developed, international calls with family members by phone or via the internet are a routine part of their daily communications. Mothers are kept informed about all aspects of everyday life at home; children can contact the mothers autonomously, share everyday joys and worries, and to some extent transcend the geographical separation by communicating that they miss one another. Everyday decisions can be discussed and taken on a daily basis. School-age children's homework sessions are now being supervised and checked by their mothers; we called this "Skype mothering" (see Lutz and Palenga-Möllenbeck 2012).

The analysis of the two projects' narratives[11] supports the thesis of Baldassar and Merla (2013b) that care in the digitalised era does not flow in one direction only, but circulates within the migrants' family networks. The internet has essentially become the central tool for "doing family" in the everyday lives of transnational mothers. Care must be taken not to idealise technologies, however. Long-distance contact has its limitations and children often do not regard virtual contact as an equivalent substitute for physical proximity. Because telephone conversations rely on expressive language skills, they are not a good option for introverted children. Furthermore, a requirement for everyone involved in long-distance contact is not only a capacity to show their feelings, but also to hide them. Bad news from school or problems in the family are often impossible to solve virtually; both children and adults must learn to spare each other news that could upset the other party. There are more asymmetries: while the mothers have often internalised the daily routines of their sons and daughters, "their children are not able to indicate what exactly their mothers do for a living" write Oleana Fedyuk and Marta Kindler (2016: 5). In addition, it was evident from the interviews with the mothers that some employers feel disturbed by phone and internet calls, either because they do not understand the language or they fear that it diverts attention away from them.

Mothers try to compensate (emotionally) for their absence by intensifying their home stays, for instance, by endeavouring to be physically present for special events (the first day of school, graduation day, religious festivals, birthdays, etc.). During the time they are present at home, they are mindful of meeting the children's needs for physical touch, as well as dealing with school and family problems that may have been neglected in their absence. Consequently, these stays at home cannot be used as recreational holiday but serve primarily to compensate for their physical absence.

MOTHERHOOD IDEOLOGIES – MATERNALISMS

Feminist historians Seth Koven and Sonya Michel (1990: 1079) have characterised discourses on motherhood in the US as "ideologies that exalted women's capacity to mother and extended to society as a whole the values of care, nurturance, and morality". Elaborating on this argument in 2012, Michel described the modern image of "Western" middle-class motherhood as "romanticised maternalism" (Michel 2012: 24), which functions as a normative standard that casts any other form of mothering (such as single motherhood, single fatherhood, grandparenting etc.) as non-conforming and deficient (see also Collins 1990; Boris 1993: 104).

"Romanticised maternalism" is an idealised motherhood that reinforces universal standards for good mothering practices by proclaiming the mother – and only the mother – to be the primary caregiver, the person responsible for bringing up healthy children and productive citizens. In her seminal work *The Cultural Contradictions of Motherhood* (1996), Sharon Hays develops a similar argument, using the term "intensive mothering" to characterise a childrearing approach that is child-centred, guided by expert knowledge, emotionally absorbing, labour-intensive and financially taxing. This historically new ideology in the United States produces cultural contradictions: "The same society that disseminates an ideology urging mothers to give unselfishly of their time, money and love on behalf of sacred children, simultaneously valorises a set of ideas that runs directly counter to it, one emphasising impersonal relations between isolated individuals efficiently pursuing their personal profit" (Hays 1996: 97). The result, in Hays' view, is a moral double standard of motherhood versus employment.

Following up on Hays' work, Cameron Macdonald (2010: 22–3) observed that since the 1990s, demands on mothers in the US have only amplified. That contemporary expert research considers "the period from birth to age three as a critical time for brain development; and the notion of child perfectibility as an attainable goal, particularly for educated, affluent mothers" (ibid: 23) has led to intensive mothering becoming a myth haunting working and stay-at-home mothers alike. A survey of parents with young children conducted at the beginning of the twenty-first century "found that 92 percent believed that their children's educational success would be influenced by their birth-to-three cognitive experiences, and that 85 percent feared that if they did not provide proper stimulation, their baby's brain would not develop properly" (ibid.: 24). Macdonald convincingly demonstrates that the primacy of the "mother–infant bond" has become the commonly accepted view since the National Institute of Child Health and Human Development (NICHD) broadcast its findings in the national media that a child's sense of security depends on the bonding with the mother during early childhood (ibid.: 23). The anxieties of working mothers leaving their children in the care of fathers, grandmothers or nannies – the latter are called "shadow mothers" by Macdonald – have been exacerbated by these "expert reports".

These observations are clearly not limited to the United States, and the fear of being labelled a "bad mother" is similarly strong in Western Europe across economic classes. It is no surprise, therefore, that motherhood ideologies have been subject to repeated questioning, deconstruction and attack in the feminist literature. French historian Elisabeth Badinter (2013) shows in her book on the new maternalism that since contraceptive pills became available for the majority of women (in industrialised countries), pregnancy and childbirth are no longer seen as an inevitable fate but a well-considered choice. Motherhood as a choice must be shaped and proactively performed; the discourse about motherhood has accordingly changed, Badinter suggests, in that women have been confronted with myriad new demands concerning the performance of good motherhood. These demands translate into various ideological struggles – ideological crusades – since the 1970s in France and other Western countries: for instance, the standpoint that a good mother should breastfeed for as long as possible to prevent allergies and illnesses (Badinter 2013: 69 ff.), or the recommendation to let children sleep in their mother's bed up to the age of four to meet the need of small children for security (ibid.: 101 ff.). Badinter suggests that these views are driven by the ideological embrace of a biologistic framework that militates against combining motherhood with paid work. This framework builds on the attachment model developed by the British child psychiatrist and psychoanalyst John Bowlby (1958), to establish that the dyadic relationship between mother and child has an exclusive and fundamental status in evolution and is therefore indispensable for the child's healthy development. In the 1980s, as Badinter shows, this mutated into the exaltation of motherhood and emphasis on maternal responsibility. Ideas along this vein, promoted by child psychologists and by health and education experts, have not disappeared despite the rising proportion of women in the workforce, and at the beginning of the twenty-first century are in fact flourishing. One manifestation of what Naomi Mezey and Cornelia Pillard call the "new maternalism" can be seen online in blogs, internet advocacy groups and discussion boards (Mezey and Pillard 2012). Unlike its predecessors, the new maternalism no longer propounds the belief that the private domain and the world of work are separate spheres, or that the place of the good mother is in the kitchen or the home; instead, it is rooted in the fundamental assumption that mothers are simply the ideal parents and irreplaceable in this capacity (ibid.). Accordingly, counter to the diagnosis of Ann Orloff (2006), maternalism has not disappeared but is integrating changing social trends, such as the quest for (self-)optimisation as women gather in mothers' forums to exchange views on (the organisation of) good mothering.

The new maternalism now also has a foothold in post-socialist Central and Eastern Europe, where pro-natalist trends have gained currency with support not only from the Catholic and Orthodox churches but also (ultra-)nationalist parties, manifesting in attempts to heavily restrict access to abortion, notably in Poland. The exaltation of motherhood is both a central element of the nationalistic symbolism of the new nation–states (Skocpol 1992; Verdery 1994; Kis 2007; Solari 2017) and a central object of family and employment policies. Today motherhood is regarded as one of women's civic duties. In place of the socialist ideal of equality – although this was never realised in the private sphere (Kałwa 2008: 124) – came a new understanding of femininity that idealised and propagated the role of the housewife and mother (Michoń 2009). According to Marta Trzebiatowska (2013: 207) this is rooted in an underlying conviction that a heterosexual relationship and the ability to bear children are essential for a woman's self-fulfilment: "Having a child means having a real, useful, purposeful and dignified femininity" (Środa 2009: 84, quoted in Trzebiatowska 2013: 208). It can be concluded that what Raewyn Connell calls "emphasised femininity" stands at the centre of a new (and yet old) conception of womanhood that "contributes to the global dominance of men over women through a social performance in which the key features are compliance, nurturance and empathy" (Connell 1987: 188).

Trzebiatowska (2013) argues convincingly that post-socialist Central and Eastern Europe has witnessed a cultural change favouring new forms and hierarchies of femininity and social performances by women of "compliance, nurturance and empathy". This shift is a culmination of changes in the political system, including the abolition of the infrastructure of care combined with an almost total ban on abortion in Poland and policies such as extended maternal leave periods in most of the post-socialist countries. Moreover, there is a longstanding history of iconography in Poland and Ukraine in which motherhood and nation are linked to symbolic figures, for example the Matka Polka (Mother Poland) and the Ukrainian mother goddess Berehynia. Idealising women's sacrifice and suffering for the sake of the nation, these emblematic figures continue to inform dominant constructions of womanhood (Korolczuk and Hryciuk 2010; Hrycak 2005).

Research on East European motherhood has often overlooked the "Western" influence on the reconfiguration of motherhood ideals. In a globalising world in which ideas and ideals cross borders via the web, or travel with markets and people, the trends described by Michel, Badinter, or Mezey and Pillard find their equivalent in post-socialism. In her article about the "new motherhood" in Poland, Malgorzata Sikorska analyses women's magazines from 1990 to the beginning of the 2000s and reconstructs heated debates about the importance of long and intensive natural breastfeeding (Sikorska 2009: 174). Investigating Polish mothers' internet forums, Marta Olcon-Kubicka (2009) characterises the new popularity of becoming a mother among young middle-class women as a "mission", not for the state, but for oneself as an individual "do-it-yourself-project". These are some of many examples from the Polish literature, and similar developments can be observed in other countries of the region. In an article about changing mothering concepts across generations, from mothers who came of age during socialism to their "post-socialist" daughters, Polish sociologists Elzbieta Korolczuk and Renata Hryciuk (2013) describe the frustration of many daughters about how neoliberal society insists on women's obligation to become happy and enthusiastic mothers even though the state has retreated from child care provision. As a result, many women juggle their dual responsibilities as workers and mothers on their own, in accordance with the prevailing ideology that greater freedom of choice implies individual responsibility for one's own success and happiness.

Poland and other CEE countries are therefore experiencing a development similar to that in the US: in the absence of state provision, mothers of young children and daughters of ageing parents turn to the "market" of migrant caregivers. For Polish mothers who are affluent, hiring a nanny – often from Ukraine or Belarus – has become a way to balance work–life requirements. Out of all Polish middle-class households that employ domestic workers, ten percent employ migrants, of which Ukrainian women make up the largest group (Golinowska 2010). In other words, Poland does not only send caregivers to countries like Germany, the UK, Austria, Italy and Spain but is also a receiving country, at the crossroads of two transnational care chains (Lutz and Palenga-Möllenbeck 2011a, 2011b, 2012, 2015; Palenga-Möllenbeck 2014).

In part, differences in these care trends in Poland, Ukraine and other East European countries reflect their differing geopolitical situations. The high proportion of female migration reflects women's and mothers' readiness to move for the sake of their families even in the context of the deterioration of state-run care facilities. "New mothering" may not be as "hot" a topic in Ukrainian society, but the "failed mothering" of migrant mothers was and is certainly an issue of public discourse (see Chapter Four on Euro-orphans).

Today we have reached a point where gender relations in Eastern and Western Europe have converged: women are trying to combine good mothering and employment even though the necessary prerequisites, notably the de-gendering of care work, are not in place. However, while members of the middle classes in affluent parts of the world or in relatively well-off parts of transition countries can enlist the support of nannies and caregivers as substitute or "shadow mothers" (MacDonald 2010) to support them in providing their children with optimal care, this is a tightrope act that the transnational mothers cannot pull off. Since both sides are measured – and indeed measure themselves – against the same ideal of motherhood, there are obvious asymmetries.

EMOTIONAL INEQUALITY – A COMPONENT OF TRANSNATIONAL SOCIAL INEQUALITY

While exponents of the global care chain approach (Hochschild 2000; Parreñas 2001) characterise the stay-behind children and family members in the sending countries as losers from care migration, the case studies of Halina and Kasia exemplify that most of all it is the migrant mothers themselves who suffer from being separated from their children and regard it as the greatest work-related burden they have to bear. Remarks such as these signal an issue that I have neglected in my previous publications. While I have emphasised in many essays (Lutz 2015, 2016) and in my last book on this theme (Lutz 2011) that transnational mothers are plagued by immense feelings of guilt, I nevertheless took the view that given the millions of women worldwide practising mothering from a distance on a daily basis, the force of reality would contribute to an overhaul of the idealisation of the mother–child relationship so that, in the long run, care-replacement solutions would be recognised as a caregiving practice of equivalent value. I espoused this position primarily as a contribution to de-dramatising an ideologically heated debate and to the repudiation of stigmatising discourses (mother blaming). Nevertheless, in doing so, I overlooked the fact that the mothers' emotions are not affected by discourses on motherhood alone and that they are indeed denied the right to look after their own children.

The right to emotionally nurture and care for one's own child and to attend to their emotional needs is, as Maria Kontos (2013) writes, a human right that migrant women have to largely forgo. The separation enforced by the work situation should therefore be considered an important element of transnational social inequality (see Palenga-Möllenbeck 2013).

The narratives of female migrant caregivers indicate that care is not just work but is based on the reciprocal exchange of emotions, reciprocal care and continuous (physical) contact. If mothers are physically absent, this exchange can be interrupted and lasting disturbances can occur. Geraldine Pratt (2012), evaluating the Canadian Live-In Caregiver Program, concludes that state protection of the needs of the middle class gives rise to geopolitical hierarchies of motherhood. She critiques the public presentation of this model as a triple-win model (for Canadian middle-class employers, migrant nannies and their families, and the migrants' home countries as the recipients of remittances). Pratt notes that while it grants Canadian families the right to protect their familial intimacy and to provide their children with optimal conditions for development, the programme denies migrant women's children any such protection and they are effectively deemed underserving of it; the underlying implication is that female migrants have made a rational choice for which they themselves must bear the consequences (Pratt 2012: 164). Pratt refers to this attitude as "normative nationalism" (ibid.). Her analysis does not map directly onto the situation of East European women migrants because the Canadian programme does not recognise circular migration and assumes migrant mothers will be absent full-time for at least two years. Comparable elements, however, are the legitimisation strategy (triple win) and the way that the care-receiving countries ignore the emotional consequences for children and mothers. Although the European Union repeatedly emphasises the human right to family life, this has not been followed up by social and governmental interventions to make the employers of care migrants aware of these rights and to support migrant women in finding a way of living with their children in one household. The sending-countries support this status quo because they are unwilling to forgo the remittances, and consider the loyalty of migrant women to their children and family as a civic duty. From what has been described as motherly dilemmas in this chapter, it can be concluded that normative maternalism results in a situation where no party supports the interests of women care workers. Emotional inequality, or forgoing the physical and emotional care of one's own children, thus remains a hidden component of transnational motherhood.

4

Euro-Orphans: Transnational Motherhood Under Pressure

One of the most tenacious instances of universalism – the belief in the universality of something – is motherhood, doubtlessly the most intimate of relationships. The current state of the allegedly globalised world makes this universalism both urgently necessary and deeply problematic. (Bal 2012: 119)

This quotation from literary theorist Mieke Bal aptly illustrates the ambivalent status of motherhood for migrant women, who as bread-winners perform a key function in improving their families' quality of life, yet are simultaneously expected – and expect themselves – to meet the normative requirements of being a "good mother". The previous chapter looked at the circumstances in which migrant mothers are compelled to combine gainful employment with care work from a distance. Ideas and practices of motherhood are by no means universal; they are not only subject to cultural, social, religious and regional norming but have also changed over time (Koven and Michel 1993; Michel 1999; Hochschild 2012). Nevertheless, the global invocation of the mother as the central figure of family and kinship networks retains its universality. This chapter sets out to examine motherhood once again, but from a different angle: it discusses the scaremongering media coverage over more than a decade about how children, dubbed Euro-orphans, suffer as a result of the physical absence of their mothers who have gone to work abroad, leaving their children in the care of family members. Although conducted primarily in the media of the East European sending countries, this debate was picked up by the Western press and continues transnationally today.

The chapter ends by analysing the Euro-orphans discourse in terms of three complementary explanatory models. First, the orphans debate is interpreted as an expression of moral panic crystallising diverse and contradictory fears, as well as resentment against social inequities and rapid social and economic change; here a historical parallel is drawn with the debate about "latchkey" children in the 1940s and 1950s. Second, the debate corresponds with negative evaluations and rejections of transnational motherhood in both sending and receiving countries. Motherhood from a distance is viewed by experts (psychologists, pedagogues, teachers) as detrimental to children's development, and mothering practices carried out from a distance are labelled as deficient. Third, the discursive figure of the orphan is being inflamed by transnational organisations and agreements (the UN convention on the rights of the child, UNESCO, World Vision, Save the Children, etc.) with the help of reports decrying the neglect of several million children worldwide by their migrating parents, mothers in particular. The conclusion to be drawn is that this debate ignores and diverts attention from the vast global diversity of upbringing contexts and child-rearing practices. Instead, the physical presence of mothers as the central figures caring for and bringing up their biological children is constructed as the indispensable prerequisite for successful family life. Their presence is thus held up as a central evaluative and normative standard for healthy and successful childhood, while their absence is identified as the cause of lasting traumatic problems.

EURO-ORPHANS AND SOCIAL ORPHANS

Children of migrating mothers are referred to variously as "left-behind children", "home-alone children", "abandoned children" (Romania), "social orphans" (Ukraine), "Euro-orphans" (Poland) and "white orphans" (Moldova). It is not possible to trace the beginning of this debate back to one Central or East European country in particular; as outlined in this chapter, the first signs are found in the Ukrainian press as early as 2005 but it is likely that the issue first came to the attention of the Western media as a result of reporting about Romania. For example, on March 25, 2007 the British newspaper *The Daily Telegraph* chose the headline "Suffering Grips Europe's Nation of Orphans" for an article in which the suicide of a child in a Romanian village was narrated in this way:

> Last March, Razvan Suculiuc walked home from school in the village of Ciorteşti, fed the chickens, went to the woodshed and hanged himself. He was 10 years old. [...] His mother, Liliane, had abandoned the bar job that paid her £100 a month and had gone to Italy to work as a maid, leaving Razvan in the care of his unemployed father [...] Maybe he missed her more than she realised. (Chamberlain 2007: n.p.)

A year later, Germany's *Süddeutsche Zeitung* published an article that cited the same case entitled "Abandoned to the Orphanage. Thousands of Romanian Parents Leave Their Children in the Lurch, Due in No Small Part to Humanitarian Assistance from the West." To quote the article:

> When Razvan Suculiuc hanged himself because his mother had left him alone in Romania, he was only ten years old. The case was all over the European press in 2006, but soon forgotten again nevertheless. And this child's lonely life is not an isolated case. More than 100,000 children and young people are currently growing up without parents in Romania. Yet hardly any of them are genuine orphans. In fact, a sizeable share of children and young people are still being left in the lurch by their parents, as in communist times. This is due in no small part to humanitarian assistance from the West. [...]. Despite being well intentioned, this assistance has fatal consequences. It motivates Romanian parents simply to give up their children, on the principle that "they're better off in the home, anyway, than with us," says René Mérite. (Brüning 2010 [2008][1]: n.p.)

The fact that Razvan had been left in the custody of his father, which *The Daily Telegraph* had mentioned a year earlier, has disappeared from the story this article tells. More will be said about the absence of fathers in media coverage in the course of this chapter. As these examples attest, the Western media tends to frame stories, particularly in the case of Romania, in such a way as to establish some link with the former regime's brutal handling of reproductive issues (prohibiting abortion, hospitalising disabled children, and neglecting children in orphanages). Neither article cites any sources, so it is unclear where the statistics about the "nation of orphans" might have come from. Rather than analysing the causes of this so-called orphaning of children in any depth, they decry crude parenting practices by pointing to their dark, communist antecedents.

The underlying reasons for the mothers' emigration are examined more thoroughly in the film *Price of Hearts*, produced with support from the US (Christian) aid organisation World Vision, along with Youth Services America and the Disney Foundation, and released online in 2009.[2] Even so, it makes the claim that 350,000 Romanian children under the age of ten were traumatised by being left behind by their parents, without analysing the families' care practices. The film is a highly professional production: accompanied by tragic music that reinforces its emotional tenor, it identifies the absence of the mother as the cause of every child's suffering and at no point turns its scrutiny on any male parent. It advocates that children accompany mothers where they are working, which is not a real option for most mothers, as multiple accounts in this book testify. The characterisation of these children as orphans in the film and these articles is factually incorrect, as the majority of the non-migrating children remain in the custody of relatives – with their mothers when fathers migrate, or with their grandmothers or other female relatives where the mother is the migrant. As already shown in Chapters Two and Three and will be explored more specifically in Chapter Five, the male partners of migrant mothers are less frequently expected to discharge this duty than female family members, including older daughters. The use of the emotive term "orphans" to characterise these children has far-reaching consequences for the assessment of female migration and the problematisation of transnational motherhood. In some sending countries, the orphan debate has already culminated in the introduction of legal measures aimed at discouraging the practice of leaving children behind. Another consequence is social pressure on mothers, who are called upon to return home.

In the following, I present the results of a comprehensive media analysis of Polish and Ukrainian newspapers between 1997 and 2008[3] that demonstrate radical changes in the public perception of Polish and Ukrainian migrant mothers.[4] This analysis covers a timespan that began a few years after the system transition, at a time when women migrants were praised as modernisers and innovators and admired as "Euro-migrants", and continued until about a decade thereafter, when the tone and appraisal decisively changed. Parents were then accused of being incapable and irresponsible, and mothers in particular were criticised for bad mothering.

The intention of the media analysis carried out in the context of the "Landscapes of Care Drain" research project was to collect articles about migration, transnational families, parenting and care in a broad sense.[5] Our assumption had been that in the first decade after the system transition, the debates in the two sending countries, Poland and Ukraine, would revolve largely around reports and assessments concerning the opening of labour markets, work opportunities abroad and the associated (positive) consequences of migration. We had also expected to find discussion of (the consequences of) female migration. The fact that the latter was reflected principally in national debates about left-behind or "abandoned children", which took off around 2005 in Ukraine and in Poland two years later, was something that we had not anticipated. In order to contextualise this shift in the discourse, I will give a short overview of the findings from the data analysis and then turn the focus to the orphans debate, starting with Poland and then moving to the findings from Ukraine.[6]

Poland

Poland has had a long tradition of labour migration from the nineteenth century onwards and particularly since the beginning of the twentieth century, both to the mining regions of Germany and the industrial centres in the north of the US. Under state socialism after World War II, the prototype of East–West migration was established by refugees from the socialist bloc who left without any prospect of returning. Meanwhile, seasonal and short-term labour migration occurred only within the socialist bloc; for instance, Polish workers did seasonal work in agriculture in the

German Democratic Republic (GDR). Following the liberalisation of border regimes after 1989, this pattern changed fundamentally; in principle, emigration to countries in the West was now possible, but circular transnational migration became the dominant form for men and women, whereby migrants commute to their places of work at intervals ranging from one week to several months while their families stay behind. Since the early 1990s, around ten percent of the Polish population has been involved in this shuttle migration.[7] This new form of work–life balance is favoured by women migrants.

The analysis we[8] carried out draws on 316 articles (1997–2008) from the following national daily newspapers: *Gazeta Wyborcza* (left–liberal), the conservative *Rzeczpospolita*, the tabloid *FAKT* and the Silesian regional newspaper *Nowa Trybuna Opolska* (chosen because of Silesia's importance as a migrant-sending region). In all the Polish newspapers that we analysed, the evaluation of migration between 1998 and 2007 was mostly approving, focusing on its positive effects on Polish political and economic life, among which were the reduction of unemployment, the easing of the burden on social security funds and better vocational training opportunities abroad, while the advantages of migrants' remittances for investment in Poland were highlighted. Depending on the ideological orientation of the newspaper, labour migration was presented as an expression of entrepreneurship, an individual and collective success story or a strategy for overcoming crisis. *Gazeta Wyborcza* (GW) focused primarily on the social aspects of migration, including complex issues such as the situation of national minorities or the negative consequences of the emigration of skilled workers. Meanwhile, *Rzeczpospolita* (RZ) was more interested in favourable coverage of the introduction of a liberal market regime, individual freedom and independent entrepreneurship, which included reporting on efforts to combat the increasing shortage of workers through employer-specific managed migration of temporary workers from Ukraine, Belarus and Russia. We found it remarkable that prior to 2007, female migration was more implicitly than explicitly addressed, for example in coverage of prostitution and human trafficking on the Polish–German border (three articles in *Gazeta Wyborcza*, one in *Rzeczpospolita*). Polish women's increasing involvement in migration was primarily taken up in stories about the marriage of "Polish brides" to partners from "Old Europe". Three articles in *Gazeta Wyborcza* dealt with Ukrainian care workers in Polish urban middle-class households, and with rising numbers of Polish women in early retirement (aged 50+) heading for Germany or Austria, but not a single article dealt with the working conditions of Polish women in households abroad.

In the autumn of 2007, a major change occurred when public discourse switched from relative silence on any negative or problematic social consequences of migration to a sudden and lively interest in the stay-behind children of labour migrants. The debate was triggered by a seemingly unspectacular event, the class presentation of a short documentary film entitled *Alex Home Alone*, produced by an 18-year-old named Aleksander Makowiak and his classmates (GW; 28 December 2007). For his final project as a student of Computer Science at the Poznan Transport School, Makowiak chose the theme of children whose parents migrate to work abroad and played himself in the film. At the time of filming, his father had left over a year earlier to work in the Netherlands to be followed six months later by his mother, his younger brother, their dog and their tortoise. This story was the starting point of the documentary, which showed Alex coping with daily life once he was left "home alone" in the family's flat. The screenplay focused mainly on humorous situations, such as Alex having to peel potatoes for the first time in his life or posting sticky notes all over the flat to remind himself to deal with the household waste, the mailbox and different foods, as well as how to operate the heating and electrical appliances. All in all, it describes an adolescent's passage to independence and the growing maturity of a young man for whom all these activities were alien because, until then, they had all been done for him – presumably by his mother. An article about this film in *Gazeta Wyborcza* sparked off a series of further reports, with the upshot that the film was uploaded to YouTube and international newspapers picked up the story. For example, the Dutch daily *De Volkskrant* (Hunin 2008) announced in an article headlined "Euro-orphan, Abandoned with Little Brother, Dog and Turtle" that hundreds of thousands of workers were leaving their children behind in Poland. In an interview with the Dutch journalist, however, Makowiak expressed a very positive view of his parents' migration and emphasised the opportunities it would give him. Moreover, he said that he – not his parents – had decided that he would stay behind and only follow the family once he had finished school.

The media furore provoked by the film cannot be explained without mentioning another event: the publication of a study commissioned by two Polish NGOs, the European Law Foundation and the European Institute in Warsaw, about the impact of labour migration on families that looked particularly at the problems of stay-behind children, identifying them as "Euro-orphans" in the report's title (Majchrzyk-Mikuła 2008: 3). The term "Euro-orphans" (*Eurosieroctwo*) made its first appearance in the article published in *Gazeta Wyborcza* about the documentary *Alex Home Alone* in late 2007 (GW; 28 December 2007). The newspaper then pursued the issue, printing 50 articles about it over a period of 17 months. The immense impact of the term "Euro-orphans" is evident from the way it advanced to become the central metaphor of the debate that has continued to rage ever since. The term rapidly became a buzzword used across both the press and research reports (e.g. Majchrzyk-Mikuła 2008: 3), although no clear definition was ever given of the precise situation it described. A representative of the Poznan education department in western Poland, for example, claimed that children living with one parent while the other parent worked abroad were exposed to the same apparently detrimental effects as those of divorced parents, while some scholars asserted that such children manifested the same behaviours as actual orphans (Hunin 2008). The prefix "Euro", which had until then been used in the press with very positive connotations in terms such as "Euro-migrants" and "Euro-labour" following the opening of Western labour markets to Polish workers in 2003, suddenly acquired more negative connotations. *Gazeta Wyborcza's* coverage of "Euro-orphans" during the first year of the debate typically featured outraged headlines such as: "Orphans Because Parents Migrated" (GW; 28 December 2007); "Almost 8,000 Euro-Orphans in the Province of Lodz" (GW; 27 January 2008); "110,000 Euro-Orphans in Poland are Expecting Help" (GW; 12 May 2008); "Who helps the Euro-orphans?" (GW;

13 May 2008); "Parents Earn Lots of Money and Their Children are Suffering" (GW; 19 July 2008); "Parents are Not Replaceable" (GW; 12 August 2008); "The Government Counts Euro-orphans; Parents Do Not Keep Their Promise to Return" (GW; 16 August 2008); "Do Not Forsake Your Children" (GW; 11 September 2008); "Read This Before You Leave Your Child" (GW; 3 October 2008). The evocative statements and moral appeals were often reinforced with images (see Figure 4.1).

The indignant tone of the articles about the situation of the left-behind children was legitimised by quotations from experts – psychologists, teachers, police officers and politicians – describing the behaviour of the children as pathological. However, in July 2008, *Gazeta Wyborcza* covered the release of a report commissioned by the Ombudsperson for Children's Rights in an article entitled "Schools Are Not Supporting the Euro-Orphans" (GW; 3 July 2008). The report summarised the findings of a survey of school children about the effects of their parents' labour migration.

To conduct the study, sociologist Bartlomiej Walczak polled 2,597 children in 110 schools. First of all, Walczak's findings refuted the staggering figure, mentioned time and time again in the press, of 110,000 Polish Euro-orphans. He emphasised, instead, that the majority of the parents living apart from their families for longer than a year were fathers, rather than mothers who were usually found to be physi-

Figure 4.1   Euro-Orphan
© Wojciech Druszcz

cally absent for shorter periods. Based on his findings, Walczak calculated that there were actually 3,000 to 6,000 children aged between nine and 18 who were living apart from *both* parents for a period of one year or more; however, as they usually spent this time in the home of relatives, such as a grandmother or an aunt, it was wrong to describe them as orphans (Walczak 2008: 32). Although this report gave the press every reason to revise its statistical exaggerations, no ensuing re-evaluation of the Euro-orphans discourse took place.

An important finding from our analysis of the Euro-orphans debate was that most of the newspaper articles begin by holding the parents responsible for the situation of the stay-behind children rather than mothers specifically, but as soon as the reporting goes into detail, the mothers are brought to the fore. Often mothers are not directly pilloried but their (physical) absence is decried in emotive terms by describing their children's problems:

15-year-old Maciek walked for three days through the streets and slept at friends' homes. While the police, his teacher and his father searched for him, his mother who had left the country for work did not. (GW; 12 May 2008)

Bartek slips into the sleeve of a blouse that his mother had left behind and falls asleep. The soft fabric smells like Joanna. [...] He pulls on the blouse and wraps the sleeves around him, as if they would embrace him. When he feels the warmth and her smell, his stomach does not hurt any more. (RZ; 22 January 2008)

Only a very small number of articles quote positive comments from stay-behind children in relation to their mother's migration. To cite one example:

Marta, 18 years old: "I have learned that even if Mummy isn't nearby, she's still close. Not just because we talk every day [via telecommunication, H.L.] about whatever was going on – we are almost telepathically in contact. When I miss her so terribly that I can't stand it anymore, she feels exactly the same; from time to time, I get on a plane and just fly to see her. Luckily, she doesn't live on the other side of the world." (GW; 21 May 2008)

Throughout the press reporting, there is a conspicuous absence of fathers. This must also have struck the journalists at *Gazeta Wyborcza* because they initiated a discussion on the theme of fatherhood published with the headline "Dethronement of the Father as God". Four female panellists – two literary scholars and two actors – debated whether fathers used to spend more time with their families than they do today, remarkably concluding that the physical presence of fathers is not significant to their fathering:

The women explained that fathers never used to be at home. The role of fathers had been limited to either fighting in the war or dying in concentration camps, or else leaving Poland completely as intellectual migrants. In the view of the women experts, the symbolic position of fathers meant that they did not need to be physically present at all, for their status and power remained intact despite their absence. Fathers had had a godlike position which was not conducive to close relationships between fathers and children. The women experts conclude that while the theme of absent parents was being taken up again in the shape of the Euro-orphans, countless examples from literature proved that it was not a new phenomenon. (GW; 7 January 2008)

While the absence of the father remains a normal characteristic of migration, it is nevertheless playing a part in restructuring the family (compared to the socialist era):

Sabina, 19 years old: Father emigrated two years ago. His friend who had found himself work in Norway persuaded him. He drove away and everything improved. Previously, he always had to stay away in Warsaw or Lublin for a whole week. He would come back on a Friday night and leave again on Saturday morning. He was always tired and slept a lot. Mum worked too – up to 12 hours a day, and at night she cooked the meals. Now she no longer has to work, she is always at home; she cleans and we always have lunch together. And we talk to Dad every day via Skype, we see each other via webcam. Every two months, he comes home for two or three weeks. Then we go for a drive and have a barbecue with Granny, walk along the Wisłok [River], and play volleyball. In Norway, he has completely changed his perspective on life, because the people there devote a lot of time to their families, and that's what he does now. (GW; 21 May 2008)

Sabina's account illustrates a coping strategy that not only normalises her father's periodic absence and evaluates it positively but also affirms a shift towards a conservative family constellation in which the father becomes the sole breadwinner and the mother is a housewife. Here, normalisation buttresses the establishment of a gender order that was an exception in the years of state socialism and its dual-breadwinner system (see Lutz and Palenga-Möllenbeck 2014).

*Ukraine**

The majority of Ukrainian labour migrants (*zarobitchany*) work as undocumented (care) workers in western and southern Europe or in Russia. While migration to Russia is dominated by male migrants from the Russian-speaking eastern part of the country, migrants from the western part of Ukraine, predominantly women, head for Poland, Italy, Austria, Germany, Spain, Turkey and Greece. As already mentioned, labour migration was not uncommon during the communist era. There were women who operated as transnational business travellers and engaged in a kind of import–export trade between countries in the socialist bloc, smuggling consumer goods that were in short supply in the other country, providing them with a comfortable (additional) income (see Lutz 2007b). However, the great majority of migrants from the Ukrainian Soviet Socialist Republic (1922–91) to other republics of the Soviet Union were male, organised as working brigades and deployed temporarily. Female migration on a large scale was a new phenomenon for Ukraine, as it was for Poland. The number of Ukrainian (commuter) migrants in 2016 was 12.5 million (IOM 2016: 10), corresponding to a population share of 30 percent.[9]

* Since the Russian invasion in February 2022, the Ukrainian situation has changed completely. This analysis, however, reflects the situation before the attack.

For the analysis of the Ukrainian press, we selected 616 articles (1997–2008) from the national newspapers *Fakty i Kommentary* (abbreviated as FiK; a populist tabloid publishing in Russian), *Ukraina Moloda* (UM; conservative–liberal, publishing in Ukrainian), the regional newspaper *Lvivs'ka Gazeta Visnyk Mista* (LG; conservative-patriotic) and the tabloid newspaper *15 Minut* (published in Russian and Ukrainian, distributed free of charge). In post-communist Ukraine, the ideological orientations of the newspapers vary between pro-Russian and anti-Russian positions, along a linguistic boundary that is generally identified as dividing the eastern (pro-Russian) and western (anti-Russian) parts of the country. We selected newspapers representing both orientations.

In contrast to Poland, there was already heightened media interest in the situation of women migrants in the early 2000s: for example, the press covered human trafficking, prostitution and white slavery as migration risks affecting women. Altogether, about 30 percent of all the articles we analysed dealt with these gender-specific dangers.

In 2004, public controversy flared up around comments made by the president two years earlier. During a state visit to Italy in 2002, then Ukrainian President Leonid Kuchma had labelled Ukrainian migrant women doing care work in Italian households as prostitutes who were too lazy to work in Ukraine (Solari 2017: 42; Keryk 2004). It was a remark that was not picked up by the Ukrainian press at the time. Only during the Orange Revolution did leading politicians associated with the uprising, Yulia Tymoshenko and Viktor Yushchenko, quote and shame Kuchma for this remark in their election campaigns, and in contrast they praised migrants as mobile, modern and diligent citizens: "It is not the sluggards who are leaving. Only the best are leaving Ukraine, those who take on responsibility for their families and those who are able to overcome difficulties" (Tymoshenko quoted in UM; 15 September 2004). For the time being, women migrants were lauded as heroines, dismissing any characterisation of them as prostitutes or victims. After taking office in 2005, President Yushchenko apologised for his predecessor's remarks and asked the Ukrainian migrants abroad to return, pledging that he would improve economic conditions. In contrast, Tymoshenko adopted a somewhat different attitude, praising the women migrants living abroad for supporting the

Ukrainian economy with their remittances. As part of her election campaign, she visited the Ukrainian diaspora in Naples and took a team of filmmakers along. In 2007 this footage was released as a 60-minute documentary film entitled *Mother–Stepmother* (Мати Мачуха) in Ukrainian theatres, cinemas and on television. Here "mother" refers to the Ukrainian state, which is not in a position to "care" for its "children", whereas stepmother Italy is wealthy and comes to the economic rescue of Ukrainians but cannot reach or feed their souls. It is addressed principally to Ukrainian diaspora voters and is organised predominantly around the figure of Tymoshenko as an icon or "a great mother goddess and the mother of the nation" (Kis 2007: 40). At the same time, the most important protagonists of *Mother–Stepmother* are Ukrainian women migrants, whose patriotism and willingness to make sacrifices for their families and their homeland are foregrounded. As the symbolic mother of the nation, Tymoshenko rails in dramatic terms against the wicked traitor Kuchma, whose "tongue she would like to cut off" (quotation from *Mother–Stepmother*). The emphasis on the motherhood metaphor is contextualised by Cinzia Solari (2017: 28) as follows: "After a Soviet state-driven ideology that celebrated unity and collectivism, Ukraine now wrestles with competing notions of morality concerned with balancing individual and collective interests and pursuit of wealth. [...] Therefore, changes in markets, moralities and motherhood are closely intertwined in Ukraine."

In the context of our press analysis, it is important to emphasise that neither in this film nor, with a few exceptions, in other articles pre-dating 2005 were migrant women blamed for abandoning their children. It was the West Ukrainian newspaper *Lvivs'ka Gazeta* that started the controversy about the neglected families of women migrants (LG; "Abandoned Children", 23 March 2005; "The Orphans Whose Parents Are Alive", 14 July 2005) and first referred to these children as "social orphans", which otherwise refers to destitute street children. Interestingly, it took another two years for the national press to pick this up. Even as it did, however, *Lvivs'ka Gazeta* has remained the leader of this debate. As in Poland, articles about social orphans were illustrated with scandalous reports about migrants allegedly leaving their children in the custody of children's homes.[10] *Lvivs'ka Gazeta* included interviews with experts to buttress its reporting. An interview with Iryna Kurevina, a researcher at the National Institute for Strategic Studies in Lviv, for example, includes the following quote:

It is important to change our legislation. For example, the passport authorities should deny those citizens who are parents of minors permission to migrate. In Stryj an investigation was conducted and it was found that children with parents abroad are bad performers in school. They miss more lessons but they have more money and can therefore afford more. This is a serious problem, which we call social orphaning. (LG; 29 August 2006)

By 2007, the nationwide daily *Fakty i Kommentary* had picked up the issue with a story headlined: "Mummy, Why Are You Working in Italy if Father Drinks Everything You Send Us? Please Come Back, Mummy, My Brother and I Will Care for You" (FiK; 14 June 2007). The story begins with a telephone call to *FiK*'s editor by a 12-year-old girl who said that her mother had been working in Rome for the last four years. Asking whether it was true that *Fakty* was read by Ukrainians abroad, she invited the journalist to visit her village so that she could tell him about her "motherless life" in the hope that mothers would read the article and finally return. The journalist presented a gripping story in which several voices were mobilised: those of the girl and her brother, their grandmother and those of teachers and regional politicians. It vividly described the rapidly changing environment and economy of a once-prosperous village that was now dependent on the flow of remittances from women migrants working in Italy, "like a patient on an intravenous drip" (ibid.: n.p.). It also highlighted the phenomenon of the total withdrawal of fathers from their care responsibilities. In the words of the girl's grandmother, Anna Stepanova:

The second problem is my son-in-law. He started drinking and going out with women. I scold him: "Why don't you work, why don't you look after yourself and the children, why don't you help in the household?" And he said to me: "Leave me in peace, mother. Why should I work when my wife sends me money?" He's always going out with friends; time after time he has seen to it that all the monthly income my daughter sent us was wasted on alcohol. And these problems affect almost all our men whose wives are earning money abroad! Almost all young married women have left the village. (ibid.: n.p.)

This article is typical of many others in the way that it portrays the mothers' migration primarily as a personal choice and not an economic necessity for the families. The misery of the children and the hardships of the grandmother, who considers herself a poor substitute for her daughter as primary caregiver, as well as the father's becoming an alcoholic, are framed as the logical consequences of the mother's migration and as contributing to the emergence of "social orphanhood". The journalist fails to engage critically with the term "orphans", meaning that there is little or no consideration of the economic and social failings of the political system.

The same facts could be presented as a story about a highly intelligent and self-reliant young girl from the countryside who, at the age of twelve, has the courage to call a journalist she does not know and ask him to tell her story. Not even a teenager, she has the maturity and capacity for insight to tell her mother that she should get rid of her husband:

Please tell our mother we love her and we're waiting for her! [...] We're very lonely and it's difficult without her. Why does she have to live in Italy when almost everything she sends home is wasted on alcohol by our father? He doesn't come home, he doesn't play with us, he never buys anything for us. He even refuses to plant potatoes in the garden, my brother and I can hardly manage. Mummy, come home, throw my father out of the house because he doesn't love you or us. My brother and I will care for you, I promise you! We are great housekeepers and good learners. Please come back, please! (ibid.: n.p.)

This story could also have been written in other ways: as one about a close and loving relationship between a grandmother and her two grandchildren, who are socially and emotionally extremely capable, good students in school and diligent helpers in the household, or one about a mother in the most challenging circumstances making an immense financial investment in her children's education, for example. It might have become a different story if the journalist had called the mother and asked for her perspective. But the mother in this story – as in almost all the others – is the great absentee; her voice goes unheard.

In the autumn of 2007, when La Strada International[11] based in Kiev published the results of a survey on "The Problems of Migrant Workers' Children", a national debate about "social orphans" was already on the ascendant. While the report took a favourable view of the migrant parents' intent to support their children, it went on to focus on social orphanhood as an undesired consequence. La Strada developed materials for distribution in schools aimed at parents planning to migrate: parents were advised to send regular monthly remittances to the family, involve the children in their decision to migrate and inform their teachers and the school psychologist about their (temporary) absences. Over the years, La Strada also organised meeting points in internet cafés where children were given access to internet telephony so that they could stay in contact with their parents. Another catalyst for a nation-wide debate was a competition for children and adolescents launched by the Institute for Education, Culture and Diaspora in Lviv in January 2008, entitled "Migrant Children about Themselves: Life in Ukraine and Abroad – Dreams and Wishes". A selection of the 156 entries, which included poems, novels, letters, short stories, fairy tales and pictures, was presented in an anthology in the summer of 2008. Even before its publication, in the spring the theme had reached the national news channel 1+1. A three-minute report, "The Children of Migrant Workers", emphasised the state's obligation to care for the left-behind children of migrant workers. The Ukrainian parliament reacted by drafting a law requiring parents to appoint a guardian for their children for the duration of their absence, and prohibiting them from leaving the country without making such arrangements. In cases where relatives could not provide care, the child had to be placed in a state institution (Yavorska and Petrenko 2007). Two years later, on 12 May 2010, a law entitled "Legal changes to combat social orphanhood in families of citizens working abroad" was passed by the Ukrainian parliament as part of the civil code and family law.[12]

Comparison of the Two Cases

Our analysis of the Polish and the Ukrainian press showed that in the majority of articles about the situation of stay-behind children, while it is migrating parents ostensibly being written about, it is primarily mothers, not fathers, who are called upon to take responsibility. The reporting from both countries thus makes it obvious that mothers and fathers face different expectations in terms of caring obligations (see also Chapter Five on fatherhood). If the negative depiction of migrant mothers in public discourse is compared with their practices of transnational motherhood (see Chapter Three and Lutz and Palenga-Möllenbeck 2012), it becomes clear that while mothers have more expansive mobility options under post-socialism, there are limits to their ability to combine paid work and caring work – both of which were integral to a woman's civic duty in the socialist era – particularly when their workplace and their family's place of residence no longer coincide. Apart from the introduction of restrictive legislation on obligatory guardianship, neither in Poland nor Ukraine are there any signs that the state is prepared to take constructive action to improve the compatibility of transnational employment and family life, such as by providing day-care facilities or care staff in schools and youth centres. Equally, there is a lack of public debate about the role that falls to fathers when their wives become the family breadwinners.

In both countries, the political leaderships are in a difficult position. On the one hand, the migrants' remittances are economically valuable sources of income, while on the other hand, the orphans debate with its mostly inflated or mistaken statistics and scandalous stories places them under considerable pressure to act. Both Poland and Ukraine took restrictive measures to deter parents from leaving the country, although it remains unclear whether and how compliance can be policed. Furthermore, in the two countries right-wing nationalist parties in alliance with conservative NGOs and the Catholic and Orthodox churches are pushing for the re-institution of a conservative model of the family and of womanhood which holds up "good mothers" as the central pillar of society; there is no place for transnational motherhood in this worldview. Apart from the media, the churches are the most important actors fanning the flames of the Euro-orphans debate.[13] Why did this controversy over left-behind children become such a relevant issue in the sending countries? Why did it emerge when it did, and what is at stake in the debate?

MORAL PANIC

My first framing of the Euro-orphans debate relates to the question of how, within a very short period of time from the viewpoint of mass media analytics, the orphans metaphor could become such a highly charged buzzword.[14] A moral panic is an expression of social anxiety and is generated when press coverage makes use of exaggerated attention, distortion and stereotyping (Cohen 1972: 31–8). However, the eruption of a moral panic cannot be credited solely to this journalistic approach; an equally necessary condition for the translation of headlines into a moral outcry is a strong reaction to these stories from the readership (Goode and Ben-Yehuda 1994: 26). The condition of children being left behind by migrating mothers was presented not only as a threat to the development of the affected individuals and families, but also as a long-lasting and serious problem for the development of society as a whole. Once the Euro-orphans or social orphans category had been used to identify a deeper-seated problem, a signification spiral (Hall et al. 1978) was set in motion which was capable of giving expression and meaning to individual experiences of crisis within a concentrated, collective anxiety. The Euro-orphans label was popularised and evolved into a genre,[15] crystallising diverse and contradictory (existential) fears, as well as resentment against the social inequities and missteps resulting from the system transition.

It is no accident that the focus of the debate is on children as symbols of the future of society, and indeed as the British sociologist Frank Furedi points out moral panics often centre on children. In his polemic, "Using Children as a Moral Shield", he writes: "Mention the word 'child' and people will listen. Raise the moral stakes by claiming that a 'child is at risk' and people will not just listen but endorse your demand that 'something must be done'"

(Furedi 2013: n.p.). It is obvious that the feminisation of migration in Poland and Ukraine was not initially identified as a potential threat to gender norms. Once the challenges faced by transnational families around the world were named as the orphaning of children, however, this term came to represent a crystallisation of the core problem, since it could be used to whip up outrage about the government's loss of control over social changes just as much as the conflicts experienced by individual families:

> When traditional norms and values no longer appear to have much relevance to people's lives then they are most susceptible to moral panics. Against this background an ordinary event like a woman leaving her children at home can assume extraordinary significance as a symbol of social chaos. (Furedi 1994: n.p.)

A historical example with particular parallels with the orphans debate is the controversy about "latchkey children" which started in the US in the 1940s. In the middle of World War II, stories published about America's latchkey children were "overwrought in their lamentations for the suffering [...] [of children who were] locked in cars, scared and lonely, or wandering the street, looking for trouble" (Tuttle 1995: 93). The term "latchkey children" is thought to have originated in an NBC television documentary broadcast in 1944, which showed the situation of children whose fathers had been called up to serve in the war and whose mothers were working in munitions factories. According to the historian William Tuttle, the government's patriotic expectations in this regard met with resistance from among the population. Working mothers faced great hostility even if they were working in a defence plant, like the famous Rosie the Riveter.[16] Tuttle writes: "Feeding this sentiment were not only long-standing gender stereotypes, but also a slew of wartime magazine articles and speeches by Father Edward J. Flanagan of Boys Town, J. Edgar Hoover of the FBI, and other defenders of father-led families in which the mother dutifully stays at home" (ibid.: 3).

Extensive sensationalist press coverage using the figure of the neglected child to discredit working mothers was the order of the day. In his study, Tuttle cites an example of public denunciation of mothers in a popular women's magazine that exhibits astonishing similarities with the orphans debate: "'Who's Going to Take Care of Me, Mother, If You Take a War-Plant Job'? So asked the curly blond-haired boy of three or four pictured in the May 1943 issue of *Better Homes and Gardens*. The boy looked sad but resigned to his fate" (ibid.: 95).[17]

Figure 4.2   Originally published in *Better Homes & Gardens®* magazine. All rights reserved.

The parallels with the coverage of Euro-orphans in the Polish and Ukrainian press are striking. Another commonality emerges in the private solutions that factory-worker mothers had to seek for their children's care. During wartime about 30 to 45 percent of working mothers relied on the help of (female) relatives or older children, according to Tuttle: "Perhaps most importantly, grandparents filled much of the void. One grandmother even suggested, 'If anyone asks for a name for this war, it's 'Grandmother's War'" (ibid.). A similar debate about latchkey children (*Schlüsselkinder*) as an expression of neglect and moral decay arose in post-war West Germany in the 1950s when many widows had no choice but to become working mothers and breadwinners for their families (see Figure 4.3).

Figure 4.3 Poster from Haus der Geschichte, Bonn

TRANSNATIONAL MOTHERHOOD AS A DEFICIENT MOTHERING PRACTICE

Transnational motherhood is not accepted in many countries as an appropriate mode of childrearing. The orphans debate ties in with the anxiety that the absence of biological mothers is detrimental to children's development. Yet scholarly work on this issue has reached no firm conclusions as to whether biological mothers are the optimal caretakers for their children and therefore irreplaceable. Some researchers focus on the disadvantages for stay-behind children and the traumas they endure due to the migration and absence of their biological mothers, while others show that the well-being of the children depends to a large degree on the competence of the persons acting as caretakers in the mother's absence (Lutz 2011; Lutz and Palenga-Möllenbeck 2012; Rerrich 2012).

In the past 20 years, there have been numerous studies examining the influence of new technologies on the communication and cultural practices of transnational family networks. One such approach is that of Baldassar and Merla (2013b), who argue that extensive use of new technologies such as text messages and interface calls can effectively establish connectedness across distance and helps to give care a multidirectionality as the emotional glue between family members who are physically separated (care circulation). Other studies (McKay 2007; Madianou and Miller 2011) come to the conclusion that the use of technologies can be conducive to mothers and children learning to articulate their feelings. They see this as yielding an opportunity for everyone involved: the sharing of emotions and intimacy between children and their mothers might even be improved by their virtual co-presence (while the hands-on daily care is provided by members of the extended family). Meanwhile, Mirca Madianou and Daniel Miller (2011) also find that among the stay-behind children they studied in the Philippines, two groups could be distinguished who had rather divergent perceptions of mobile communication: children whose contact with their mothers had been sporadic or had dried up before the diffusion of mobile phones viewed mobile communication as superficial and did not see it as a substitute for deeper relationships, whereas younger children who had been socialised in the use of mobile phones and used them from the first time that their mothers went away took a positive view of virtual communication for the most part.

Ultimately research shows that the absence of mothers cannot be assessed as wholly negative or positive. Kristine Zentgraf and Norma Chinchilla (2012) underline the paramount importance of reliable and resilient care arrangements for transnational families (see also Hondagneu-Sotelo and Avila 1997; Wirz 2021). Moreover, the age and health of the stay-behind children are important variables that contribute to the success or failure of caregiving arrangements. In their survey of stay-behind children of Ghanaian migrants, Miranda Poeze and Valentina Mazzucato conclude that the 90 minors they interviewed in no way saw their parents' absence as the failure of a social ideal, and were generally accepting of the substitute caregivers consisting of relatives from the extended kinship or neighbourhood network. The social norms surrounding parenthood are seen as particularly helpful in this context: "The flexible and inclusive childcare and family norms in Ghana help children to cope with and even value their lives in a transnational family context" (Poeze and Mazzucato 2014: 166). With reference to the orphans debate in Eastern Europe, this observation seems to me to be of crucial importance, because by insisting that mothers are irreplaceable, an inclusive view of caregiving arrangements that alleviate the absence of mothers in transnational families is precluded. In that case, any comparable positive comment by children on their mothers' migration remains not just unspoken but unspeakable, because a congruous narrative that might draw out the positive aspects of transnational family life is marginalised in the orphans discourse.

THE GLOBAL LEFT-BEHIND CHILD

My third explanation comes from a different direction. The debate about left-behind children is by no means confined to Eastern Europe but has become one with global dimensions. Rosalia Cortés (2007: 14) estimated that the number of children left behind in Ecuador by migrant parents was 150,000 in 2000, while F. K. Coronel and Frederic Unterreiner (2007) arrive at an estimate of 1.5 million children left behind in the Philippines. The anthropologist and historian Annika Pissin (2013: 5) even quotes a report which states that in China those classified as left-behind children (*liushou ertong*) number as high as 58 million.

In China, these are children of internal migrants moving from the countryside to the emerging megacities, where lack of housing in the main centres of employment forces parents to leave them behind in the custody of older relatives (Biao 2007: 180). In a finding that coincides with our analysis of the orphans debate in Eastern Europe, Pissin acknowledges that the quoted figures are not hard facts but estimates based on guesswork. As in Eastern Europe, the term *"liushou ertong"* is not reserved for children left behind by both parents due to migration but is also applied to those whose mothers have moved to the cities alone. Under China's current pattern of migration, they constitute the majority of migrants. Much like in Eastern Europe, grandparents or members of the extended family take on the hands-on childrearing and day-to-day care of the children. Anthropologist Xiang Biao interprets the left-behind children debate as a reaction to the rapid pace of social transformation, which has been accompanied by social disorientation in both rural and urban China. In contrast, Pissin (2013) highlights the emergence of the orphans debate in very different countries and regions around the globe, whose myriad of differing childrearing practices astonishingly seem to have no influence on the treatment of transnational mothers. She therefore concludes that the rapid spread of the metaphor and its global use at a particular historical point in time originated with global organisations.

Pissin traces the debates in various organisations and actions of the United Nations, starting from the Year of the Child in 1979. She also points out that the United Nations Convention on the Rights of the Child (UNCRC) in 1989 generated a standardised definition of childhood and children's rights for the first time. According to Pissin, these idealised universal standards for children all over the world stem from the Western middle-class model. They define childhood as the period between birth and the age of 18, a definition that is entirely at odds with the everyday lives of the majority of children in many global regions because it disregards cultural, class, race, ethnic and gender distinctions that affect the realities of children's lives. Since then, the Western nuclear family model has been established as the benchmark for the assessment of children's well-being worldwide. Consequently, children growing up in fragmented or in migrant families are now considered to be an "at risk" group. Since 2005, UNESCO has produced reports on an almost annual basis about left-behind children on all five continents, which inform the work of globally operating NGOs. Pissin's observations resonate with our own research findings on Eastern Europe, where numerous transnational or religious (mostly Catholic-based) NGOs, notably La Strada, the Tree of Life Foundation and Patrizio Paoletti Foundation, based in Italy, have specialised in the issue and are producing reports, launching campaigns and establishing offices in the sending countries. These organisations consider themselves to be defenders of children's rights and have been able to establish themselves as advisors in organisations like UNESCO and UNICEF; they are also pressing the European Union to take action on behalf of left-behind children, for example via the Brussels-based network Children Left Behind.[18]

This gives us good reason to concur with Pissin's conclusion (2013: 12) that the phenomenon exceeds regional or national dimensions and the left-behind child must therefore be analysed as a discourse produced in a global context. The debate is closely linked to an expert language that has come into use across national borders and languages. Pissin also interprets China's family policy with its (former) focus on one-child families[19] and a good education as an indicator of the regime's intention of creating a "quality population" (2013: 9) by means of optimisation. Although the dimensions of China's system transformation are vastly greater than in Eastern Europe, in both cases biopolitics can be observed in the spread of global capitalism (see also Randeria 2009). Demographic crises tend to be linked to reproduction and motherhood all over the world, but in post-socialist Europe where an additional dimension is the formation of new nation–states, the role of mothers in the symbolic construction of the nation comes into evidence (see Solari 2017 for Ukraine; Yuval-Davis 1997). Their departure abroad symbolises the disintegration of the state, and consequently special pressure is exerted on them, leaving little space for acceptance of alternative care arrangements. By pathologising transnational forms of motherhood, alternative care arrangements are seen as norm violations and breaches of the universal norm of "good motherhood". This kind of stigmatisation brings us back full circle to the words of Mieke Bal: "One of the most tenacious instances of universalism – the belief in the universality of something – is motherhood, doubtlessly the most intimate of relationships. The current state of the allegedly globalised world makes this universalism both urgently necessary and deeply problematic" (Bal 2012: 119).

5
Masculinity and Care in Post-Socialism: The Fatherhood of Stay-Behind Partners

It is very important for a father to teach his son about a real man's life. And when Kolya [my youngest son] turned one year old, I took him by the hand and brought him to a steam room. Of course, he complained and ran out. But now that he is four years old, he can endure temperature differences from 100f to 28f in the swimming pool. Plus, he endures ice baths. In Belarus, this is called fatherhood. Everywhere else it is called child abuse.[1] (Alexander Lukashenko, quoted in Novikova 2012: 95)

The above quotation is taken from a 2009 *Financial Times* interview with the president of Belarus, Alexander Lukashenko, and is quoted by Irina Novikova (2012) in her excellent essay on fatherhood in the post-socialist context. Countering what he sees as an effeminised discourse of masculinity prevailing in other parts of the world, Lukashenko presents an ideal of tough, heroic manhood trained in physical strength and the endurance of physical challenge. It is not insignificant that the speaker of these words has for decades been the president of a dictatorial regime;[2] he sees himself as the defender of a communist system and his demonstration of manly strength is important in that context.

It is interesting to consider the notion of fatherhood propagated by Lukashenko alongside that put forward by another powerful (former) president, Barack Obama: "Fathers [need] to step up, to realise that their job does not end at conception; that what makes you a man is not the ability to have a child, but to raise one" (interview with *Parade Magazine* 2009, quoted in ibid.: 95). Read together, the two quotations stand as antipodes for idealised, stereotyped ideals of masculinity: a loving, caring masculinity and responsible fatherhood versus an atavistic, physically strong masculinity and severe fatherhood.

While the Western side of the debate gladly attests to its own modern, attentive fatherhood, "the East" is constructed as backward and traditional in its gender relations and ideals of fatherhood. Meanwhile, the same dichotomy is mobilised by the new nationalists and the Catholic and Orthodox churches in Eastern Europe to affirm opposing values. The European Union's antidiscrimination policies protecting the rights of women and gay people, for example, are attacked as a "gender ideology" imported from the West to dismantle the family (Graff 2014).[3] The anthropologist Katherine Verdery (1994: 251) argues that the political discourses that arose throughout Eastern Europe after the fall of communism had their roots in the opposition movements that preceded the system transformation. The (re-)introduction of traditional family models was presented as an alternative to the socialist model; men were urged to stop thinking of themselves as being disenfranchised by the state and to overcome the "socialist matriarchy".[4] In the post-socialist period, the new religious–nationalistic parties and movements that rose out of the anti-communist opposition made use of this line of argument to call for an overhaul of gender relations in order to eradicate the stigma of "effeminised" masculinity. The Hungarian sociologist Joanna Goven, for example, writes: "Socialist mothering made men weak and lacking in authority, and to alter this requires restoring autonomy to the family and authority to the father: mothers should be dependent, not on society but on their husbands" (Goven 1993: 234). Bourgeois family norms are reintroduced and espoused as the new family ideal appropriate to the restoration of capitalism, she argues, particularly the valorisation of masculine authority and the male breadwinner model (ibid.). Goven's analysis suggests that the societies of Eastern Europe have come back full circle to a place they were decades ago.

This chapter deals with ideas and practices of masculinity and fatherhood among stay-behind fathers – the partners of women migrants – and considers where these can be located in relation to discourses of hegemonic masculinity. In this analysis, I seek to avoid the antipodal East–West discourse because it usually implies an analytical framework in which the West/the North are presented as the norm and the East/the South as deviations. The aim here is rather to make use of sociohistorical contextualisation to reconstruct aspects of the transformation of the gender order in Eastern Europe.[5] In contrast to the currently influential studies on modern fatherhood,[6] which generally begin with the establishment in the course of the nineteenth century of the male breadwinner model and its erosion in contemporary societies, my analysis focuses on the social legacy of the socialist experiment of gender equality. I consider its impacts on masculinity and fatherhood, and its mixed repercussions on gender debates in the post-socialist era.

More than just clarifying how fatherhood and motherhood are differentiated and given meaning by migrants from East European sending countries – and how they are reconceptualised in the course of migration processes – the following analysis also explores hegemonic gender systems, particularly in relation to the reciprocally conditioning relationship between fatherhood and masculinity (Hearn 1987). I take up Lynne Segal's (1990) convincing proposal to investigate this relationship with reference to fathering practices and to assess the social transformation of masculinity by how men act as fathers. Michael Meuser, who takes up Segal's thesis, conceives of fatherhood as the litmus test for the social transformation of masculinity and ascribes paramount importance to the organisation of the division of labour in the family, the mainstay of the bourgeois gender order (Meuser 2014: 160). However, the analysis of fatherhood in post-socialism must begin where socialism starts: with the framing of an explicit countermodel to the bourgeois gender order, which I turn to in the following section.

"SOCIALIST MATRIARCHY" AND "EFFEMINISED MASCULINITY" IN STATE SOCIALISM

The Russian sociologists Elena Zdravomyslova and Anna Temkina (2007) have characterised the gender regime in the USSR as "etatcretic", a term they use to refer to the state's control of gender relations by means of diverse institutional interventions and statutory regulations. Tetyana Bureychak distinguishes several historical phases in the period from the beginning of the twentieth century to the fall of the Iron Curtain. The goal of the first phase (1918–30), the "Bolshevik experiment", was the destruction of the traditional bourgeois family in favour of a life of sexual freedom. The second phase (1930–50), roughly identical to the Stalinist era, was characterised by two developments: the reduction of male authority through the replacement of the sole breadwinner principle with the co-breadwinner principle, and a simultaneous move towards pronatalist policies and family relationships (Bureychak 2011: 326). The intention was to counter the orientation towards sexual freedom of the Leninist period. The third phase (1950–80), was "characterised by liberalisation of gender politics and the emergence of criticism of gender relations, much of which, however, was censored" (ibid.).

Initially, the abandonment of the sole breadwinner model and the concomitant emancipation of women were viewed as core elements of a modern, non-capitalist social order in which women's employment represented the first, necessary step in the direction of gender justice and equality. In the Soviet Union between 1920 and 1930, the new household family model advocated "comradeship of men and women in the collective of workers and as part of the great Soviet family" (ibid.), and in the Stalinist era mothers were given more control and rights than fathers in relation to children (ibid.). While the state repeatedly attempted to curb male misconduct such as excessive drinking, marital infidelity and violence, and invited women and children to cooperate with these attempts (Bureychak 2011: 327), there was never any programme or policy that aimed at increasing fathers' participation in childrearing or in the household (Gerasimova and Chuikina 2004; Koshulap 2007). A debate about the liberalisation of gender relations erupted during socialism's third phase from 1950 to 1980, but this was also controlled and censored by the state (Zdravomyslova and Temkina 2007; Rotkirch 2000).

The picture painted by these authors assumes a high level of female activity in the household in addition to their full-time employment, in contrast to what Zhanna Chernova describes as men's alienation from their families and absence from the private sphere (2007: 166). The role of the new Soviet man was to seek success in paid employment and in the public sphere (Koshulap 2007: 364). As the counterpart to the working mother, a new hegemonic image of masculinity celebrated the man as a soldierly hero (defender of the country), as a physically and morally steeled, selfless worker pressing forward with the establishment of communism and socialism, and as a wise teacher and strategic genius steering the fate of communism and socialism (Bureychak 2011: 329 ff.). The practical implementation of women's participation in the labour market, which Lenin had advocated for in the early Soviet years, was taken up relatively quickly post-1945 by most Central and East European countries, including the German Democratic Republic (GDR), and established as a two-earner model. The income of a male breadwinner was reduced, or in other words, replaced with a co-breadwinner income as the new standard, which led to a massive influx of women into the labour market, generally as full-time employees. The new constitutions guaranteed women equal rights to access education (through women's quotas at universities and technical colleges) and the labour market, as well as in divorce and property law (Fodor 2011). Many authors assert that state socialism led to the "effeminisation" of men (Goven 1993; Verdery 1994; Imre 2001) and that fathers were socially "marginalised" by state policy (Ostner 2002: 152). I find such an analysis unhelpful because it continues to be oriented towards the ideal of the nineteenth-century, authoritarian bourgeois patriarch, from which the socialist father normatively differed. There are few empirical studies dealing with fatherhood from the socialist period, and as such it seems to me that there is no adequate evidence of either paternal marginalisation or effeminisation (see also Scholz 2004). What is certain, however, is that such an account was already espoused and promoted by opposition parties throughout Eastern Europe prior to the system transformation and, for that very reason, played an important role in the post-socialist transformation.

Changing Gender Orders in Post-Socialism

The implosion of state socialism was followed by the state's retreat from social protection and care obligations and the relocalisation of these tasks to the family, accompanied by an ideological upgrading of the status of motherhood (Novikova 2012). As Irina Novikova argues:

> The breakdown of the socialist system was perceived as "heroic" and like all "heroic" acts, masculine, with the emphasis on the importance of bringing men back from their "feminised" condition to their natural power positions in both the family and the economy (father and breadwinner) as the bedrock of order and rationality in a nation encountering globality. (Novikova 2012: 98)

Through the elimination of state-guaranteed and financed social safety nets, demands were made of the entire population to reground themselves and find their feet in a market economy. This induced a collective shock or, as Pjotr Sztompka (2000) writes, brought in its wake traumatogenetic shifts for large groups in society unable to cope with the pace of change, nor its impact on associated basic values (see also Alexievich 2013). Although this change in values was not strictly related to the order within the private household, millions of people – primarily women, but also a sizeable share of men – lost their jobs as a consequence of reforms of the economic system; an experience that had previously been almost unheard of unleashed deep existential fears. Moreover, the economic changes accelerated the abolition of state forms of provision, particularly in the care sector. It is noteworthy that after the fall of the Iron Curtain, the prevailing hegemonic gender orders in Eastern and in other regions of Europe manifested more common ground than in the preceding 50 years (Palenga-Möllenbeck and Lutz 2016).

Men in Eastern Europe found themselves in a paradoxical situation: at the very moment that the male breadwinner was proclaimed as the new ideal of hegemonic masculinity and male citizenship, it became a difficult ideal to fulfil because of the economic transition (Mazierska 2008: 12). Large-scale migration of men from Eastern Europe can therefore also be understood as an attempt to conform to the new standards of male citizenship. The migration of women does not fit into this schema but, as described in previous chapters, can be seen more as a continuation of the co-breadwinner identity than a break with the new gender regime (Lutz and Palenga-Möllenbeck 2012, 2014). But how do the husbands of these women experience the temporary absence of wives and mothers? What does it mean for these men when their partners take over as the main breadwinners? Does it awaken fears of giving up or losing their masculinity? Does departing from the ideals of hegemonic masculinity leave them feeling emasculated? What ideals of fatherhood are relevant for them?

The case examples presented below are selected as ideal types: the involved, caring father and the authoritarian head of the family, who leaves the everyday care work to the grandmother (see also Lutz and Palenga-Möllenbeck 2012). Also described in the literature – but not found in our sample – is an absent father, who leaves the shared home while his wife is working abroad, a practice found among businessmen (Walczak 2008). Our sample contained a high proportion of widowed and divorced female migrants (around 50 percent). However, we did not find a single case in which a divorced father took charge of caring for the children. In the following sections, three ideal-typical cases emerging from our analysis will be described.[7] The first two cases (Pawel and Sergij) are based on interviews with fathers, their children and their wives, while the third case (Costica) is taken from a documentary film.

INVOLVED FATHERHOOD AND CARING MASCULINITY

Case Study 1 – Pawel: "I just have to manage alone now"

The case of Pawel (40), father of Dawid and husband of Klaudia, comes from our Polish sample.[8] At the time of the interview, Pawel's wife Klaudia had been migrating to Germany to work for seven years. Pawel was 33 years old when, in 2000, his wife first stood in for her cousin as a domestic worker in Munich, staying there for three months. This was the first time he had been left alone to run the household and care for their then five-year-old son Dawid. When asked whether he supported Klaudia's decision, he said: "Ye-es. I was in favour and we made our minds up together, Klaudia wanted to as well. For sure, there was a minor conflict because I didn't know how we were supposed to manage here, but – somehow it has worked so far."

At the time, he had just started a job as a foreman in a firm working on pre-assembly for a big-brand German car manufacturer. Pawel was responsible for rostering and supervising 52 people. Shift work, particularly the night shifts, made caring for Dawid especially difficult: on those evenings he would put his son to bed and leave the house. Pawel had visible difficulty talking about the fact that he left his child alone: "I did all I could to get him off to sleep before I had to leave." The unspoken element is that this did not always work. When interviewed at age twelve, Dawid related that he had often been afraid and cried when his father left the apartment. In the earlier period of Klaudia's absences, Pawel's mother came by in the morning, woke the boy up, made breakfast, took him to school, and picked him up afterwards, while Pawel took charge of all the remaining tasks once he returned home. He had difficulties in combining his full-time job with his caring responsibilities:

> The work was to blame for all that. I must admit, it's still the same today. But now I try, I've learnt to get on top of the stress so that I can separate the world of work from my home life. Somebody upsets me at work, and I vent about it at home. Sometimes Dawid takes the brunt of it, because instead of talking to him calmly I'm still wound up from work when I get home, and when Dawid comes to me with his problems on top of that – it's too much. But – that's just how it was sometimes, and Klaudia also used to get cross with me for coming home so furious, and so on.

A major reason for his stress level at work was that at the beginning of a shift he would often realise that around a quarter of the workers were absent. The men would take leave to do seasonal jobs abroad, which he could understand in view of the low pay, but which put him under pressure because his responsibility was to keep the production line running – 290 cars had to be finished by the end of each shift.

Klaudia's migration was not the family's first; in the 1990s Pawel had also tried his luck abroad. Born in a mining region of Poland, he had become a car mechanic and later completed a two-year programme at technical college, graduating with a vocational baccalaureate majoring in Social and Political Studies. After college, he found no work appropriate to his qualifications and ended up working in mining for two years. He then took on seasonal work in France, Austria and Germany before following his wife's brother to the UK in 1997, where he worked without documentation for British firms, first on building sites and later as a craftsman. He sent Klaudia the money, they financed an apartment, and after eleven months he broke off his stay in England, explaining his return by saying that the exploitative working conditions and the "lifestyle of the English" did not appeal to him.[9]

Klaudia, 35, was a skilled shoemaker. At the time of the interview she had been working for seven years in Munich, where her work consisted of cleaning homes everyday, in addition to providing all-day care for older people on weekends. She rented a small apartment with her sister, with whom she alternated on a two- or three-month cycle. Her preference would have been to emigrate to Germany, but her son vehemently resisted the idea. Klaudia was in daily telephone contact with Pawel and Dawid, sometimes helping Dawid with his homework over the phone. She proudly reported that upon her arrival at the family home on Christmas Eve, Pawel had already cleaned the house and prepared twelve dishes for the Christmas celebrations.

At some point during the first two or three years that Klaudia was away, Pawel fell out with his mother and had managed without her help since then: "And at some time or another it reached the point where I felt, I just have to manage alone now, and I would rather she stopped coming over to our place." After that, he taught Dawid to use the telephone to call him whenever he was afraid at night. If Dawid called him when he was at work, Pawel then contacted the neighbours who took care of the boy. Pawel emphasised that his son's needs came first for him, and that he always responded to his calls immediately, even if it meant interrupting his work:

I always found a few minutes for him, so I never pushed him away or said, "Why are you phoning? Stay indoors, don't let anyone in and that's the end of it! Don't call me at work – we'll talk when I get home". I never did that. It was clear to me that as a child on his own, he could get frightened.

Dawid confirmed that the neighbours in the building supported him during his father's absences.

When asked how his colleagues and friends reacted to his wife being away and his lone parenting, Pawel reported that there were no comments; in any case, he was reluctant to give his colleagues the impression that he might quit at any time because his wife's earnings were several times higher than his own. This statement is very informative for an understanding of the relationship between fatherhood and masculinity, because presenting oneself among other men as earning less than their partner or as a main caregiver may potentially invoke a loss of masculinity (Meuser 2014; Behnke and Meuser 2012). However, Pawel's remark that he took his work just as seriously as his fathering duties enabled him to deflect or compensate for loss of masculinity by emphatically locating his identity in paid employment. Furthermore, he insisted on a clear separation between working and private life, saying that the subject of wives and families was not generally spoken about at work. Pawel was proud that he was capable of doing both things: bringing up his son *and* holding his own at work.

Pawel's routine on workdays was as follows: He would get up at 3:45 am and make Dawid some tea, which was kept hot in a thermos; put cornflakes and milk on the table and lay out his clothing ready; drive to work; wake Dawid at 7 am by phone and make another call shortly after to check whether he had actually got up. He used to prepare Dawid lunch which he left in a plastic lunchbox, but Dawid now took care of that himself. Dawid's first task of the day was to let the dog out; Pawel would check whether he had done so by calling after another half hour, and remind his son that he needed to lock the door and feed the dog before going to school. Dawid ate lunch at school, and after school Pawel would phone to find out if Dawid was home yet; he would worry because Dawid had to cross some very busy roads, "so I check up on him almost constantly". Once he returned home, between 3:15 and 3:30 pm, Pawel would cook; he commented, "I can cook, too, life has forced me into it." From 5 pm, Pawel would devote himself to household chores like "paying bills, tidying up, cleaning, washing up, just normal life".

Pawel and Dawid's daily routine seemed to be organised very pragmatically; Pawel went to great lengths to normalise his everyday life with Dawid, and from his point of view it was working very well. When asked whether there had ever been difficulties with Dawid, the following exchange with the interviewer unfolded:

Pawel: No, the only difficulties that come up are because I don't like his wailing, that he's such a wimp; he knows that she'll come back, but for a child it's a really big deal when Mum's away, because Dad scolds him more and that really upsets him, and that's why he cries. And if he were grown up then you'd just say to him, "You've been alone before, be brave, you'll get through it just fine". And he did get through it. Sometimes it did annoy me when he wailed or whined like that, but what can you do...

Interviewer: And how did you react to that? Did you just talk with him?

Pawel: No, sometimes, well yes, a few times, but I had to control myself because after all it's not his fault. Then either I shut the door to be on my own, or I went outside for a cigarette or something like that. But if he caused trouble, then he got a beating, end of story.

Interviewer: And what about affection? Did you try to take the place of his Mum by hugging him?

Pawel: Yes, of course. When he came to me, we sat down and watched children's programmes, had some fun, played a game, normal things. I can't say whether that was enough for him or not, whether I should have devoted more time to him, I don't know, he doesn't complain, unless he did complain [laughs]. You'd have to ask him.

The interview with Dawid[10] had already taken place before Pawel's interview, which is the context for the remark "unless he did complain". Dawid said that during his mother's absences, he sometimes slept in his father's bed. The fact that Pawel did not mention this himself indicates that he preferred not to be open about this form of intimacy. At one point, however, Pawel hinted that sometimes he was not equal to his self-assigned task of replacing the boy's mother:

> I always spoke to Dawid as I would to an adult. We sometimes annoyed each other. Because there were problems at school. I kept in contact with his teacher the whole time and so on. She phones me, I phone her and so on. Dawid behaves quite erratically, he has good grades, I'm pleased with him, but the behaviour itself, like a boy basically – one time he had a fight, another time it was spitting, and I just couldn't take it anymore. I said to him, "I come home and I wish for just one thing: that once in a while you're not in trouble at school. I'd rather not be getting angry letters home, and so on". And I don't have time for so many phone calls with the teacher.

Pawel did not describe Dawid's problems at school in detail. From the interview with Klaudia, however, it emerged that because of his behaviour at school she had taken Dawid to a psychologist, who diagnosed the child with hyperactivity said to be caused by the mother's absence. In a defiant tone, she commented, "*I'm* supposedly to blame".[11] The parents looked for solutions in consultation with the psychologist and a teacher. At first Dawid was sent to a sports club to release his energy and tensions; at the time of the interview, he was going to judo four times a week, had tutoring once a week and had just started to play the guitar that was a gift from Klaudia to Pawel. Dawid's computer game consumption was strictly limited and supervised.

Pawel felt burdened by all this. Nevertheless, Pawel had chosen to raise Dawid without help. This began when Pawel argued with his mother over aspects of the child's upbringing and he asked her to stop coming by. After that he briefly employed a young woman as a housekeeper and babysitter, but soon terminated the arrangement because the neighbours started to "gossip" and Pawel worried that people assumed he was having an affair with the young woman. In any case, the babysitter did not do the housework to his satisfaction:

So I told Klaudia on the phone that I'd prefer to do it alone. I'd rather work myself to death and work alone than pay somebody else to do it and then still have to put it right. I didn't want that. I'd much rather wait until Klaudia comes home and complains that I haven't done something properly. Then I can just say "right" and give it another wipe. But if that happens, it was me, and not having to deal with somebody else as well. That's how it is.

Pawel tried to uphold standards of cleanliness and order in the home, presenting himself as the "apprentice" of his wife, who instructed him on how he should do the cleaning. Cleanliness in the house had an important function for him, giving structure to his daily life. Pawel, unlike almost all the other men interviewed,[12] did not leave the domestic chores to his wife when she was home for six to eight weeks, indicating that he did not share the mainstream gender-coding of this work as female. Pawel was not constantly monitored by his wife but was able to develop his own everyday practice, which he did in frequent interaction with the transnational mother. Fathers whose care work is controlled by their wives are referred to as "perpetual apprentices" (Jurczyk and Lange 2009: 13). Dawid described the different division of work when his mother was home as follows: "Because when Mum is there, everything is shared out between three, and otherwise between two."

Pawel was not unhappy with his situation. He emphasised that although he missed Klaudia very much during her absences, his love for her had actually been strengthened by the shuttle migration. They communicated daily, not only by SMS and "love arrows" (emoticons and a code system of their own invention) but also with phone calls every evening. He proudly related that he would also "check" on Klaudia as a way of protecting her: he knew her daily routine, and since she travelled in the evenings and he worried about her safety, they exchanged text messages when she would leave and return to the Munich apartment and, if possible, in between as well. Klaudia said she enjoyed this "protection" and reported with laughter that when she came home, Dawid and Pawel would argue over whose bed she should creep into in the evening. As long as there was still a "battle" over her, she said, it's a good thing.

Pawel did not complain about having to take on Klaudia's tasks, and while he said he was happy with the situation, it was not one that he would have chosen: "If I were a millionaire, then she wouldn't have to do that [working abroad] [laughs]. But unfortunately I'm not, or – if she, if she had a good job here, yes, somewhat better paid." Like the majority of the male population, Pawel cannot give up the ideal of the male breadwinner. Instead, he endeavours to be an involved father, a co-parent and a good "apprentice" to his wife, although according to his own assessment, he cannot replace her as a mother. His remark "if she had a good job here" also suggests that he upholds the socialist co-earner model and in no way desires to be the sole breadwinner. Another sign of his egalitarian understanding of partnership is evident in the fact that all decisions about money are taken jointly by the couple.

At the time of the interview, Klaudia was two months pregnant and planning to give up her work in Munich for a period after the birth of their second child. Klaudia was worried about how Pawel would cope with two children alone once she went back to work, while Pawel was considering whether he might try a new babysitter, or else involve his mother in the childcare again.

Their son Dawid, who made a very adult impression for a twelve-year-old, also knew that changes were ahead. To the interviewer's question of what he thought of his mother's shuttle migration, he replied, "Well, it's both good and bad. Good, because – good, because – well, then we have money and that. And bad, because it's more difficult at home." Dawid had realised that his mother's break from work would bring financial constraints, but hoped that they would not affect him too much because he wanted a laptop and was saving up for a PlayStation. He spoke openly about how much he missed his mother. As soon as she would come back, what he wanted most of all was physical closeness to her, which Klaudia considered a legitimate need. While this is still acceptable behaviour in a twelve-year-old, she said, it shocked her to observe the same need in the 21-year-old son of her female cousin who, like her, worked in Munich.

Dawid had largely adapted to or normalised the transnational migration that operated within the family. For instance, he said that his tasks included caring for the dog, "because Dad is at work and Mum is – too." As he saw it, what both parents had in common was that they worked, even though his mother's workplace was over 800 kilometres away. This is a family in which the normalisation of the mother's (periodic) absence was treated as a joint project, and Dawid made his contribution to coping with the situation on a day-to-day basis by resolutely not talking to friends about his mother's absences. Dawid was also dealing with a migration issue of his own: he had a girlfriend who had emigrated to England with her family. He would Skype with her and meet her when she visited her grandparents. It is no surprise that he said he would rather emigrate to England than Germany.

I have labelled the model of fatherhood practised by Pawel as "involved" since this father did indeed take full charge of childcare and domestic chores in addition to his employment whenever his wife was away. In this regard he developed his own form of practical coping, which does not fundamentally differ from motherhood and can be characterised as caring masculinity. This involved fatherhood was not in any way a consciously practised, carefully legitimated alternative model, nor was it presented as such. Pawel's fatherhood practice was affirmed and appreciated by his wife. He also symbolically assured himself of his masculinity in the partnership by protecting and monitoring her virtually. The finding from a Norwegian study by Berit Brandth and Elin Kvande (1998: 307) that involved fathers can better manage to uphold their masculinity with caring work than with housework does not appear relevant for Pavel and his fatherhood and masculinity. This may indicate the presence of a social class difference between the fatherhood practices of middle-class fathers and those with more manual jobs. A further issue is that the migration situation calls for methods of coping with everyday life that differ from the model of modern fatherhood in which both parents are available and living in one place. In the case of the caring masculinity of the stay-behind father portrayed here, housework was not neglected. However, the men interviewed in our sample struggle to show their own feelings and to deal with their children's emotions, as demonstrated by Pawel calling his son a wimp when he cried. All the fathers interviewed tended to treat emotions as taboo, and discussed them only hesitantly when the interviewers persisted in enquiring. This is an indication that the interviewees wanted to protect themselves against losing emotional control, or feared distancing themselves from a hegemonic ideal of masculinity.

If allowing a range of feelings and dealing communicatively with emotions are considered a core element of caring, as is often the case in the debate about involved fatherhood, this is one area where shortcomings must be noted. However, for Pawel it is the verbal articulation of emotions that is subject to a taboo but not emotions themselves, since both his son and wife reported that he did engage emotionally with his child's moods. It follows that there is a discrepancy between paternal practices and a discourse of masculinity that insists on emphasising differences from femininity. Meanwhile in both East and West, femininity is discursively associated with care and nurture, which is stipulated as the norm for maternal care. Here the question that must be posed is whether fathering has to be a replica of these mothering ideals, or whether it is not rather the naturalised linkages between care, women and motherhood that should be put up for question. In her study "Can Men Mother?", the sociologist Andrea Doucet warns against considering the experiences of fathers through a maternal lens, since this overshadows and obscures other forms of nurturing (Doucet 2006: 222). Furthermore, as Meuser notes, the characterisation of caring men as "mothering fathers" symbolically reproduces the connotation of care as feminine (2014: 163). Pawel, like the vast majority of men whose wives are involved in the shuttle migration system, prevents the loss of masculinity by such actions as not giving up his paid work and trying to do things perfectly. Requesting a reduction to part-time hours would not be possible for him, in any case. This form of *involved fatherhood* has thus far been given no social recognition in post-socialist societies, and it is to be feared that this will remain so for the foreseeable future.

Case Study 2 — Sergij: "I take it upon myself to command the troops"

The following case describes a family living in western Ukraine in which the husband managed the two children with the help of his mother. It has already been noted that in the overwhelming majority of stay-behind families, grandmothers take on the mother-substitute function in practical everyday life and fathers assume a more assistant-parenting function (see also Lutz and Palenga-Möllenbeck 2012). This case contrasts with that of Pawel in multiple respects: how ideals of masculinity were presented, how the husband coped with the structural impossibility of living up to the ideal of being the sole breadwinner, and how the everyday practicalities of running a household were handled.

Sergij, 43, had a qualification as a teacher and was self-employed running his own video rental store. His wife Nadja, 37, a former bookkeeper, spent a period of three years in Poland (2004–07) as a domestic worker, and the interviews were conducted two years later. As a shuttle migrant, Nadja generally stayed for two months per visit and worked seven days a week doing several families' housework (washing laundry, tidying, cleaning and minding children), returning to her own family for two months cyclically. Her monthly pay amounted to the equivalent of $150, almost all of which she sent home. Sergij and Nadja's sons were ten and 17 years old at the time of Nadja's first migration.

When the interviewer[13] asked Sergij to recount how his wife came to travel to Poland as a domestic worker, Sergij answered that he would not have sent her but Nadja wanted to help her sister, who was already working in Poland and needed a reliable partner for her cyclical employment. In this way, Sergij presented migration as a generous gesture. In addition, it was facilitated by him, because Nadja was an employee in his business. It mattered to him that he had the authority to allow his wife to work abroad: "She would travel for a month or so; I didn't allow her to go for longer because even that way I'm already overworked." Although Nadja's transnational migration was only two years in the past at the time of the interview, Sergij could no longer remember how long Nadja would be away. He emphasised that her absence was an annoyance for him, disrupting his normal routine ("even that way I'm already overworked"). Accordingly, he felt empowered to place limits on the duration of this disruption. He commented, "Mostly she went for a month. That's all. And, well, if someone goes abroad for two or three years, I would never accept that."

Sergij distanced himself from families in which the wives are away for several years. He obviously wanted to avoid any impression that he encouraged her labour migration; instead, he claimed to have *tolerated* Nadja's work abroad. Asked about the division of work in the household during Nadja's absence, he told the interviewer that his eldest son, aged 17 at the time, took charge of cooking: "*He* did the cooking. I never cooked, and I never would. I actually got married so that I wouldn't have to cook."

His contribution to the housework consisted of loading the washing machine in the mornings and making fruit preserves in the summer. "And otherwise, everyone pulled together... I only gave instructions, pointed my finger, I... I take it upon myself to command the troops."[14] In addition to his sons, he probably also included his parents – especially his mother, who took charge of most of the household chores – among the troops. His self-presentation as a man who retains authority and control even in difficult times, steering the family's fortunes as head of the household, permeated the interview. When asked what problems he could recall during Nadja's absence, he said:

Oh well... the problems... I have difficulties everyday in any case; I [barely] noticed [she was away] because I have a very mixed heap of problems in any case. When I've solved one problem, the next one comes along right away. I think about three things within a minute, and then I also have to do the right thing. Hmm. I'm not the kind of person [to talk about problems]... I'm sitting here now [laughs] and my thoughts are somewhere else.

Nadja's absence was presented by Sergij as an additional problem, certainly not as a solution to financial difficulties. The last sentence, addressed to the interviewer, suggests that he considered this interview a waste of time. It is likely that Sergij only made himself available for the interview because he could not check or influence the narrative told by Nadja,[15] and it was clearly important to him to present his own version. His very aggressive presentation also created the impression that he did not enjoy facing the memories of that time, perhaps because it would undermine the image he had of himself as a man in control, always acting rationally and "command[ing] the troops" with a cool head. This self-understanding shows astonishing similarities with the ideals of both bourgeois and soldierly masculinity (Mosse 1996), where any loss of control is to be avoided. In this light, then, it is no surprise that Sergij played down Nadja's financial contribution to the family income. When asked how he communicated with Nadja, he said, "Oh, the telephone rang everyday. I probably spent more on that than she earned in Poland [smiles]."

Nadja also talked about how she phoned Sergij daily particularly at the beginning when she found the separation hard to endure and often cried on the telephone. That Sergij would comfort her fits well with Sergij's self-image as the head of the family who remains in emotional control. When the female interviewer insistently asked how the money earned by Nadja was spent, Sergij emphasised once again:

> There wasn't that much money, don't you understand. When the money came home, it was automatically...you know, I didn't wait around for her to bring money home; because the money she earned paid the telephone bills, that's how we soothed her mood swings, her anxiety.

This statement contradicts Nadja's account of how her earnings were used to buy an apartment, which her husband had presented as his own accomplishment. Nadja also reported having invested in household goods such as the washing machine, and in the children's education in the form of extra tutoring: "The elder son had already completed the eleventh grade, hmm, and was having extra tutoring. We needed money for that. My money had already been spent before I'd earned it. Hmm, that's how it was."

Both sons had now gone to university, to their parents' pride. Even Sergij's nerves were not as robust as he would have people believe; that much is evident from his own narrative of how Nadja's migration came to an end:

> Well of course I worried, because it was a stay abroad. And then she wanted to go back once more, and I fell ill. And she didn't go back anymore, and won't go back, because the state of my health no longer allows it. It's all worry and anxiety; she worries more than I do. To my mind. That's my opinion.

Nadja's version of how it ended was somewhat different: "And he decided… well, he just didn't let me go anymore." She said nothing about her husband being ill. Yet two sentences later, what she had characterised as a ban on going abroad is presented as a joint decision:

> And we decided that Mum needs to be with the children. My opinion is that a husband and a wife, a family has to be together because… if one of them is away for a length of time, various situations start to turn into conflicts, they stop trusting each other, that's why they have to be together, that's my opinion.

Sergij, in contrast, did not mention migration causing any relationship conflicts, and when asked what had changed in their relationship, he responded:

> Nothing has changed. The relationship was fine, just like it used to be. I have a good relationship with my wife, I have a very good wife and she's the only one I want [smiles]. And the relationship has not changed at all. There was no time for the nonsense that other people have time for. Not least because I was busy.

The reference to other people's "nonsense" suggests that he interpreted the question about change in the relationship as being a question about his sexual activity. Sergij clearly did not believe that his wife would cheat on him, while an extramarital fling of his own would be unfeasible due to lack of time. With this self-presentation, once again he underscored his (ability to control his) virility.

Since Nadja described her work in Poland as more of a sacrifice than an act of self-determination, it can be assumed that she suffered more from the separation than her husband. At the same time, it seems a reasonable assumption that her migration to earn income for the household was at odds with Sergij's ideal of the male breadwinner. It is in this light that we can perhaps read Nadja's investment in a traditional discourse of femininity or maternalism that complemented her husband's narrative. In the course of the interview, Nadja ultimately presented the decision to end her migration as the gift of an empathetic husband:

I have a husband who understood everything. He simply saw how I was before I set off, and when I returned I was exhausted, worn out…and he made a decision. He didn't want me to go abroad ever again. Other job offers came in; they [the Polish employers] asked me to go back, and sent me the invitation. But he had simply tried it for a while and then understood that enough was enough. And that was how it ended.

The numerous ambivalences in this quotation are characteristic of a partnership in which there were certainly yearnings for self-determination on Nadja's part. Indeed, as she recounted at the start of her interview, in her youth she was keen to be independent. This changed, likely as a result of the marriage to Sergij, as she now largely shared Sergij's traditional and patriarchal notions of gender roles – he got married "so that [he] wouldn't have to cook" while in return, she expected him to protect and provide for her. Sergij found it hard to admit that he was not in a position to meet the expectations he had of himself, and Nadja supported his version of events: her decision to improve the family's financial situation by working abroad was ultimately presented as an experiment on her husband's part, one that did not work out. This narrative deprived Nadja of the possibility of being proud of the income she had generated.

The younger son Ilja had difficulty processing the story of his mother's migration even two years later. Initially he stated that he could not remember all that well, yet began to cry when asked how he felt about it at the time. Nadja herself emphasised that her sons missed her very much, although her absence also had positive aspects:

Because they realised what it's like with a mother and without a mother, they started to appreciate their Mum's work more. This daily work at home that every woman does, that nobody ever appreciates unless they have to do it themselves [smiles].

Nadja described a learning process that led to the recognition of her daily work as a housewife as a positive outcome of her labour migration, perhaps the only one. This also underscores the gendered division of responsibility presented by Sergij: paid work as the husband's terrain, the home as that of the wife. Sergij and Nadja's model of partnership, which is dominated by Sergij's traditional ideals of masculinity, does not seem compatible with a positive evaluation of female shuttle migration.

In a constellation in which the husband masks the fact that he is effectively incapable of earning the family's income, this shame dominates the narration of the female migration as well: in the circumstances, it can only be presented as a failed project – a mistake (Sergij) and trauma (Nadja and the children) that they do not enjoy talking about. At this juncture, a third party enters the frame as a target of both partners' complaints, namely the Ukrainian state, which compels people into migration instead of providing adequate employment opportunities in their own country. It is astonishing that the family agreed to the interview at all and it is conceivable that the comments made by Sergij and Nadja were also meant to be understood as a protest about social conditions in general.

Case Study 3 – Costica: "I'm robbing my children of their childhood"

Migration studies scholars, such as Saskia Sassen (1998), have long argued that where female migrants became the family breadwinners, they would gain power and influence within their families, eroding the traditional gender order and even culminating in complete role swaps. On the surface this is precisely what we see in Romanian filmmaker Thomas Ciulei's award-winning documentary *The Flower Bridge* (2008), which follows the daily life over a period of several months of Costica Ahir, a university-educated Moldovan farmer in his mid-forties. Costica lives with his three children, caring for them alone since their mother left for Italy as a migrant care worker "three years and four months ago" (Ciulei 2008). In our own sample, there were no women who were physically absent from their family for a period of several years, although cases such as these are apparent in the literature. The plan was that Costica's wife would return after two years, but the family is still far from reaching its financial goals (covering school fees for the children, renovation and extension of their house and expansion of the farm). The mother is evidently unwilling to bar herself from legal re-entry to Italy, so at the time of filming she is still in Italy "waiting for her papers".[16] She sends parcels regularly and phones now and again. The family has a telephone and a PC that the children use to write letters to their mother. The film superbly demonstrates the textured experience of a father caring for his children alone: it begins with a scene in which Costica is applying a tincture for chickenpox to his son Alexi's face while saying to the camera that, particularly at moments like this, it is very difficult for him to take the place of his wife.

Costica organises everyday life in a way that seems somewhat regimented: the children, Alexandra (15), Maria (about 13) and Alexi (8), line up in front of him and he assigns them tasks. There tends to be a gender-specific division of work since the girls are mainly responsible for housework, while the boy is assigned to tend to the animals and keep the yard clean. But in principle everybody is equally involved in the chores: between them, they sow corn and turnips and the flower seeds sent by the mother, bake bread, fetch water from the well, wash laundry by hand, slaughter a chicken and shovel snow. They even save money on hairdressing: the father cuts the children's hair – much to the visible chagrin of his daughters, who would prefer to go to the hairdresser's – and they cut his. Costica knows that his children are (over-)burdened by all this: "The children work a lot. As hard as I try, something is missing. I'm robbing my children of their childhood, they work much, much too much."

Although he feels guilty, he does not know how he can change the situation. The only leisure pursuit the film shows is Costica teaching his children to handle an air rifle. In the evenings he reads them sad, heroic nationalist poems. As a greeting ritual, he questions the children daily about their school grades, which incidentally is also the first question the mother asks the children when they have calls. This reinforces the impression that the children's education is valued highly by both parents. The children write their mother letters in which they report news from the farm (the birth of twin goats) and their achievements at school, but they do not upset her with any emotional "scenes" and nor do they tell her that they miss her.

It is striking that apart from Costica, no other adults appear in the film. The filmmaker Ciulei described this in an interview

(Ciulei and Ott 2008) as a device to make the absence of the mother "palpable". It is a family without any sign of a grandmother, female neighbours or other men (grandfathers, friends or work colleagues).[17] At first glance, Costica cannot be characterised as a particularly nurturing father because he comes across as loud and severe, barking orders and barely demonstrating affection. But when Costica insists that his son must not show how upset he is about his mother's absence, Costica's explanation is that this would make him cry too. In other words, he struggles against a loss of emotional control, although he does also communicate this to his children. The film does not feature militaristic fatherhood practices and ideals such as those described by Lukashenko. There is no indication that Costica fears a loss of masculinity or social denigration for taking on "motherly" care work. At one point in the film, torrential rain is shown flooding the farmyard and Costica remarks laconically, "We're sinking in the mud but the children are fine". His attention is devoted primarily to his children and they react to his orders obediently, but often laugh about him and point out his mistakes. It is clear that the children have scope for negotiation and that the father depends on the children both emotionally and practically: if the mother sends a parcel from Italy, the children translate any machine instructions from Italian, which is a language that Costica does not understand. Overall, this portrait of a stay-behind husband and his children differs in many ways from ideals of nurturing care as found in the middle classes of Western countries, especially concerning emotional support and the children's need for affection (see Flaake 2014). But here the question arises of whether the mothering done by fathers under such conditions can only be valued as an equivalent and complete replacement for the mother if it corresponds in every respect to the way mothers do – or are meant to do – motherhood.

CONCLUSION: CARING FATHERHOOD AND UPHOLDING THE IDEAL OF THE SOLE BREADWINNER

From the synopsis of the three case studies, there are evidently many differences between the fatherhood practices of the *involved father* Pawel, the authority-minded *father-commander* Sergij and the *lone parent* and farmer Costica. Common to them all is that they continue with the same income-generating practices as before their partners started to work abroad and attempt to keep fulfilling the hegemonic ideal of fatherhood, even if this has been eroded and is no longer financially necessary. Pawel and Costica take charge of care tasks without seeing the feminine coding of these as a problem. However, Pawel's daily caring responsibilities collide with the demands of his workplace, and in this sense his experience is comparable to that of lone-parenting working mothers who must deal with a double workload.

Costica does not cast doubt on the care he provides to his children, but emphasises his inability to perform it "like a mother". From the outset, Sergij rejects any hint of role swapping or attempting to replace the mother, and thus corresponds to a type which Iryna Koshulap (2007: 371) labels as "breadwinners despite themselves". I refer to it here to mean that Sergij upholds the masculinity ideal of a sole breadwinner, which he cannot fulfil under the given economic conditions. In the meantime, the media in many East European countries have begun to present an ideal of conscious fatherhood (ibid.), although it essentially entails fathers being more involved in leisure time or at weekends rather than swapping roles or sharing equally in care responsibilities. It is a habitus that can also be found among male migrants whereby they emphasise the value of spending leisure time with the children when they are home (see Palenga-Möllenbeck and Lutz 2016).

I contend that the fatherhood practices of Pawel and Costica can certainly be understood as a form of alternative fathering because the tasks being done in practical terms are very much those expected of a mother. Nevertheless, it is not a new phenomenon as it was not uncommonly found in the co-breadwinner families under state socialism, not necessarily as an ideal, but as a practice. In this respect, the partners of female migrants continue to be oriented towards the co-breadwinner model by which they lived under state socialism. However, the post-socialist period saw the erosion of this model as a social paradigm, as well as the dismantling of the institutional arrangements that made it possible, notably the slashing of state care provision. Given the new hegemonic ideal of fatherhood – the father as the family's breadwinner

– the stay-behind fathers of families engaging in transnational migration who take primary responsibility for the care of their children have little chance of being recognised as pioneers of modified fatherhood practices or agents of change. Instead, they must protect themselves from emasculation in the eyes of others and themselves, and relatedly they do not proactively question the current hegemonic model but are subject to it.

All in all, these cases illustrate two aspects of care migration. The first relates to the emotional burdens and practical strains that family members face in the context of geographical fragmentation of families. What happens in practice turns out to be very far removed from the hypothesis that fathers would automatically assume the feminine-coded care responsibilities as soon as women became the main wage-earners. Since most Central and East European countries regard the shuttle migration of women as temporary absences and refuse to acknowledge the contribution they make to the national economy, support programmes for the relatives of shuttle migrants in the sending countries continue to be rare. Equally, little action is being taken by the receiving states, which ignore the emotional costs and struggles faced by the (relatives of) female care workers (cf. Lutz 2011, 2015, 2017a).

Second, the narratives of the stay-behind husbands and fathers bring to the fore an aspect that remained in the shadows during decades of migration research addressing male labour migration: the unpaid provision of care for children and older relatives by stay-behind female partners, which was regarded as self-evident. Only when women become breadwinners working abroad do the sending societies realise that their absence causes care gaps back home. The upgrading and recognition of fathering as valuable and dignified care work could be one part of an adequate response to this social phenomenon; one which, unfortunately, is nowhere to be seen.

6

From Socialist Utopias to the Global Commercialisation of Care: New Answers to an Old Question

My aim in this chapter is to embed the phenomenon of East European care migration historically within the framework of care theories and debates. To understand the specific context of post-socialism, I will first go to the sources through re-reading works by socialist utopians, before turning to questioning the implementation of these ideals in real state socialism. Subsequently, the feminist critique of capitalism, which had its heyday in the 1970s and 1980s in Western industrialised countries, will be reconstructed on the basis of texts by Socialist Feminists. In particular, I will discuss the Wages for Housework campaign and the debate on the subsistence economy. The political and theoretical debates from these two periods are then compared with the new feminist critique of capitalism in the early twenty-first century.

Are the issues today the same as 120 years ago? What are the continuities and differences? How is the care question discursively framed today? What is the role of Marxist analysis and its revision, for example by Nancy Fraser, who rediscovered – as did several others – Karl Polanyi's 1944 work *The Great Transformation*? What is the status of migrant care work in the feminist debate today? Are alternatives to the globalised commodification of care work being discussed? Or will the expansion of the market result in a situation where every reasonably well-off citizen in a rich country will at some point adopt the status of a migrant's employer? Will this be considered an acceptable solution to care deficits, or are there alternatives? Is the universal caregiver model, a thought experiment Fraser (1994) conducts, an alternative or merely an idea without a place, a utopic idea? My main concern in this chapter is to bring together debates that are not usually connected with each other. In the debate on the globalisation and transnationalisation of care work, discussions on the rediscovery of socialist utopias and their scope have so far found little resonance; conversely, globalised care migration has so far been rather underrepresented in the debate on neoliberalism.

SOCIALIST UTOPIAS

In European socialist utopias of the nineteenth and early twentieth centuries, the question of women's emancipation was framed as one of changing the gender-specific division of labour in bourgeois societies through the reorganisation of wage labour. Notably, Friedrich Engels' 1884 work *The Origin of the Family, Private Property and the State* emphasised the connection between the allocation of domestic and reproductive labour to women and the emergence of private property. According to Engels, bourgeois society contributed to the cementing of male domination, and only if women are able to escape domestic labour might emancipation be possible:

> The domestic labour of women was considered insignificant in comparison to men's work for a living. The latter was everything, the former a negligible quantity. At this early stage we can already see that the emancipation of women and their equality with men are impossible and remain so, as long as women are excluded from social production and restricted to domestic labour. The emancipation of women becomes feasible only then when women are enabled to take part extensively in social production, and when domestic duties require their attention in a minor degree. This state of things was brought about by the modern great industries, which not only admit of women's liberal participation in production, but actually call for it and, besides, endeavour to transform domestic work also into a public industry. (Engels 1974/1908: 196)

This quotation indicates the direction the revolution was supposed to take: by including women in the labour market, their social position would necessarily improve. However, this argument presupposes a great deal. It anticipates a radical model of a labour society (*Arbeitsgesellschaft*) that, as Hannah Arendt (1960: 80) writes, glorifies labour as the source of all value, which rests fundamentally on a distinction between productive and unproductive labour. According to Arendt, the economists Adam Smith and Karl Marx shared a "contempt for the domestic servant" and a view of their work as parasitic, "as if they were dealing with a kind of perversion of labour, which only deserves its name when it increases the stock of the world" (ibid.). Accordingly, all activities in the private household were categorised as unproductive labour, as leftovers from the past (ibid.: 81). Here, while productivity is performed at the workplace and in public space, private space is determined by consumption. This dichotomy of productive versus unproductive work (consumption) has remained an organising economic principle and has now become entrenched in the adult–worker society, in which people are socialised primarily through their participation in gainful employment (see Lutz 2010).

The relevant point is that this asymmetrical valuation of paid work on the one hand and domestic and care work on the other was already present in the cradle of socialist utopias. Furthermore, there was no agreement among the protagonists on what the liberation of women from the unproductive private sphere should look like. Following the publication of Engels' seminal work, the socialist branch of the women's movement across Europe demanded women's right to access paid work and discussed different modes of female employment. Socialist thinkers and advocates of women's rights such as Rosa Luxemburg, Clara Zetkin and August Bebel assumed that this would require a change in the economic–political system. They discussed women's full-time employment and their liberation from household and care duties as the key to gender equality, which would take place automatically through the system change from capitalism to socialism. In this vein, the Russian communist and feminist Alexandra Kollontai wrote in 1909:

Specific economic factors were behind the subordination of women; natural qualities have been a secondary factor in this process. Only the complete disappearance of these factors, only the evolution of those forces which at some point in the past gave rise to the subjection of women, is able in a fundamental way to influence and change their social position. In other words, women can become truly free and equal only in a world organised along new social and productive lines. (Kollontai 1977 [1909]: 58–62)

In a famous speech in 1919, Vladimir Lenin characterised housework as "the most unproductive, the most barbaric and the heaviest work that women do" (Lenin 1961 [1919]: 26), quoting Kollontai by adding that "women can become truly free and equal only in the world organised along new social and productive lines". He said that, according to the socialist ideal, "exemplary institutions, dining-houses, crèches [will be created] which are to liberate woman from domestic service [...] these institutions, which liberate women from domestic slavery, [will] come into being wherever there is the slightest possibility of doing so. [...] Our task is to make politics accessible to every working woman" (ibid: 27).

A somewhat different form of women's liberation was proposed by Lily Braun, who, as a member of the Social Democratic Party in the German Empire, was active in both the bourgeois and proletarian women's movements and advocated cooperation between the two. Her 1901 publication *Frauenarbeit und Hauswirtschaft* (Women's Work and Home Economics) laid out a model of a "one-kitchen house" as a way of life for emancipated women. In this political programme, Braun took up ideas that were already being discussed in the US under the rubric of a "domestic revolution" and that had inspired collective experiments such as the Cooperative Housekeeping Association (Hayden 1981). Her project envisaged the expansion of household-specific technologies, as well as new forms of collective economic activity. As Braun wrote:

In a complex of houses enclosing a large nicely planted garden there are about 50–60 flats, none of which contains a kitchen [...] Instead of the 50–60 kitchens which an equal number of women used to manage, there is a central kitchen on the ground floor, equipped with all modern labour-saving machines. (Braun 1901a: 7)

However, the main feature of the one-kitchen house consisted of enabling middle-class women to engage in professional activities, while a community-funded staff of cooks and maids in the basement of the house would prepare meals, clean housing units, do the laundry, ironing, errands, shopping and caring tasks. In short, they would provide the whole ensemble of a middle-class household's services, dubbed by Bridget Anderson (2000) the three Cs – Caring, Cooking, Cleaning. Braun's goal was to replace the "prevailing dilettantism" of the bourgeois household through the efficient use of technology and service personnel. Only in this way could family and life forms reach a "higher cultural level". By this she meant a "family trinity – man, woman, children" (Braun 1901b: 535) – in other words, the nuclear family form. Critics of her proposal suggested that it was not so much based on a progressive idea, but rather a reaction to the so-called servants crisis, which made it no longer affordable for individual households to pay the rising wages and respect the work regulations that the servants' unions and associations had fought for at the beginning of the twentieth century.

What is certainly important about this model is the fact that the servants or maids, as members of the working class, were to receive a wage from which they could live independently and thus domestic and reproductive activities were considered work. The model provoked fierce opposition from Clara Zetkin, a leading member of the Independent Social Democratic Party – who criticised the fact that the single-kitchen model provided for far too few workers and that this would create a heavy workload for the employees (Zetkin 1901) – and especially from Rosa Luxemburg, co-founder of the Communist Party Germany. Luxemburg directed her criticism in particular against the employers of these servants, the women of the exploiting class:

The women of the property-owning classes will always fanatically defend the exploitation and enslavement of the working people by which they indirectly receive the means for their socially useless existence. (Luxemburg 1971 [1912]: n.p)

In principle, Luxemburg shares the view of Engels, Marx and Lenin in that she agrees with their assessment of class contradictions and the significance of productive labour; however, she points out that this analysis applies primarily to the dominant capitalist system:

> As long as capitalism and the wage system rule, only that kind of work is considered productive which produces surplus value, which creates capitalist profit. From this point of view, the music-hall dancer whose legs sweep profit into her employer's pocket is a productive worker, whereas all the toil of the proletarian women and mothers in the four walls of their homes is considered unproductive. This sounds brutal and insane but corresponds exactly to the brutality and insanity of our present capitalist economy. And seeing this brutal reality clearly and sharply is the proletarian woman's first task. (ibid.)

Luxemburg rails against the fact that proletarian women's work in the private household is considered unproductive; Lenin had called it just that. This confrontation exemplifies analytical distinctions that reverberated through socialist thinking over the decades.

ASYMMETRICAL GENDER JUSTICE IN PRACTISED STATE SOCIALISM

The vision of women's liberation from domestic labour and their participation in productive gainful work, not only in (collectivised) agriculture but also in factories and offices, was gradually implemented in the course of the first half of the twentieth century, in particular in the socialist and communist systems. Men and women were to perform gainful work side-by-side for the benefit of the community, while domestic and reproductive work was to be outsourced from the private household through the creation of collective infrastructure, thus facilitating the participation of women in political life. At the same time, this infrastructure – all-day crèches, kindergartens, canteens, laundries, cleaning staff – would create jobs that women in particular could use to support themselves. Jobs available primarily to women would be created. In this sense, it was already recognised in the visions of that period

that the dependency relationship between productive and reproductive labour lies at the base of a labour society, because without
reproduction there is no production and vice versa.

It is not surprising that a utopic project that prioritised women's
labour force participation made great efforts precisely in this area:
training women in social, as well as technical, professions to inte-
grate them into the labour market. The success of this policy meant
that until the system transformation of the 1990s, the proportion
of women in full employment in state socialist countries was barely
below 75 percent. However, although protagonists like Kollontai
advocated for a rethinking and questioning of (hetero-)sexual-
ity and gender relations, these revolutionary works and thought
hardly reached the socialist private household: the lion's share of
reproductive work continued to be in women's hands.

Since the emergence of state socialism, women thus functioned
as (co-)breadwinners, as within this political system women's
labour market participation was the rule and not the exception.
The dominance of the housewife marriage model in the West
was countered by state socialism with the model of compulsory
employment for all adults, which a part of the Western women's
movement long considered progressive (cf. Menschik and Leopold
1974). The adult–worker model has now also found its way into
late and post-Fordist societies.

Since the early 1990s, formerly socialist countries have undergone enormous changes, not only in regard to their state system
but also in terms of gender relations. In the course of neoliberal
reforms in all countries of the post-socialist bloc, the state has withdrawn from many of its previous tasks and delegated responsibility
for care work to (the female part of) families. A characterisation
of this development as a "stagnating welfare state" (Aulenbacher
2015: 36) overlooks the massive restrictions in access to social
rights and the resulting glaring social problems. Thus, the general
trend towards a re-familialisation of care policy, which Éva Fodor
(2011: 34) appropriately calls a "return to domesticity", is better
understood as a radical marketisation of former welfare state tasks.

Due to massive cuts in family policy benefits and the rapid loss
of jobs in female-dominated fields of employment (Kałwa 2007:
208; Klaveren et al. 2010), many women were compelled to leave

the labour market. This corresponds to the conservative ideology of "new motherhood" (Szelewa and Polakowski 2008: 117). At the same time, the economic transformation led to increased pressures to migrate as families could barely survive on the remaining income of the men. Migration to Western countries, considered as a temporary solution, created new dilemmas that permeate living conditions in the region today.

FROM SOCIALIST FEMINISM TO THE NEW FEMINIST CRITIQUE OF CAPITALISM

In the Western social movements of the 1960s to 1980s – the Black Civil Rights Movement in the US, the transnational student movements and the internationally oriented feminist movements – the critique of capitalism experienced a high point as it turned towards Marxist theory. However, the autocratic practice of Marxist-inspired state forms in Eastern Europe, Asia and Africa has contributed to the fact that the implementation of socialist ideals in real socialism and communism can no longer be regarded as a successful alternative form of social organisation. This disillusion was also shared by the grouping of Socialist Feminists (Soc.Fem) anchored in the US and Europe, who combined the demand for gender justice with a critique of capitalism.[1]

In my re-reading of these movements, I am primarily interested in showing, on the basis of some striking positions of different protagonists, what points of contact can be found for the current debate relating to the new feminist critique of capitalism. The socialist–feminist theorists started from Marxist class theory, but their vision of revolutionary social transformation extended beyond the elimination of class hierarchy and the change of property relations, to include the overhauling of gender relations. In other words, they were concerned to give Marxist theory a feminist orientation (Himmelweit 1995: 2) by focusing on a "feminist materialism postulate" (Beer 1990: 77). At the core of this vision was the status of reproductive labour, and the concern of socialist feminists was above all to make visible and thus redefine unpaid domestic work as labour.

Counter-planning from the Kitchen – Wages for Housework

The Wages for Housework[2] campaign was initiated by Italian feminists in the early 1970s and taken up internationally by the rapidly growing women's movements in countries of the Western bloc. Based on the thesis that the private character of services in the household is an illusion, the campaign sought a social redefinition of "the private" and of housework. Mariarosa Dalla Costa, one of the intellectual leaders of the movement, saw the demand for payment of wages for domestic work as testing forms of struggle,

> that immediately challenge the whole structure of domestic work, through which we refuse this immediate work, refuse ourselves as housewives, and refuse the home as the ghetto of our existence; for the problem is not so much, and not exclusively, to throw down all work, but to destroy the whole housewife role. (Dalla Costa 1973: 43)

Some of the public demands went so far as to call women a class:

> Half the world's population is unpaid – this is the biggest class contradiction of all! And this is our struggle to wages for housework. It is the strategic demand; at this moment it is the most revolutionary demand for the whole working class. If we win, the class wins, if we lose, the class loses. (Polga Fortuna quoted in Edmond and Fleming 1975: 18)

The Wages for Housework movement conceptualised the housewife as the creator of labour power, which the members of her family then offered as a commodity on the capitalist labour market. In this arrangement, housewives are denied recognition of their contribution to capitalist production, as their labour is not renumerated and wages reach them only indirectly through the income of the husband or children. The view of women as a class of their own was advocated in particular by French feminists such as Christine Delphy (1984); two groups of actors – capitalists and (married) men – were considered to be the exploiters of this class. As an extension of this argumentation, a debate arose in

West Germany that went down in the history of feminism as the Bielefeld approach and was disseminated in the English-speaking world mainly through the work of Maria Mies.

The Bielefeld approach, represented by Mies, Claudia von Werlhof and Veronika Bennholdt-Thomsen, saw the blind spot of Marxist economics in the omission of all those areas that do not function according to the laws of exchange of capitalist commodity production, such as the preparation of food, household work, the daily maintenance of vital activities, and caring for children and old and sick people. They introduced the concept of the "subsistence economy", an economy that could be found both in private households in industrialised countries via what they called "Hausfrauisierung" (Housewifisation) and in the peasant communities of the "Third World":

> The housewife emerges with the citizen and the wage worker. This is a fundamental and general capitalist relation of production, which is also produced in the peasant economy of the so-called developing countries together with their transformation by capitalist commodity production. [...] The separation into socially relevant public and majority-paid work on the one hand (mainly men) and "irrelevant" private, unpaid work linked to immediate subsistence on the other (women's work is no longer considered socially relevant here) only takes place with the generalisation of commodity production and wage labour. (Bennholdt-Thomsen 1988: 48)

Here a homology of women and the "Third World" was created: "It is not women who have the status of colonies, but colonies who have the status of women. The relationship of 'First' to 'Third' World corresponds to that of man to woman" (von Werlhof 1978: 30). In their work, the Bielefeld group referred to Luxemburg's theory of imperialism (2003 [1913]) and in particular to the colonisation thesis, which posits that a perpetual original accumulation of capital and a progressive expansion of capitalism must always incorporate territories and areas in the societies of the world that do not (yet) function according to the laws of capitalist commodity production. The subsistence approach pointed out above all that colonisation outwards (the subjugation of colonies) was accompanied by colonisation inwards.[3] From the beginning, however, there were objections to this argumentation. African–American Marxist and feminist Angela Davis, for example, not only called into question the notion that women should be defined by their domestic function, regardless of class or race, but also critiqued how domestic labour was conceptualised:

> If the industrial revolution resulted in the structural separation of the home economy from the public economy, then housework cannot be defined as an integral component of capitalist production. It is, rather, related to production as precondition. [...] In other words, the capitalist production process presupposes the existence of a body of exploitable workers. (Davis 1982: 234)

This characterisation of domestic and care work as a prerequisite for the exploitation of human labour power was taken up in the debate under the term reproductive labour, but was later also heavily criticised as a male ideology on the basis that the separation of production and reproduction went hand in hand with the separation of the male (public) and female (private) spheres. Alison Jagger and William McBride (1985), instead, argued that production and maintenance should be characterised as two sides of the same coin. Davis, in her 1982 paper on the approaching obsolescence of domestic labour, pointed out that an analysis that declares all housewives in the world to be an exploited class is mistaken because it obscures differences between women, overlooking the racism faced by Black women as domestic workers in the US, for example:

> Because of the added intrusion of racism, vast numbers of Black women have had their own housekeeping and other women's home chores as well. And frequently, the demands of the job in a white woman's home have forced domestic workers to neglect her own home and even her own children. As paid housekeepers, they have been called upon to be surrogate wives and mothers in millions of white homes. (Davis 1982: 238)[4]

Davis remained sceptical about the Wages for Housework campaign, and argued that the socialist–feminist movement would be better off calling for the abolition of housework:

> The abolition of housework as the private responsibility of individual women is clearly a strategic goal of women's liberation. [...] The only significant steps toward ending domestic slavery have in fact been taken in the existing socialist countries. Working women, therefore, have a special and vital interest in the struggle for socialism. (Davis 1982: 243–4)

Her recourse to the rejection of "domestic slave labour" as articulated by Lenin, Zetkin and Kollontai underlines the political project: "In the final analysis, neither women nor men should waste precious hours of their lives on work that is neither stimulating, creative nor productive" (ibid: 223).[5] Seen from this perspective, housewives are unemployed workers (ibid.: 239). Davis also imagined that housework could be replaced by technical devices in the future and therefore it would become almost obsolete, a position that today, unfortunately, we can see was misguided. Another aspect overlooked by Davis was the fact that the Italian feminists saw their campaign above all as an intervention in the debate of the left that questioned the reduction of the political subject to the male wage worker; they were convinced that this refusal itself represented a form of struggle. Silvia Federici (2012 [1975]), for example, criticises the left for thinking that women as housewives do not suffer from capital, but from its absence:

> The left has accepted wages as the criterion by which to distinguish labour from non-labour, production from parasitism, and potential power from powerlessness. Thus, the immense amount of non-waged labour that women do for capital in the home escapes their analysis and strategy. From Lenin to Gramsci to Juliet Mitchell, there is agreement throughout the left tradition on the marginal importance of domestic labour for the reproduction of capital and of the housewife for revolutionary struggle. (Federici 2012 [1975]: 107)

Dalla Costa and Federici were not ultimately concerned with real wage demands, but understood the Wages for Housework Campaign as a necessary contribution to the reorganisation of society, to the change of the capitalist system. From this perspective, the "migration" of housewives into wage labour could also be seen as an act of refusal of housework. In her excellent re-reading of the works of socialist feminism, Kathi Weeks writes:

> As a project dedicated to mapping capitalist economies and gender regimes from a simultaneously Marxist and feminist perspective, the tradition was focused on understanding how various gendered labouring practices are both put to use by and potentially disruptive of capitalist relations of production. (Weeks 2007: 235)

In her famous essay "Marxism and Feminism: An Unhappy Marriage", the US socialist-feminist Heidi Hartmann (1981) pointedly argued that the Marxist degradation of women's emancipation to a secondary contradiction and the concomitant refusal to join the struggle against patriarchy must lead to a divorce of feminism from Marxism:

> As a general rule, men's position in patriarchy and capitalism prevents them from recognising both human needs for nurturance, sharing, and growth, and the potential for meeting those needs in a nonhierarchical, nonpatriarchal society. But even if we raise their consciousness, men might assess the potential gains against the potential losses and choose the status quo. *Men have more to lose than their chains.* (Hartmann 1981: 32–3; emphasis added)

In this quotation we find the anticipation of what 15 years later was characterised in feminist-inspired masculinity research as male symbolic capital or male complicity (Connell 1995; Bourdieu 1998). At the same time, Hartmann was critiqued for ignoring the situation of Black women in the US: Gloria Joseph (1981) rightly insisted that their living situation cannot be analysed without including racism in a Marxist and feminist conceptualisation. The question of race and racism continued to be neglected in continental Europe theorising. Nevertheless, the Soc.Fem. movements have had an enormous influence on feminist activism and theorising. Above all, the establishment of a new or expanded concept of labour emerged from these debates.

However, the revisiting of Soc.Fem. arguments cannot do without an examination of the failure of the movement and the theoretical approaches that emerged from it. While the German sociologist and social psychologist Frigga Haug (2011: 350) is of the opinion that Socialist Feminists to this day continue to employ the basic formulation of Marx and Engels in *The German Ideology* (Marx and Engels 1990 [1846]) to determine productive power by neglecting reproductive work, my re-reading shows that the references are much broader and that borrowings can be found not only from the pioneering works of Marx but also Engels, Lenin, Luxemburg and other thinkers.

Weeks explains the failure of the domestic work debate in terms of what she calls the fixation on the "dual system" or the question of whether domestic work should be grasped inside or outside capitalist production. She suggests that "by the late 1970s, the domestic work debate itself had become bogged down in the shoals of the 'inside or outside' controversy" (Weeks 2011: 16). In her view, the debate about whether domestic labour should be defined as unproductive and existing outside of capitalist production, or else as a precondition for capitalist production, is historically outdated because it related to and was limited to the world of Fordism. It seems important to me to conclude from these debates that from today's perspective, the exegesis of Marxist theory that generations of feminists and gender researchers – myself included – have undergone exposed the weaknesses of Marxism, but has not been able to initiate a broad popular debate on the recognition of reproductive/care work, its decoupling from femininity and its economic re-evaluation or upgrading.

Instead, with the help of feminism, the opening of the labour market for women was pushed forward and resulted in the adult-worker model (Lutz 2010), which not only suggests that women of working age will take up employment but also establishes it as a citizen's duty. Nevertheless, every time budget study of the past decade shows that the distribution of domestic and care work in private households is only extremely slowly beginning to change towards men taking over home and care work (see Eurostat: Genderstatistics[6]).

THE NEW FEMINIST CRITIQUE OF CAPITALISM

The new feminist critique of capitalism partly takes up the understanding of the "production of life" developed in *The German Ideology*; this includes all social activities that are necessary for the maintenance of human existence (Aulenbacher et al. 2015a: 18). The debate thus picks up insights from the early work of Marx and Engels, which is no longer to be found in the later works on value chains. At the beginning of the twenty-first century, it is rather the "carelessness" (Aulenbacher et al 2015b) of neoliberalism and financial capitalism that is critiqued. The financial economy is now considered to be an independent sector, and value creation imperatives extend to the whole of life and coexistence in qualitatively new ways.

The sociologists Brigitte Aulenbacher, Maria Dammayr and Fabienne Décieux (Aulenbacher et. al. 2015b) centralise "care" and "carelessness" in the terms of their analysis, which they link to the care debate. Their argumentation contains a new turn: the problem of the undervaluation of care work is no longer only considered in relation to unpaid domestic and care work, but also in relation to poorly paid work in the care professions. This analysis makes a revolutionary demand for the visible valorisation of care work by questioning the standard economy's notion of the human, which is oriented towards "homo economicus". Accordingly, care is not only seen as subordinate to one's own interests, but is defined as a social good in a new way (see Aulenbacher et al. 2015a).

As their work makes clear, research on care and care work must be conducted from within a critique of capitalism. That also means that in a feminist consideration of care, the redistribution of care work – in which middle-class households in the Global North engage in "disposing" unprofitable care activities to workers from poor regions of the world (Apitzsch and Schmidbaur 2010) – must be a central topic of analysis. The merit of this argument is that it escapes the nation-state container and shows how an analysis of care in the twenty-first century urgently needs to take into account transnational migration, as well as transnational care regimes and globalisation effects. The sociologist Gabriele Winker's (2015) book *Care Revolution*, on the other hand, remains entrenched in the nation-state framework, largely ignoring transnational aspects. Winker outlines a socialist utopia in which citizens are not only socialised through their gainful employment, but in which care for others is central, in a way that is not dissimilar to Nancy Fraser's model (1994) discussed below.

Winker's "guide to a social transformation based on solidarity" completely excludes from the proposed collective solution the dilemma of care migrants who have to leave their families behind and thus deprive them of care, and who on the other hand are dependent on their income as care workers. Winker also explains that her utopia ultimately relies on the abolition of private ownership of the means of production so that the sale of labour power as a commodity can be overcome (Winker 2015: 170), bringing us back to the socialist utopians of the nineteenth and twentieth centuries.[7] Philosopher Cornelia Klinger also draws on the production of life from *The German Ideology* and develops the concept of "life care", which is understood as a critique of a new form of capitalism that claims the whole person:

> [...] thus, also heart and soul, feelings and commitment, beauty and love, fantasy and dream, in short: from creatureliness to the creativity of the I in all dimensions and facets of a subjectivity. The commodification of everything and everyone, juxtaposed with the marketisation of everything that has been kept away from the rational operations of state and economy as contingent and irrational, makes the boundaries between the spheres and sectors of society permeable. (Klinger 2012: 272)

Summarising Klinger's argument, one could say that care is relevant to all spheres of society, no longer only to the private sphere in which the Socialist Feminists embedded it.

Alienation, Emotional Surplus and Deep Commodification –
The Erosion of the Boundaries between Paid and Unpaid Work

The thesis put forward by Klinger that service and finance capitalism is dependent on emotional labour, which is itself a constitutive element of post-Fordist forms of production and society, is by no means new. This idea has been put forward by Arlie Hochschild since the 1970s in what Ursula Apitzsch describes as her "sociology of emotion" (Apitzsch 2013). Hochschild begins where the US sociologist Charles Wright Mills (1951) left off in his study *White Collar: The American Middle Classes*.

Mills described the new middle class in the US as a class between the proletariat and the bourgeoisie, whose white-collar jobs required a new form of deployment of (feigned) emotions, which he sees as selling out one's personality. Hiring criteria for these jobs, according to Mills, were based on personality assessment in terms of appearance rather than qualifications. He analysed the expanding market as a new form of (self-)commodification of the working subject. While Mills' focus was male white-collar workers, Hochschild sees emotional labour as a characteristic of late capitalism. She understands emotional labour as the showing or suppression of feelings with the aim of maintaining the outward posture that has a desired effect on others (Hochschild 2003: 7). Hochschild thus not only understands emotional labour to be a new form of labour, but also considers it to be socially necessary labour.[8] Weeks (2011: 20) rightly sees this as "a compelling analysis of the constitutive effects of immaterial labour", a description of the production of subjectivity, with a focus on the process of producing it; efforts to love or enjoy their customers help employees to identify with their job (Hochschild 2003: 6). The production of gender, i.e. the production of a gender-normed habitus, is part of this labour and, according to Hochschild, represents an added value for employers. Following Marx's concept of reification and alienation, Hochschild draws parallels between the forms of alienation of child labour in the nineteenth century and those of workers performing emotional labour in contemporary post-Fordist service society:

For all the differences between manual labour and emotional labour, there is a similarity in the potential cost of the work: the worker can be removed or alienated from the part of the self that is used for the work – whether it is the body or the psyche. (Hochschild 2003: 31)

In the production of emotional labour, both the separation between inside (I as self) and outside (I as worker) and that between consumption and production are eroded. The dissolution of labour boundaries is thus inherent in "emotional capitalism" (Illouz 2007), and accordingly also manifests itself in an interaction of commodification and decommodification processes: the lifestyles and demands of middle and top earners drive the growth of a market of service providers who take over (part of) the formerly unpaid work. This includes care and provision work in all phases of life: childcare and care of the elderly and sick, wedding and child planning, cleaning, tutoring, training dogs, the leisure and events management of family celebrations and children's birthdays; this and much more is handed over to service providers. Emotional work is demanded of workers in a comprehensive way and their success is measured by the provision of emotional added value (Hochschild 2012). One could draw the conclusion from Hochschild's work on the sociology of emotions that a process of feminisation of labour competences is taking place through the spread of emotional labour. However, she does not go that far herself, but points out that the production of gender is to be understood as a kind of (self-)commodification. In summary, the new feminist critique of contemporary neoliberal capitalism starts from an expanded concept of labour which remains in or exceeds Marxist theoretical frameworks, and that was fought for by the feminist movements.

My impression is that Marxism is being rediscovered today for the feminist care debate, and that it is being discussed, supplemented and revised in much more unorthodox and creative ways than was the case in previous generations. So far, the tendency towards exegesis that characterised some of the old debates has been absent, which in my view is very welcome. There are, however, two problematic elements that should be briefly outlined here. First, the expansion of the concept of affective or emotional labour in both Hochschild's and Klinger's versions threatens to level down the connection with social class if migrant care workers, as well as CEOs of large companies, can be seen to be required to do emotional work alike. In this commonality, the differences between these groupings in terms of pay, working conditions, social security, racism and alienation disappear. With regard to migrant care work, this analytic framework would neglect the dimension of domination, as well as the social and emotional costs of migrant women and their families having to live apart from each other for months and years, a fact that I have described as a component of transnational social inequality (Lutz 2018b). Second, with a few exceptions, feminist critiques of capitalism continue to lack a serious examination of the central importance of racialisation for the care debate. This oversight compromises its analytical usefulness given that transnational migrant women today, just like Black women in the US, South Africa and other (post-)colonial societies over a period of centuries (see Davis 1982; Romero 1992; Cock 1989), were and still are found in the private households of the (white) middle classes as cheap care workers in precarious employment situations; at the same time they have to leave the care of their own children to substitute mothers, grandmothers or older children (Romero 2013). Therefore, it becomes clear that "care" has at least two faces, one for the care receiver and one for the (migrant) care worker; the relationship between the two is characterised by mutual dependency under the conditions of asymmetrical power relations (see Lutz 2007a, 2011).

Another neglected aspect of care is articulated in studies of (post-)colonial, racist discourses. For example, the Swedish sociologists Diana Mulinari and Anders Neergaard (2013) analyse the racist discourse of members of the right-wing populist party Sweden Democrats, in which care is used as a linguistic cover. These politicians are concerned with care and support for "autochthonous Swedes", while also arguing that immigration to Sweden has disadvantages not only for the autochthonous Swedes, but also for migrants and refugees themselves:

Care may be extended to the racialised other arguing that their migration to Sweden (while of course not being good for Sweden and the "Swedes") is also bad for the migrants themselves. In this sense, caring racism is also formulated as helping migrants by sending them back to their "true" home. (Mulinari and Neergaaard 2014: 52)

Mulinari and Neergaard see this care rhetoric as a continuation of a colonial discourse of care in which the superiority of colonial rule was expressed and consolidated with the help of "care for the colonised", a form of epistemic violence in which so-called care for others is clearly used as power over the other(s).

POLANYI'S RECONSTRUCTION OF CAPITALISM

As already indicated, several authors engaged in critiquing contemporary capitalism refer to Karl Polanyi's 1944 work *The Great Transformation* (Fraser 2013; Aulenbacher et al. 2015a; Aulenbacher et al. 2018; Safuta and Degavre 2013; Lutz 2017b). His analysis focused on market fundamentalism, or the so-called self-regulating market. Although Polanyi's analysis drew from Marx's early writings on money and alienation, he argued that exploitation had diminished over the course of the industrial revolution. While Marx saw exploitation as the central experience of capitalism, Polanyi located this experience in commodification (Burawoy 2015: 127–8). He describes the compulsion generated by capitalism for the expansion and autonomisation of markets, along with the demand for (social) protection from the excesses that this compulsion triggers. At the centre of his "moral indictment of unregulated commodification" (ibid: 127) lies the deconstruction of the myth of the self-regulating market, which first emerged, according to Polanyi, in the years of the burgeoning industrial revolution around 1830–40 in England. There, for the first time, land, labour and money had been commodified, or turned into "fictitious commodities", with the consequence that these fundamental elements of human life could be casually bought and sold. According to Polanyi, the historically preceding mercantilism, despite its pronounced tendencies towards commercialisation, had not known such excesses but had protected the fundamental elements of production, labour and land from being transformed into objects of trade (Polanyi 1978: 104). In contrast, the credo of the self-organised market was the prevention of state intervention in market conditions:

> The mechanism of the market is interlocked with the various elements of the commercial economy through the concept of the commodity. [...] Meanwhile, labour, land and money are not commodities: the assertion that everything that is bought and sold had to be produced for the purpose of sale is clearly false in relation to these factors. In other words, according to the empirical definition of the commodity, it is not a commodity. [...] The designation of labour, land and money as commodities is thus entirely fictitious. (ibid.: 107–8)

Polanyi added that no society could bear the effects of such a system for even a short time "unless its human and natural substance as well as its economic structure were protected against the ravages of this diabolical mechanism" (ibid.: 109). He identifies a dual movement in the nineteenth century in which market organisation was expanded in relation to real commodities but restricted in relation to fictitious commodities, and distinguishes a controlled (embedded) from an unleashed (dis-embedded) market system. Nancy Fraser highlights the importance of Polanyi's conceptualisation of the commodification of nature for feminists' critique of capitalism, in particular the way that it integrates into the analysis of the ecological dimension of life: controlled markets develop comprehensive social protection mechanisms that protect humans and nature from destruction, whereas market systems externalised from the lifeworld context – unleashed markets – require humans and nature to swim naked in the ice water of selfish calculations (Fraser 2013: 143).

According to Fraser, Polanyi's distinction between controlled and unleashed markets is noteworthy in that he does not – unlike many others – anticipate a system collapse, but rather presents a critique of crisis that does not reject the entire market system, but only its dangerous and unleashed variants (ibid.: 139, 143). Fraser adds a third dimension to Polanyi's distinction that does not leave the task of protection to a benevolent democratic state, but which is enabled by the emancipation movements of civil society. Their goal is not the humanisation of market systems, but the abolition of domination (ibid.: 145, 148). She criticises Polanyi's model for its lack of analysis of gender hierarchies or of colonial and racist exploitation, which are important axes of power for the status quo of the ruling classes. She writes:

> Emancipation fires the passion of successors to the new social movements, including multiculturalists, international feminists, gay and lesbian liberationists, cosmopolitan democrats, human rights activists and proponents of global justice. (ibid.: 156)

Fraser's credo differs from other critics of capitalism in that she does not fundamentally question the existence of markets, but primarily their excesses. It is in this framework that emancipation movements have a key role in mediating between marketisation and social protection. Nevertheless:

> Equally, however, conflicts between protection and emancipation must be mediated by marketisation. Thus, the critique I have made of Polanyi can also be turned against the adherents of emancipation [...] [as they] have neglected the impact of marketisation projects on conflicts between social protection and emancipation. (ibid.)

Here, Fraser is clearly committed to a market system overseen by the welfare state. Interestingly, in these remarks she does not go back to the alternative care model she designed in the early 1990s, the universal caregiver model, which is presented in detail below.

NANCY FRASER'S POST-INDUSTRIAL THOUGHT EXPERIMENT: THE ORGANISATION OF LIFE FROM A CARE PERSPECTIVE

In her seminal article "After the Family Wage: A Postindustrial Thought Experiment" (Fraser 1994), Fraser questions the logic of how the connection between work and private life is organised in late capitalist societies. She is particularly critical of the fact that the resource demands of the workplace (time, flexibility, mobility) have escalated to become the clock of private family life. She addresses the situation in many post-industrial welfare states where although gender justice is enshrined in law, care work continues to be culturally regarded as a female obligation, with men expected to function largely as family breadwinners. Fraser lays out various options to resolve these contradictions: a) the universal breadwinner model, b) equal distribution of care, and c) the universal caregiver model.

Fraser sees the ideal of the universal breadwinner as an ambitious scenario, the implementation of which is crucially dependent on whether employment-promoting services such as day care, child care, or care for the elderly are available, and thus whether women – freed from their care responsibilities – can take up full-time employment on similar terms as men (ibid.: 51–2). Job reforms and macroeconomic policies to create high-paying and permanent full-time jobs for women would be needed. Governments would have to make care work services available as a public good, or finance their marketing through vouchers, which would then, however, be delegated to migrant and Black women, usually at low pay (ibid.: 52). Such a scenario hardly leads to overcoming androcentrism: "It valorises men's traditional sphere – employment – and simply tries to help women fit in" (ibid.: 54). Thus, the universalisation of the male half of the breadwinner/housewife couple would be realised and with it the demand on all adults of working age to perform this service.

With regard to the second model – the equal distribution of care – the aim, according to Fraser, is not to equalise women's lives with men's, but to make the differences "cost-free": child-rearing, housework and care are equated with formal paid work (ibid.: 55). While in the universal breadwinner model, care work is outsourced to the state and the market, in the parity distribution model it remains in the household and is supported by the state with public funds. The advantage of this model is that care is valued and there is no demand that women conform to the male norm. Apart from many complicated aspects of legal implementation, however, Fraser sees the main problem in the fact that the valuing of care work does not go so far as to demand it of men and nor does it require men to change (ibid.: 59).

Both models, Fraser summarises, require major political and economic restructuring, such as public control over corporations, and the ability to tax profits and wealth to fund quality social programmes, the realisation of which in turn would require broad public support. However, neither model would fully address the care dilemma. Fraser presents the universal caregiver model (UCG), which would make women's caring responsibilities the norm for all, thus enabling both men and women to combine parenthood, care for the elderly and gainful employment. This would be accompanied by new articulations of masculinity, as well as a radical change in the co-organisation of life and work (ibid.: 62). As a consequence, all workers would also be caregivers and all would be entitled to assistance through employment-supporting services. Care work would not be passed on to social services, babysitters and carers, but would be carried out by relatives and friends in households where people with children and elderly people live (ibid.: 61). Achieving such a situation, Fraser notes, would require the deconstruction of gender relations, undermining the gendered division of labour and reducing the importance of gender as a structural principle of social organisation. This requires a thorough rethinking and redefinition of the role of care in the post-industrial context where, so far, the world of work sets the pace while activities that threaten to disrupt this pace are outsourced to the market. Given the extent of change required, such a model seems rather utopian. Fraser is aware of this when she writes: "But it is the only imaginable post-industrial world that promises true gender justice. And unless we are guided by this vision now, we will never get any closer to achieving it" (ibid.: 62). I agree with this sentiment, as I think utopic thinking is all the more important at times that cynicism prevails. We need a re-evaluation of the entire world of work services from the point of view of sustainability and care with an aim to abolishing social inequality. The latter implies an implementation of this model not only in the existing welfare states, but also in a transnational regime involving the migrating actors from the countries of origin.

CONCLUSION

This chapter has focused on the relationship between unpaid care work and paid gainful employment, an issue that has been on the agenda of several social movements since the mid-nineteenth century. Women's right to access paid work was discussed and demanded in different branches of the women's movement. However, from the beginning there were fierce disputes about what implementation should look like. The bourgeois and social democratic women's movements preferred the commodification of reproductive and care work, which was in essence the continuation of the bourgeois servant model, albeit in the form of gainful employment secured by labour law. Their vision thus continued to rely on the undervaluation of household and care work compared to other activities. While a range of models were discussed among socialists, the implementation of women's equality under state socialism/communism consisted primarily of declaring full female employment as the norm (co-earner principle) and regulating it through state-imposed financial restrictions (such as low salaries for single-earner households). In addition, a comprehensive infrastructure contributed to the relief of women (crèches and kindergartens, all-day schools, school canteens, old people's homes, early retirement etc.) and to the reconciliation of work and family life. However, the radical project of transforming the gender order called for by Kollontai (1977 [1909]) and her contemporaries was side-lined, and gender relations remained largely unchanged within private households.

The Western socialist–feminist movements adopted the demand for women's right to access the labour market and called for the state provision of care infrastructures, primarily for childcare. With the exception of France and the Nordic countries, these demands were implemented only very hesitantly and ultimately inadequately in most European welfare states, with the result that full female employment was only rudimentarily realised and for most working women translated into a double burden. The sociologist Paula England (2010) has appropriately described this development as a "stalled revolution". In principle, access to the labour market has been achieved, but a cultural and economic re-coding of care work away from female responsibility to a societal one is no closer.

Since the mid-1990s, a so-called social investment approach in OECD[9] countries has made investment in good education and training of children the primary investment goal of the future (OECD 1997), and in this framework has promoted the expansion of kindergartens, preschools and parental support. However, it is evident that this policy does not focus on gender equality at all, but on the contrary promotes a child-centred perspective that demands a renewed maternalism that places increased and new demands on good motherhood: "By focusing on the mother-child-dyad, this new maternalism within national and international discourses renders invisible the gender equality goals carried by national and international feminist mobilisations" (Jenson 2017: 281; see also Aulenbacher et al. 2018). The demand for gender-equitable policies in relation to the care of the elderly and sick has also not been adequately addressed by the social policies of most welfare states. Although there are drafts and also a couple of partly realised new models, for example in the association of pensioners in residential care communities in Austria and Germany (Riegraf and Reimer 2014), or the foundation of alternative living communities in the form of commons (Widding Isaksen et al. 2009), the major social debates that would enable such alternatives to emerge from the margins have so far been absent. Instead, the increased introduction of cash-for-care policies in European welfare states since the beginning of the twenty-first century (cf. Williams 2010) continue to promote the commodification of care, giving it new relevance as a fictitious commodity.

The care work performed by migrants fulfils a specific function in the care economy. They fill the gaps that have arisen in state regulations: flexibility for a limited period of time and at low wages (see Lutz 2017b). The universal caregiver model designed by Fraser has not been publicly discussed, nor have there been any serious debates on the preconditions for its implementation. One of the few attempts in this direction was made in 2011 by the European Social Platform, an association of 46 European NGOs (European Social Platform 2011). The European Social Platform critiqued the imbalance in the relationship between gainful employment and care work from a gender democratic perspective, framing the one-sided transfer of family care work to women as a violation of equality law and principles. The platform considers the entitlement to care as a universal human right and calls for a paradigm shift that rejects the current profit motive in the care sector. These demands go in the direction outlined by Fraser, as they challenge the common gendered division of labour and the meaning of gender as a structural principle of social organisation. It has become clear that there are social forces that want a change in this direction, but social movements that carry these demands into the public sphere and into (political) parties are not yet strong enough. In addition, the questioning and readjustment of common values in the evaluation of work is an extraordinarily complex project that penetrates the comfort zones even of those who are committed to transformation.

I was puzzled by the comment of one of my students who said that she was very sympathetic to the universal caregiver model and could go along with it, but only on the condition that political work would be counted as care work. In my response to her, I pointed to the famous disputes between men and women in the Socialist German Student Union in 1968, in which the female members problematised the way that political work was valued higher than care work and that the latter was left to women. Each generation needs its own approach and a relevant utopia on these questions. I say this in the spirit of the philosopher Ernst Bloch who argued that concrete utopias develop in the process of realisation and are brought forth through attempts: "On the way to the new, one must usually, if not always, proceed step by step. Not everything is possible and realisable at all times; a lack of conditions not only inhibits but blocks" (Bloch 1978: 235–6).

For care workers, whose perspective is the focus of this book, the reorganisation and redesign of care work according to the universal caregiver model would represent progress only if it took into account the transnational interconnections of economy and society, and promoted a redistribution of wealth in a global context. Nevertheless, pending any utopic project, the working and living conditions of those affected need to be improved urgently.

7

The Care Economy after COVID-19: Vulnerability and Resilience

This chapter will consider the impact of the COVID pandemic on care for the elderly in the German-speaking countries, which is a field that depends on the mobility of migrants. Did COVID-19 change the view of care and of care migrants' working conditions and payment? Has the public perception of care work shifted towards a greater appreciation of migrant women's work? What have the consequences of the pandemic been with regard to the transnational care economy?

The reaction of most states to a microscopic virus with enormous mobility, crossing borders unnoticed and settling all over the world, was to close their borders. However, this governmental action of sealing national borders and obstructing the mobility of people ultimately turned out to be ineffective at keeping the virus at bay. Instead, these measures had enormous negative effects in particular for socially disadvantaged groups, including welfare recipients, single working-class mothers and refugees. With regard to the women who are the subject of this book, it had a negative impact on the (circular) migration of (care-)workers as the lockdown of inner-European borders created enormous problems in the households of care receivers and caregivers. Migrant care workers were initially either denied entry to the receiving countries or faced quarantine restrictions, whether in the receiving countries or their home countries. Sending countries such as Poland imposed a 14-day quarantine on returning migrants, compliance with which was monitored by the state, for example through police controls. These conditions, as I will show, put many migrant caregivers in situations where they were compelled to make difficult decisions.

The pandemic sparked debates in migration studies about whether it would be a turning point for the better leading to greater globalised labour force mobility in the long term. Some, including myself,[1] were rather sceptical and feared that the economic and social focus on growth and markets would quickly readjust after the end of the coronavirus pandemic in societies committed to financial capitalism, which has indeed been the case. The International Labour Organisation, for example, noted in 2022 that as COVID-19 waned, a whole series of multiple crises were intensifying (civil wars, inflation, new epidemics, environmental problems such as drought, flooding, etc.): "These crises are likely to further increase labour market inequalities due to the disproportionate impact on certain groups of workers and firms, while contributing to a growing divergence between developed and developing economies" (ILO 2022: 1).[2]

In the first part of this chapter, I will present the voices of care migrants. I will then give an overview of the way the German-speaking receiving countries dealt with the Corona crisis in regard to migrant caregivers. The final part will deal with sociological attempts to conceptualise the COVID-19 crisis and its consequences.

VOICES OF MIGRANT WOMEN

Polish migrant caregivers were interviewed during the summer of 2020, six[3] months into the pandemic.[4] The interviewer started by asking how they were doing and how they had spent the last few months, before going on to ask whether they had received any help from their placement agencies, the families of the care-receivers, or elsewhere, and finally whether they expected a change of working conditions once the pandemic was over.

Mala – "We are a grey zone"

When it comes to my working in Germany – well, that's difficult, in the sense that I actually worked for two and a half months without having any time off. The person I was looking after no longer went to day care.[5] This is a person who really needs care. Well, without having time off, I protested a bit at the end. Because

I had *two people* to look after and, and well, the man died on 16 May. He'd just been lying there for the last few weeks. This is someone who was almost 190 cm, not slim, the weight plays a role here. I was simply no longer able to help him to the toilet. And well, he didn't sleep at night either. So, for three weeks, I didn't sleep much, I worked a lot, and I just couldn't stand it.

During these weeks, Mala had the task of looking after two people in the same household all day. The number of hours she spent caring for both care receivers, in particular helping the man, had changed dramatically.

And I think I should have been paid extra for that. You know, my contract says that I work 160 hours a month, yes? So, an average of 40 hours a week. If you convert that to seven days, then I should effectively work about five and a half hours each day, because, generally speaking, those are all working hours, yes? … That means I clean, tidy up, cook, wash. The rest, that's on-call duty, so to speak. I should have been guaranteed one break daily, two to three hours. I should have at least one full day off guaranteed. I should have, let's say, eleven hours of uninterrupted sleep [on a rest day]. Well. So, I say to the agency it would be right to pay a little extra! On top of the salary. They replied: 'Well, it's a hard time for everyone', and that they weren't going to turn to the families for a pay rise. Whereas when the man I was looking after died, they cut my salary all the more quickly, of course, because there was now one person less.

Like most of her colleagues, Mala received no financial recognition for her extra work, not even for the end-of-life care, neither from the clients' families nor from her agency.

I am on these digital portals for carers, and I can see that the salaries have gone up. Yes, for caregivers. They may not be high amounts, but they have gone up, whereas my agency hasn't increased the salaries. While the Germans have given their carers something on top – bonuses – during the pandemic, but there's no mention of us. We are a grey zone.

Mala had learned from television and digital media that care-givers in German retirement homes and hospitals received a financial bonus for their work. None of our interviewees were offered bonuses, in large part due to the structure of the employment relationship. Since the Polish agencies are responsible for recruiting and sending care workers, they did not consider it their responsibility to negotiate a bonus with the German agencies with which they cooperate. The German agencies, for their part, consider themselves primarily responsible for the communication with care worker-employing relatives. This model ignores to a large extent the employers' duty of care towards their employees. As a result, care workers have little manoeuvring space between these two agencies; instead, a "grey zone", as Mala appropriately calls it, emerged, for which neither the Polish nor German agencies claimed responsibility.

Asked whether she expects an improvement of working conditions and better pay once the pandemic is over, she responded: "I'm waiting for that. I'm sure I won't live to see it, maybe at some point it will finally be sorted out. [laughs] Because for the time being, Poland isn't trying to do anything like that, it's just as if we don't exist." She added that she had no hope for the improvement of her own working conditions in the future: "I don't see anything! You know, it's the kind of work where you can't change too much, yes? Well, you go to old, sick people and you have to do your job, whether there's coronavirus or not."

Malwina – "If they would ask just once"

All care workers interviewed emphasised that they lacked information and support from the Polish agencies. They mentioned that the agencies had gone to great effort to deliver care migrants to their places of work, usually by providing small buses, in order to minimise the risk of infection. Apart from this, they were unsupported by the agencies. The interviewees reported that they had been left alone to solve the new tasks they faced in their clients' households. To protect themselves and their clients, the carers had to buy sanitisers, gloves and masks, often paying for these out of their own pockets. Most of them mentioned their understanding for the initial problems of the sending agencies, notably finding carers willing to prolong their stay and recruitment of new care workers willing to function as replacements. They confirmed that at the beginning of the pandemic, the agencies did not know if they could deliver the care workers to the households of their clients.

"They begged us to stay longer," Malwina reported. Once the migrants had either agreed to extend the originally arranged working period or to travel to the clients despite the difficult circumstances, risk of infection and difficulties with border controls, hardly any attention was paid to the problems faced by the carers.

Mawlina returned to Poland, before coming back to Germany later for another placement. The Polish state required that returning migrants undergo a 14-day quarantine. She did not want her husband to be tied to the house with her for 14 days, explaining:

> I rented a flat, so that my husband didn't have to live in prison. I don't know, a man of that age, he's 74 years old, if he can't even walk across the street, that would be a tragedy for him. That's why I paid for a flat out of my own pocket, I rented it. With the help of friends, of course. And I lived there on my own for a fortnight.

Compliance with the quarantine obligation was strictly monitored by the local Polish authorities, and Malwina accepted additional costs in order not to "force" her husband into quarantine. She did not receive any money from the agency to cover these costs; apparently the agencies assumed that the migrants and their relatives would find a solution.

When asked whether she saw any advantages in working with an agency, she replied: "Absolutely none. Absolutely none. If that's the point, then unfortunately not. I only heard the words 'Thank you' and nothing else."

All interviewees reported numerous examples of specific difficulties caused by the pandemic that they were left to handle on their own without additional support. For example, a large number of the senior clients suffered from dementia, and in most cases the task of explaining the effects of the pandemic fell to the migrant care workers. Malwina described how she dealt with the client she was supporting at the time of the interview:

She doesn't understand. I have to keep explaining to her why it's like this – what's going on, why she can't receive visits from her friends. Because she was always visited by her friends who are the same age, and now they can't come, both to protect themselves and to protect her. She has to walk at least a bit; she has no other exercise than these walks. It's a good thing that we live on a housing estate with small houses, where people give us a wide berth when we go for a walk. But you can't go to the park. That makes it even more difficult, because it's hard for a person of this age with Alzheimer's to understand why that is.

The German government considered elderly citizens the "most vulnerable" group of the population, and as such, relatives of seniors were advised not to visit them during the pandemic, in order to avoid exposing them to infection. The interviews show that this advice led to a situation in many cases where clients received no visits at all. Most of the interviewees reported that children and friends of the care recipients gave telephone instructions on how to deal with the situation, for example with regard to shopping behaviour or giving the care recipients exercise by taking them for walks. There were a few exceptions, including the family for which Mawlina worked. She recounted:

Where I am now, I've been working for 16 years. This family is very friendly. The daughter of the man I was looking after came to visit me. They came to see if I was okay. [laughs] Whether they could help in any way…. So, I'm very happy. The only thing I've lost is free time. Time that I have for myself. Because I can't leave my client alone for long. So, I don't have any free time. That means, I do have some, but only on site. I can go to my room, but I have to stay in the house. Her family asked me to go outside with her, go for walks, things like that.

Even if the family members – as in this case – were grateful and supportive, they generally did not offer a bonus of their own accord. When the staff of Malwina's agency had difficulty finding replacements for the gaps left by other migrant women who feared infection at work or during the journey, she agreed to replace a colleague in another client's home. She was not offered a bonus or salary increase.

Like all other interviewees, Mawlina confirmed that she did not receive important information about COVID-19 from her brokering agency, but rather from Facebook postings. She commented: "If they would ask just once, inform us when it comes to the questions of quarantine or anything else. They somehow don't care! My agency isn't interested in that at all."

Lidwina – "Because if the Contract Says '24 hours', Then That Means She Has to Work 24 hours"

Lidwina, a woman in her early 70s, had been working as a caregiver in private households of German senior citizens for 17 years. Over this time, she designed an unusual arrangement: her husband accompanied her to work and stayed with her in the household. He took care of repairs, mowed the lawn and accompanied his wife and her clients on outings. She explained: "The employment contract is in my name, my husband just has some kind of minijob, for any kind of work: gardening, clearing leaves, clearing snow, any heavy work."

Lidwina and her husband decided to work exclusively directly through German labour contracts and companies, because these include the payment of social insurance contributions. She accused Polish agencies of lying, explaining that these agencies assure the care workers that the agency's obligation to pay pension insurance contributions in Poland is adhered to, but they never pay the contributions or pay less than they are supposed to. Lidwina commented: "And then they take a lot of money every month [from the families] for the carer. Well, for me that's damned unfair, it's almost a crime. And that's why we've never worked with a Polish agency."

At the time of the interview, the couple was in their home in Poland, and had been waiting for five long months for the carer whom they were supposed to replace to return to Poland.

The carer who was already there didn't want to go home when the restrictions were imposed in our country: she couldn't do the 14-day quarantine because she lives with her family in a large house, with children, with grandchildren. And she was afraid that she might infect someone. .... And that's why she extended her stay so long that she's still there today. And we stayed in Poland, yes. [laughs] So our situation has become more complicated and for the time being we're at "zero", because the woman hasn't said anything about wanting to go back home.

As a result of the other caregiver's decision to stay in Germany, the couple lost their income.

And we also got a fright in a certain sense, because we don't know what the future holds, what it will look like. We've really limited our private plans.... We're afraid of spending money or planning anything at all.

Lidwina describes very well the situation of many live-in caregivers who had to make difficult, almost impossible decisions. Asked whether she thought that there would be an improvement in working conditions and better support of the working conditions on the part of the agencies in the future, she said:

I am on one of the portals where I get these newsletters.[6] And it turns out that nobody suffers from a shortage of carers, and on some portals, I even read that Polish companies, or companies that have something to do with Poland and are active in Germany, have simply adapted and sent coaches so that the carers have no problems. Someone organises, let's say, a group of carers locally in Romania, in Ukraine, in Bulgaria, and the company sends a coach to pick them up and drive them to Germany. And they simply switch to these countries[7] – well, because the women there have even fewer demands, so to speak, because of the living conditions in the respective country. In other words, there will certainly always be many willing women in these countries who previously had no work permit in Germany. As long as this market has not somehow filled up. Well, I don't see that the agencies have suffered from this coronavirus, because I can see that the demand [for live-in carers] is there all the time.

Here, she refers to the fear of being replaced by a cheaper labour force, something that has indeed been accelerated by the pandemic. Lidwina's criticism was not only directed at the problematic Polish agencies, firms and authorities, however, but also German employers and their escalating requirements of live-in caregivers: "The moment a caregiver comes to someone, to a father or mother who is already so ill that they need 24-hour care, the cleaning lady or domestic help is dismissed, because then the caregivers are supposed to look after all of that work."

Apart from the only male caregiver we interviewed, all our interviewees reported that their work was often not limited to caring for, supporting and looking after the needs of the senior person, but also cooking, washing, cleaning and maintaining the household. As Lidwina put it:

> Normally, there is a cleaning lady in these households. But when it turns out that there's a carer from Poland, she does all that. The carer simply must divide up her working day so that she can do it all. Because if the contract says "24 hours", then that means she works 24 hours.

Clearly, migrant caregivers found themselves in the dilemma of either submitting to these demands or giving up the occupation altogether.

"ESSENTIAL" WORKERS AND APPLAUSE FOR THE CAREGIVERS?

In the first weeks of the pandemic, doctors and nurses were applauded from balconies in many countries for performing life-threatening care work for infected citizens. The commitment of medical staff was publicly celebrated. By contrast, none of this recognition applied to migrant care workers who looked after senior citizens. There are several reasons for this, including the invisibility of migrant senior care in private households, the lack of public recognition of household and care work in the intimate sphere, and the unclear legal situation linked with the existence of a legal grey area.

During the first couple of months of lockdowns in 2020 there was a danger that the rotation system would break down due to border closures. As already mentioned, one of the first reactions from the placement agencies was to ask migrant caregivers to overstay in "their households", as their replacement would not be able to travel due to border controls. In Austria, which has long implemented the legal regulation of care workers' placements in private households through brokering agencies, the government introduced a one-off, tax-free bonus of €500 for those caregivers who extended their working period for at least four weeks.[8] Unfortunately, it turned out that many carers were not able to benefit from this bonus because the state restricted the transfer to Austrian bank accounts.

Shortly after this action in Austria, the German association of placement agencies, VHBP, unsuccessfully called on the German government to make the same offer (VHBP 2020a). However, a couple of weeks later, when farmers resisted the closing of the national borders for asparagus-picking seasonal workers from Central and Eastern Europe, the government gave in and opened the border for this group of workers and then also for workers in the meat processing industry. Interestingly, when the trade unions drew attention to the hygienically unacceptable accommodation and working conditions in these occupations, the state forced employers to improve labour and living conditions, including the payment of higher salaries. The VHBP referred to these regulations and protested against the state's inflexibility with regard to domestic/care workers (VHBP 2020b), initially with little success.

The Austrian government started negotiations with sending countries, including Croatia, Slovakia and Romania. In some Austrian provinces, the local placement agencies, in collaboration with local chambers of commerce, organised charter flights and flew in 355 caregivers from Romania, Bulgaria and Croatia. In addition, special night trains were allowed to bring 2,000 care workers from Romania, and the same trains were used for the return journey of the care workers being relieved (see Leiblfinger et al. 2020: 145–6). Although this showed that collaboration between the government, local chambers of commerce and brokering agencies was possible, the implementation revealed major deficits, for example no instructions or information were provided in the migrants' home languages.

Meanwhile, the German government's first official response to the COVID pandemic was to facilitate family members' caring roles for their elderly dependents by offering wage compensation for short-term absence from work in order to fulfil care obligations. The accompanying leave provision was doubled from 10 to 20 working days. In addition, the government flexibilised unpaid family care leave (BMSFJ, n.d.). Such measures were introduced when families reported difficulties in finding care workers for their parents. These moves underlined the essential familialism of the German care system; at the same time, they demonstrate that from the government's point of view live-ins and family members are interchangeable. As mentioned above, options were sought for the admission of female migrant carers, and the government finally responded by relaxing border regulations, for example between Poland and Germany. The border police refrained from checking minibuses transporting migrant carers to and from Germany on the condition that the brokering agencies issued documentation. Despite some confusion arising from diverging practices between the German federal states, there appeared to be an unspoken consensus that care workers were not obliged to quarantine in Germany before being allowed to enter their "work places". However, none of this was publicly announced. It can be assumed that the practice of tacitly allowing care workers to enter the country was a way to pacify the employing families of an estimated 500,000 to 800,000 live-ins (see also Safuta and Noack 2020).

The Swiss government generally permitted the entry of migrant carers for work purposes as long as families were able to present a valid work permit. No further work restrictions or regulations were introduced, which may have something to do with the fact that live-in care for the elderly in Switzerland had not yet reached the same level as in Germany or Austria (see Chapter One).

This analysis of the COVID-19 state interventions in the three German-speaking countries shows that the living and working conditions of migrant caregivers were barely acknowledged. As demonstrated by the extracts from the interviews above, the work itself became even more demanding when friends and family members no longer visited their (grand)mothers and (grand) fathers, because they were advised by the government not to. Working conditions became more precarious and care workers faced additional burdens, both physical and emotional, when for example the outpatient care services no longer provided support or the care labour distribution between carers and family members collapsed. Instead, the caregivers were not only made responsible for managing and organising household and care work, but also for additional tasks, such as organising the provision of medical care. As we can see in the interview extracts, in many cases family members were no longer present or providing support, and so the migrant carers, whose rest periods were already restricted before the pandemic, had to take over all physical, psychological and mental care.

The interviews show that migrant carers were faced with difficult decisions: either they prolonged their stay from usually six to eight weeks to extend to several months, which necessarily led to an extended separation from their families, friends and homes, or they exposed themselves to risks connected with travelling. If they decided to stay in their home towns, this led to a loss of income and as a consequence to financial hardship in the long run. In cases where migrants decided to extend the usual working period and remained in the care receiver's household, the rotation system was interrupted and their colleagues could not take over. The latter group was disadvantaged and, as a result, often faced financial difficulties. Ultimately, for many of the carers, this decision entailed a consideration of how to minimise the physical and social costs for themselves and their relatives left behind. As governments did not take their living and working situation into account, they had to bear the consequences themselves. In addition, the pandemic not only harmed the flow of migrant workers but accordingly interrupted the flow of remittances.

Although rhetoric during the pandemic repeatedly emphasised how "substantial" the services of nurses and caregivers were, with the exception of the one-off Austrian bonus payment, migrant workers were generally not offered a pay rise or bonus for (over-) staying in this critical situation, neither by the agencies nor their employers. As Chiara Giordano (2020: 8) writes: "While they were given the possibility to save their jobs – in return for the intensification of their effort (working extra hours, performing health tasks which were not allowed in normal times, renouncing their time off, etc.) – they were locked down with a family other than their own". As a result, they had to deal with a particular burden of emotional and psychological isolation. The hope that this group of migrant caregivers would be rewarded for their efforts and dedication, and that working conditions would be improved, did not materialise.

While the pandemic was often portrayed in mainstream rhetoric as a virus that targeted its victims indiscriminately, not differentiating between wealthy and poor, it was by no means a social equaliser. To the contrary: social differences have rarely been as poignantly clear as they were during this period. As the sociologist Didier Fassin (2020) underlined, it is a dangerous illusion to think that the virus affected people equally or in the same way:

> The COVID-19 pandemic has done something unprecedented: Threatened by a potentially deadly virus, life suddenly became our most precious commodity, so precious in fact that it could be sacrificed, at least in part, for another commodity that many considered of higher value, namely growth combined with limits on public spending. By reversing our values, biological life was prioritised over economic life. Health over wealth, as some say..... However, it is clear that not all lives are of equal value.... The coronavirus-induced celebration of life does not have the same meaning for everyone, and it is even likely that the epidemic will further exacerbate the pre-death inequalities that undermine our society.

In other words, far from being an equaliser, the pandemic deepened existing structural social and economic inequalities.

BIOPOLITICS, VULNERABILITY AND CARE EXTRACTIVISM

Already during the coronavirus pandemic, a range of sociological critical analyses of the healthcare system and the pandemic were utilising two philosophical concepts: biopolitics associated with Michel Foucault and vulnerability as configured by Judith Butler.

Foucault's essay on the origins of modern state power traces the emergence of forms of power in the context of new (state) governing technologies and modernisation (Foucault 2014). What Foucault conceptualises as biopolitics includes the control of populations' health profiles, the regulation of birth rates, as well as guidelines for the preservation of public health, that is to say health checks over the course of a lifetime (from the cradle to the grave). As Sonja Gassner (2020) points out, Foucault's conception of biopower/biopolitics is not only connected to the state's ability to sustain or enhance lives but fundamentally to the state's right to differentiate between population groups, through practices of hierarchisation, distinction and exclusion. Included here is the ability to enforce racist measures by focusing attention on specific population groups considered more valuable than others. The use of the term "essential", which suddenly appeared during the early days of the pandemic to refer to medical personnel, including doctors, nurses, and carers in retirement homes, is also an operation of biopower. Following Foucault's analysis (2014: 104), such changes in terminology go hand in hand with what he described as a caesura: the making of distinctions between citizens that are useful and whose life is valuable and those whose lives are rather redundant. Applied to the COVID-19 pandemic, this includes the far-reaching acceptance of the fact that devalued individuals and socially excluded groups can be exposed to increased (death) risks (Gassner 2020: 423–4).

Biopolitics was a fundamental form of colonial governmentality – most notably in all the practices that effected a differentiation between a "master" race and "lesser races" – and continues to be key to the governmentality of nation–states which, as sociologist Stephan Lessenich (2020) points out are now considered the standard form of states. Lessenich references several examples to make this point. During the corona pandemic the nation–state's governance was particularly evident, for example, in the rapid closure of borders to non-citizens as applied in virtually every state in the world. The intensification of border controls and its associated biopolitical differentiation between important and unimportant groups of people followed the exclusionary logic of citizenship status. This was reflected in the fact that governments considered it their duty to rescue their own citizens from abroad. One typical example is the evacuation of 200,000 German tourists from their vacation destinations to be brought home to the realm of the functioning German health system, while less than 50 unaccompanied minors from Greek refugee camps were allowed to enter Germany (Lessenich 2020: 457).

The systems put in place to manage the pandemic identified certain population groups as particularly vulnerable, meaning they deserved special attention and protection from the state. In this context, the concept of vulnerability became important in governmental actions and rhetoric, and at the same time vulnerability made a "career" as a key concept for sociological and philosophical investigations of the pandemic with many commentators making use of Butler's configuration of the concept as a key term for the understanding of (human) life. Vulnerability is contrasted with the hegemonic neoliberal notion of a subject as an autonomous and sovereign entity (Pistrol 2016: 238). Butler's understanding of vulnerability is not only concerned with the fragility of bodies and life, of physical and emotional human existence, but also with the interdependence of attention, care, and various forms of emotional and physical support in different life situations. This support is necessarily mutual as family, friends, colleagues and co-humans will need help themselves at different points over the course of a lifetime. These considerations go to the heart of human survival. Far from being organised around interdependence, mutuality and survival, in the contemporary world – both within nation–states and globally – an unequal distribution of concrete vulnerabilities of damaged life prevails, leading to a "differential allocation of grievability" (Butler 2006: xiv). Here vulnerability is understood not only as a fundamental element of human life, but also a socially produced condition which generates different types of social vulnerabilities[9] (Dowling 2022: 210).

In his essay "Make Live and Let Die: The Politics of Vulnerability", Lessenich (2020: 454) argues that while the German state (and this applies to many other states in Europe) repeatedly emphasised that "saving lives has become the definitive governmental rationale – whatever the political and economic costs",[10] the state's commitment ultimately was not about protecting and saving all members of a nation–state, but about the saving of certain lives: "In the corona crisis, the sovereign was the one who could decide on the state of vulnerability" (ibid.: 455). Among those who made the decisions, there were of course no representatives of those who were vulnerable.

In Germany, from early on in the crisis, senior citizens living in nursing homes were marked out as particularly deserving of protection, and they remained a highlighted group in vulnerability policies. As a result, residents in retirement homes were quarantined and relatives were denied access for many months.[11] The government recommended that relatives of senior citizens refrain from visiting their parents and grandparents to avoid exposing them to the risk of infection.

The "selectivity of vulnerability diagnoses" (Lessenich 2020: 458) was reflected in the government's double standards when, for example, it came to the scandal around the non-hygienic conditions in refugee accommodation or the lodging of East European contract workers in the meat industry and working as asparagus cutters. The selectivity in the labelling of vulnerable groups was also revealed in the fact that certain systemically relevant jobs were hardly mentioned in this context: public transport workers, supermarket cashiers and parcel deliverers, for example, were all forced to accept a situation where contact with many people was inevitable. The vulnerabilities related to the nature of their work were of little interest to politicians and policymakers. The same applies to the situation of welfare recipients and low earners. In this sense, vulnerability became a term for categorising lives rather than a policy for life, "where the question of recognising or not recognising the vulnerability of social groups and subject positions takes on the character of domination" (ibid.: 459).

Interestingly, many authors, including Lessenich, concluded their analysis on the hopeful note that the corona crisis should be understood as an "opportunity" in view of the fact that the vulnerability debate was being discussed in public (the press, organisations and reports by health and ethics committees) and in various social disciplines. It was assumed that in the future the increased focus on vulnerability would catapult various forms of social disadvantage into the public discourse, and that, accordingly, intersectional discrimination would be given greater consideration.

During the pandemic, very different scenarios for the post-pandemic period made the rounds:

1. The care economy, in Europe and globally, prefers a "self-regulating" market, but the lockdowns represented a step towards a preference for nation–state governmentality, which impedes on market rules of buying and selling cheap labour. Some argued that there might be new restrictions and rules for the care economy, including a stricter regulation of labour regulations, or that caregivers' wages might be raised to national minimum wage levels. The desired result would be that caregiving would become more attractive for native care workers.

2. The second scenario was a return to the pre-pandemic situation as soon as the virus was under control, and borders within the EU labour market were re-opened. This would imply a comeback of the cheap labour supply and return to the former deregulated care worker system. A valorisation of care work, as in the first scenario, was not implied here.

3. The third scenario has already been pushed by some countries, including Japan. As in other sectors of the economy, such as digital teaching, COVID-19 gave a boost to emerging technologies in the field. The care robot development industry, which aims at replacing human caregiving and so removing the need to pay them along with any other labour considerations, remains a very cost-intensive sector, but it is conceivable that some countries will intensify their investment.

At the moment of writing (Spring 2024), it appears clear that we are back to the pre-pandemic status quo. With regard to elderly people in need of care, the improvement of working conditions for migrant caregivers continues to be neglected. Although the German government announced its intention to legalise and improve care migrants' status and working conditions in 2021 in the coalition agreement, nothing has as yet materialised. Progressive lawyers, such as Barbara Bucher (2018), Eva Kocher

(2014) and Kirsten Scheiwe (2014), have repeatedly pointed out the legal untenability of the current situation, but there have been few efforts to change this. Trade unions often point out that this group of potential members is difficult to organise. This is true to a certain extent, as the mobility of transnational migrant carers is very limited due to their employment conditions. However, the staff at Fair Mobility, a union-affiliated organisation, offers advice services mainly by telephone, and is extremely supportive.[12]

NEW ECONOMIC GOVERNANCE AND CARE EXTRACTIVISM

To understand why there has been a return to pre-pandemic behaviours and practices, we need to focus once again on the rules and regulations that characterise the care economy. In their study providing an overview of the European Union's interventions in the health sectors of its member states, Sabina Stan and Roland Erne (2023) argue that while in the aftermath of WWII and at the time of the EU's founding, the policy of decommodification of health systems was pursued, this has fundamentally changed, in particular since the financial crisis of 2008. What they call a "new economic governance regime" has been introduced. As Stan and Erne explain, the commodification of healthcare became a "script" which followed "a common commodification logic" (ibid.: 2). They trace the development of liberalism in the EU from the 1970s onwards, during which a new phase of capitalist expansion gradually developed, following the logic of "accumulation by dis-possession" (Harvey 2004). They state that "this included attacks on the commons of public services, leading to their increasing commodification" (Stan and Erne 2023: 3).

The consequence of the creeping commodification of public services is – as already described by Karl Polanyi (1944) in *The Great Transformation* – the erosion of not only users' rights, but also of (health) workers' rights. Stan and Erne argue that in the 1990s, the constantly driven expansion of the EU market and its monetary integration placed constraints on member states' public expenditure, and similar pressures were exerted as acces-sion criteria for the new member states from Central and Eastern

Europe (Stan and Erne 2023: 5). In the wake of the 2008 financial crisis, it became clear that the consequences of this policy approach for the populations of the Central and East European states were "macroeconomic imbalances that threatened to break up the EU" (ibid.), and so new laws for policy monitoring were introduced, so-called country specific recommendations (CSRs) for every EU member state. Their aim was – and continues to be – the reinforcement of an Excessive Deficit Procedure based on a Stability of Growth Pact (ibid.: 6), which means that the EU requires all member states to regulate their deficits in the healthcare sector by introducing market mechanisms. Stan and Erne investigated the German, Irish, Italian and Romanian healthcare systems from 2009 to 2019, and came to the following conclusion:

> We argue that commodification became a script not only because commodifying prescriptions were more numerous than decommodifying ones, but also because their uneven deployment across countries and years followed a common commodification logic. By targeting national health systems individually (through country-specific prescriptions), EU executives sought not so much to address these systems' specificities (e.g. in terms of healthcare financing) as to intensify commodification in countries that lagged in this respect. (ibid.: 2)

Although European trade unions in particular opposed health commodification, the new economic governance regime prevailed. Stan and Erne describe how healthcare commodification measures have a direct impact on healthcare workers: "Privatising measures, such as the outsourcing of ancillary services, lead to the segmentation of wages and employment conditions. Measures such as the introduction of performance-based pay replace collective wage-setting arrangements with individualistic market-like ones" (ibid.: 4). The European Commission monitors each state's implementation of CSRs and "accesses its progression in country reports, which thereafter inform the next yearly round of CSRs" (ibid.: 6). Like many other EU states, Germany was obliged to curtail resources for health services on the grounds that it needed to "enhance the cost-effectiveness of public spending on health and long-term care" (Council Recommendation 2011/C 217/09),[13] and the government was advised to "focus on prevention and rehabilitation and independent living" (ibid.). The German state passed this pressure onto the federal states, which pushed ahead with the privatisation of hospitals claiming that this would reduce costs. This approach ultimately led to healthcare multinationals being subsidised and financed by the German state. During the same period the growth of private home care services, including informal employment arrangements and precarious contracts offered by brokering agencies to migrant workers, became a booming business. The conclusion that can be drawn from Stan and Erne's study is that until the new economic governance regime is challenged across the EU, there is little hope of formalising and monitoring current practices under a labour law that does not control employment relationships.

So far, the attention to (social/bodily) vulnerabilities has not generated new ways of dealing with fragility and interpersonal dependency. The repression of these experiences is being addressed by various research teams (on the pandemic experience of schoolchildren; the situation of long COVID patients, and on the long-term psychological impact of the pandemic on children and adolescents), but no or few lessons have materialised in practical action.

Concerning the sector of live-in migrant caregiving, it can therefore be assumed that care extractivism will continue to prevail in the search for cheap labour. This concept was developed by Christa Wichterich, who explains that:

Care extractivism can be used as a space- and time-diagnostic tool to politicise care and analyse power relations in the organisation of social (re)production and care work.... It marks the intensification and expansion of the ongoing economisation and commodification of labour and resources in arenas that were not commercialised until recently. Extractivism is a reckless and careless exploitation and depletion of resources assuming that they are growing naturally and are endlessly available. The concept of care extractivism with its focus on reproductive and affective work is an analogy to the concept of resource extractivism, however countervailing its productivistic and industrialistic focus of value creation. (Wichterich 2019: 15)

The concept of care extractivism is useful in explaining how care workers are made to be cheap workers. This dynamic is refined and concealed by hegemonic discourses that construct workers not as workers, but rather as actors who invest in their "entrepreneurial self" (Bröckling 2007). These employment relationships include the dissolution of boundaries in the relationship between "work and life" (Voss 1998). Ultimately, the new economic governance regime conceptualises migrant care workers as actors who "optimise" themselves, meaning that they must bear the risks and costs. Transnational care markets are organised along social hierarchies of gender, class, race, and North–South inequalities that are the result of colonial and post-colonial exploitation. Transnational care extractivism, writes Wichterich, can be perceived as a manifestation of an "imperial mode of living" based on neo-colonial power relations, with which the global middle classes secure their level of production, consumption and own reproduction by recruiting, appropriating and extracting care capacities from less prosperous regions, within a nation–state and increasingly from outside (Wichterich 2019: 15).

It should be noted that care extractivism in relation to transnational migrant care workers from Eastern Europe has rarely been publicly questioned. The lucrative agency sector is constantly growing and this is unlikely to change given increasing demand. In Germany, for example, the number of people in need of care from the "baby boomer generation" in the coming years is expected to grow rapidly from 4.1 million at present to almost 8 million in 2070. It is hardly to be expected that care extractivism will not be exploited as a "solution" to this crisis. There are already signs that other East European countries are being considered in the search for new caregivers, including Moldova, Romania, Bulgaria, Georgia, Kazakhstan, Kyrgyzstan, Armenia and Azerbaijan. As long as large parts of these populations face significant economic hardship, these countries will be treated as suppliers of labour and their economic conditions exploited.

However, some authors are more optimistic about future developments. In her essay, "The Covid Care Fix", Emma Dowling argues in favour of a break with economic thinking in the care sector. She suggests:

Instead, what will be needed is cross subsidisation from the more productive parts of the economy to the less productive ones. One model here is public investment in the care sector on the basis that it is an important social infrastructure that is the background condition of economic activity and in itself generates economic activity through job creation. (Dowling 2022: 226)

Dowling argues that "care would be the arena where first experiments with post-growth economy could be made" (ibid.: 227). Collective care, she writes, "allows for the redistribution of wealth across a population so that everyone can have the same access to care" (ibid). Dowling believes that the organisation of giving and receiving care encourages the reallocation of resources like money, energy, space and time.

A change in the care economy in this direction would of course be very welcome. But where are the collectives that can bring this reorientation into the public debate and implement it? Such a turnaround would require a radical rethinking of the connection between health and the care economy, and, unfortunately, many more decades will be needed to put these ideas into practice. At the same time, migration research should urgently expand and improve its contribution to this topic. As Isabel Shutes (2021: 117) writes: "Research on migration continues, often, to decouple labour from care, migrant workers from the care relations in which they are embedded, and in doing so to reproduce rather than interrogate the division between productive and reproductive labour."

Notes

PREFACE

1. See Aulenbacher et al. 2024; Emunds et al. 2022; Aulenbacher et al. 2021; Emunds et al. 2021; Rossow 2021; Wirz 2021; Scheiwe 2021; Auth et al. 2020; Hielscher et al. 2017; Leiber and Rossow 2017; Emunds 2016; Satola 2015; Krawietz 2014; Haffert 2014; Kocher 2012; Scheiwe and Krawietz 2010; Karakayali 2010.
2. https://www.youtube.com/watch?v=CJP9hk9Ycqc. Websites cited in the Foreword were last accessed 15 August 2024.
3. The founders were Yugoslav President Josip Broz Tito, Indian Prime Minister Jawaharlal Nehru, Egyptian President Gamal Abdel Nasser, Ghanaian President Kwame Nkrumah and Indonesian President Sukarno.
4. https://www.bpb.de/themen/migration-integration/laenderprofile/english-version-country-profiles/160106/albania.
5. https://de.statista.com/statistik/daten/studie/870218/umfrage/polen-in-den-laendern-der-eu.
6. https://data.unhcr.org/en/situations/Ukraine.

CHAPTER 1

1. Two extensive research projects are the empirical basis of this book: 'Landscapes of Care Drain: Care Provisions and Care Chains from the Ukraine to Poland, from Poland to Germany' (2007–10) and 'Decent Care Work? Transnational Home Care Arrangements' (2017–21), both funded by the German Research Foundation (DFG). The second project also received funding from the Austrian Science Fund (FWF) and the Suisse National Fund (SNF).
2. https://globaldialogue.isa-sociology.org/articles/caring-across-borders-the-transformation-of-care-and-care-work. Websites cited in this chapter were last accessed 15 August 2024.
3. The Organisation for Economic Co-operation and Development.
4. According to the legal definition of the SGB XI, persons in need of care are "persons who have health-related impairments of independence or abilities and therefore require assistance from others. This involves people who are unable to compensate for or cope independently with physical, cognitive or psychological impairments or health-related stresses or demands. The need for care must be permanent, probably for at least six months, and at least as severe as defined in § 15. (Section 14 (1) SGB XI)" (Statistic Austria 2020: 6).
5. This estimate is from May 2024. https://www.24h-pflege-check.de/24h-betreuung/pflegekraefte-aus-osteuropa/.

6. Migrant women repeatedly report that they often do not realise until many years later that pension and health insurance payments were not made on a monthly basis.

7. In 2019, 800 agencies with a trade licence for the organisation of personal care were registered in Austria (see Benazha et al. 2021: 31).

8. In German-speaking Switzerland, there were 60 specialised agencies in 2019 (see Schillinger 2024).

9. https://vpod.ch/themen/gesundheit/das-netzwerk-respekt.

10. https://www.faire-mobilitaet.de/en.

11. https://www.caritas.eu/fair-care-mobility-and-migration-in-europe.

12. http://www.vij-faircare.de.

13. https://www.diakonie-wuerttemberg.de/abteilungen/gesundheit-alter-pflege/pflege-im-eigenen-zuhause/faircare.

14. In Europe, only the following countries have signed the agreement, also known as Convention 189: Finland, Sweden, Belgium, Germany, Ireland, Italy, Portugal, Spain and Switzerland. See: https://www.wiego.org/ratification-countries-domestic-workers-convention-c189.

CHAPTER 2

1. Ingo Dell, *Die Karawane der Pflegerinnen* (The Caravan of Caregivers), see: https://www.youtube.com/watch?v=kxFDz1GXC2s. Websites cited in this chapter were last accessed 15 August 2024.

2. This is associated with a devaluation of skills, which also contributes to the legitimisation of poor pay.

3. See also the documentaries *Der Pflegeaufstand* (The Nursing Revolt) by Ariane Rieker and *24 Stunden Pflege: Ausbeutung oder letzter Ausweg?* (24-Hour Care: Exploitation or Last Resort?) by Maximilian Wilhelm.

4. See *Destatis*, Statistisches Bundesamt 2023: https://www.destatis.de/DE/Presse/Pressemitteilungen/2023/03/PD23_124_12.html.

5. IBS Policy Paper 2/2017: http://ibs.org.pl/app/uploads/2017/10/IBS_Policy_Paper_02_2017_en.pdf.

6. In 1995, 54.8 percent of the unemployed in Poland were women, in 1997 the figure was 61.2 percent (Fuszara 2000: 268) and in 2013, despite a significantly improved economic situation, it was 42.4 percent (Kindler et al. 2016: 5).

7. https://www.qualtrics.com/blog/countries-ranked-by-female-workforce/.

8. Such comparisons usually refer to full-time employment, which in turn leads to distortions, as mothers of young children in particular do not usually work full-time.

9. See also: https://en.wikipedia.org/wiki/Migrations_from_Poland_since_EU_accession.

10. https://de.statista.com/statistik/daten/studie/530499/umfrage/auslaender-aus-polen-in-deutschland/.

11. http://www.ukrsat.gov.ua.
12. https://www.ceicdata.com/de/indicator/ukraine/monthly-earnings.
13. https://data.worldbank.org/indicator/SP.POP.TOTL?locations=UA.
14. https://data.unhcr.org/en/situations/Ukraine.
15. According to calculations by Ambrosetti et al. (2014: 178, 205, 49) and Ratha et al. (2011), 14.4 % of the population was abroad in 2010, putting Ukraine in fifth place among emigration countries worldwide.
16. See: https://finance.ec.europa.eu/system/files/2022-09/220927-joint-statement-remittance-ukraine_en.pdf.
17. In 2007, a bi-national agreement was introduced regarding Ukrainian labour migrants in Poland, which since 2012 has included the mutual recognition of social insurance. A "simplified procedure" has been in force since 2015, according to which a work permit is no longer required for a period of 6–12 months. Although Ukrainians have been exempted from visa requirements in the rest of the EU since June 2017, they are not entitled to take up gainful employment. However, Ukrainians employed in Poland are now increasingly being sent to Germany to fill the widening gap in care.
18. This is also the argument used by Renate Föhry, the owner of a care agency, who is probably best known for her appearances on talk shows and whose company SeniorCare 24 places care workers from Poland in German households.
19. The Association for the Promotion of Germanness in the Eastmarken was founded in 1894. Eastmarken refers to German property in Eastern Europe. The aim of the association was to promote Germanisation and the "strengthening of Germanness".
20. The "state" here refers to the German Empire.
21. The Polish intelligentsia was systematically persecuted by the National Socialists with the aim of removing "undesirable Polish elements" (Schenk 1990). Reinhard Heydrich, SS-Oberscharführer (Chief Squad Leader) and head of the security police, was in charge of the "Final Solution of the European Jewish Question" and the "extermination of the Polish intelligentsia" (Harten 1996).
22. On this first genocide of the twentieth century in German South West Africa in 1904, see the collection edited by Helma Lutz and Kathrin Gawarecki (2005).
23. The question of which of the two containers Central and East European states fall into is rarely addressed. I argue that the CCE region should be seen as containing deviations from these container categories.
24. For a discussion of the concept of fictitious commodities, see Chapter Six.

CHAPTER 3

1. The interviews presented here are drawn from two research projects, both of which received funding from the German Research Foundation. The first

interview comes from "Landscapes of Care Drain: Care Provisions and Care Chains from the Ukraine to Poland, from Poland to Germany" (2007–10), while the second and third come from "Decent Care Work? Transnational Home Care Arrangements" (2017–21).

2. Halina was interviewed by Ewa Palenga-Möllenbeck in 2008. For earlier presentations of this interview, see Lutz 2016.

3. The German Institute for Human Rights estimates the number of migrant women at 700,000, while others believe it could be as high as 800,000, see: https://www.institut-fuer-menschenrechte.de/im-fokus/haeusliche-betreuung-harte-arbeit-wenig-schutz [Accessed 15 August 2024].

4. Kasia was interviewed by Iga Obracka in 2018.

5. Agencies often seek migrant caregivers to cover the Christmas period to replace those caregivers returning to their relatives over the holiday period.

6. Reference to the household of a 94-year-old woman where she was working at the time of the interview.

7. She assumes that other interviewees also talk about this phenomenon.

8. This is equivalent to A-levels.

9. Mateusz was interviewed by Iga Obracka in 2018.

10. A reference to the situation with his former client in another federal state.

11. Interviews conducted in 2008 and 2018.

CHAPTER 4

1. The article was first published on 26 May 2008, and again on 17 May 2010.

2. https://www.youtube.com/watch?v=PpJ2J1NMzqk. Websites cited in this chapter were last accessed 15 August 2024.

3. This analysis was carried out in the context of the research project "Landscapes of Care Drain. Care Provision and Care Chains from Ukraine to Poland and from Poland to German" (2007–10). In total, 969 newspaper articles from the daily press in three countries – Germany, Poland and Ukraine – were analysed. The German debate, which took less notice of Euro-orphans and dealt more with the so-called care crisis, is disregarded here.

4. The following references to Polish and Ukrainian newspaper articles, their titles, publication dates and contents are taken from our unpublished research reports "Migrationsdiskurse in Polen" (Migration Discourses in Poland; Palenga-Möllenbeck 2010) and "Migration und Care in der ukrainischen Presse" (Migration and Care in the Ukrainian Press; Wirz 2009).

5. The idea was to create a complementary and comparable collection of articles from two sending countries, Poland and Ukraine, and from one of the main destination countries for female care migrants in Western Europe, Germany. The period of inquiry from 1997 to 2008 was chosen against the background of the accession negotiations which led to Poland joining the European Union in 2004.

6. Our methodological approach made use of critical discourse analysis, as established by Siegfried Jäger (2012).
7. See: Kicinger and Weinar (2007) https://www.econstor.eu/bitstream/10419/140810/1/573872252.pdf.
8. The press analyses were conducted as a team in collaboration with Ewa Palenga-Möllenbeck and Yevgeniya Wirz.
9. In 2020, shortly before the outbreak of COVID-19, the IOM estimated the number of migrant women living abroad at 3 million, still close to 30 percent of the population (IOM 2021: 13).
10. The figure of 7.5 to 9 million stay-behind children has been circulating since 2007. In an effort to trace the source of these statistics, we found a survey which estimated the number of Ukrainians working abroad at seven million, of whom only six percent reportedly do not have children (LG; 5 July 2006).
11. This is a network of NGOs supported by the Global Alliance Against Traffic in Women.
12. This is called the Feldman Law after the member of parliament Oleksandr Feldman, then chair of the Parliamentary Commission for Human Rights.
13. See the report on the 2023 conference in Katowice about the Euro-orphans phenomenon: 'How Much Does it Cost to Have a Better Life?' https://www.leuenberg.eu/cpce-content/uploads/2023/06/Euro-orphans-Katowice-article.pdf.
14. For a similar interpretation, see Urbańska (2015).
15. Numerous films on the issue were found on YouTube and other social media; for examples, see the filmography section in the bibliography.
16. See: https://www.defense.gov/News/Feature-Stories/story/Article/1791664/rosie-the-riveter-inspired-women-to-serve-in-world-war-ii/.
17. *Better Homes and Gardens* has existed under this name since 1925 and is one of the most important women's magazines in the US.
18. See http://www.childrenleftbehind.eu/ and UNICEF https://www.unicef.org/media/83581/file/Children-Left-Behind.pdf.
19. The one-child-policy is no longer in place and China is now pursuing policies that increase the fertility rate.

CHAPTER 5

1. In Celsius, this is a temperature range from minus 2 to plus 38.
2. Lukashenko was elected president on 10 July 1994 and at the time of writing has been in this position for 30 years.
3. One prominent example is Father Tadeusz Rydzyk, a Catholic Redemptorist preacher and owner of a media empire that includes the influential radio station Radio Maria. He warns his audience of millions against the "homo lobby" and the "gender tsunami" that is descending on Poland, and opposes abortion and assisted fertility alike (see Brill 2014: n.p.).

4. An allied claim was that socialism encouraged women to be sexually aggressive and "that they have ceased to be affectionate and understanding" (Goven 1993: 227–8).
5. See Chapter Six for further discussion.
6. See "Fatherhood and Masculinity" by Joseph Pleck (2010) and "Understanding Contemporary Fatherhood: Masculine Care and the Patriarchal Deficit" by Jemimah Bailey (2015).
7. The fathers were interviewed without their partners present in order to avoid the co-narrativisation of history. Fathers were questioned with the help of semi-structured narrative interviews. Beginning with the decision-making phase and initial experiences with their wives' migrations, the interviews focused on how the fathers coped with everyday family life.
8. Each family member – Pawel, Klaudia and their son Dawid – was interviewed alone. All the interviews with this family were carried out by Ewa Palenga-Möllenbeck in 2008.
9. This account points to a collective empowerment strategy that has been noted several times in research on the situation of Polish workers in Britain (cf. Datta and Brickwell 2009).
10. Depending on their age, the children were surveyed using structured questions, such as what differences they notice when their mother is at home or absent.
11. On the stigmatisation of mothers that occurs especially in press and expert discourses, see Chapter Four.
12. A total of 41 guided interviews were conducted with Ukrainian and Polish relatives (grandmothers, friends, caretakers), 15 of them with husbands.
13. The interview was conducted by Oksana Kis in 2009.
14. This could be an ironic remark; however, Sergij did not laugh and neither did he qualify the comment.
15. As stated above, married partners were interviewed individually.
16. This presumably refers to a legal work and residence permit.
17. It can be assumed that there were relatives who probably visited the family occasionally, but the director did not want to include them.

CHAPTER 6

1. Readers will forgive the author for not being able to reproduce the entire breadth of Soc.Fem. positions here.
2. This was the title of an essay by Silvia Federici published in 1974.
3. See Luxemburg's concept of land grabbing (2003 [1913]), which has been taken up by Klaus Dörre, Martin Ehrlich and Tine Haubner (2014) to explain why capitalist logic is adopted in the ideology of post-socialist states.
4. This part of Davis' analysis was taken up ten years later by Mary Romero (1992) in her pioneering work on (migrant) domestic workers, *Maid in the USA*.

5. On the Marxist aporia of productive and unproductive labour, see Lutz 2010.
6. https://ec.europa.eu/eurostat/statistics-explained/index.php?title=How_do_women_and_men_use_their_time_-_statistics. Websites cited in this chapter were last accessed 15 August 2024.
7. In her book, Winker also presents contemporary initiatives and activities that are already working on such a reorientation.
8. Parallels can be drawn here with the work of the French sociologist Jean-Claude Kaufmann (1999).
9. Organisation for Economic Co-Operation and Development.

CHAPTER 7

1. See: https://wideplus.org/2021/03/09/video-slides-and-answers-available-of-webinar-webinar-global-care-chains-and-vulnerabilities-in-the-covid19-crisis-3-march-2021/; https://helma-lutz.de/aktivitaeten/pflegearbeit-im-sperrmodus/ and https://minor-kontor.de/die-vierte-saeule-der-pflege/. Websites cited in this chapter were last accessed 15 August 2024.
2. https://www.ilo.org/wcmsp5/groups/public/---dgreports/---dcomm/---publ/documents/briefingnote/wcms_859255.pdf
3. Although the spread of the virus had started earlier, in particular in China in 2019, the outbreak was characterised as a pandemic by the World Health Organization in March 2020, and it was only after this that counter-measures were first taken in most European states.
4. Ten migrants were first interviewed in 2018 by Iga Obrocka and then re-interviewed by Tatjana Jewsiejewa in the summer of 2020.
5. Day care is a form of care in which senior citizens are collected from their homes and taken to a care facility where they can chat with others, have lunch and are kept busy by occupational therapists.
6. The platform *mypolacy.de* (We Poles) was launched by Polish and German entrepreneurs. The site offers information, services and networking opportunities for the Polish community in Germany.
7. To find new migrant care workers.
8. For more detailed information, see Leiblfinger et al. 2020.
9. And in connection with this, of course, also physical vulnerabilities.
10. Notwithstanding this rhetoric, it soon became apparent that certain sectors of the economy, such as the pharmaceutical industry and medical technology, were profiting significantly from the pandemic.
11. My own mother, who was then over 90 years old and living in a nursing home, described the increased isolation during the pandemic as one of the worst things she had experienced in her life.
12. See also the analysis in the report 'The Fourth Column of Care' https://minor-kontor.de/die-vierte-saeule-der-pflege.
13. https://eur-lex.europa.eu/LexUriServ/LexUriServ.do?uri=OJ:C:2011:212:0009:0012:EN:PDF.

Bibliography

Alexievich, Svetlana (2013): *Secondhand Time. The Last of the Soviets.* New York: Penguin Random House.

Ambrosetti, Elena; Eralbal, Cela; Strielkowski, Wadim; Abrhám, Josef (2014): Ukrainian Migrants in the European Union: A Comparative Study of the Czech Republic and Italy. In: *Sociology and Space* 53 (2), pp. 141–66.

Ambrosini, Maurizio (2013): *Irregular Migration and Invisible Welfare.* London: Palgrave Macmillan.

Ambrosini, Maurizio (2016): From "Illegality" to Tolerance and Beyond: Irregular Immigration as a Selective and Dynamic Process. In: *International Migration* 54 (2), pp. 144–59.

Amelina, Anna (2017a): *Transnationalizing Inequalities in Europe: Sociocultural Boundaries, Assemblages and Regimes of Intersection.* London/New York: Routledge.

Amelina, Anna (2017b): After the Reflexive Turn in Migration Studies: Towards the Doing Migration Approach. In: *Working Paper Series Gender, Diversity and Migration* 13. www.fb03.uni-frankfurt.de/67001816/amelina_doing_migration.pdf [accessed 1 May 2024].

Amelina, Anna and Lutz, Helma (2019): *Gender and Migration. Transnational Intersectional Prospects.* London: Routledge.

Anacka, Marta; Brzozwski, Jan; Chaupczak, Henryk; Fihel, Agnieszka; Firlit-Fesnak, Grayna; Garapich, Micha; Grabowska-Lusiñska. (2014): Spoleczne skutki poakcesyjnych migracji ludnosci Polski. Raport Komitetu Badan nad Migracjami (Social Effects of Post-Accession Migration of the Polish Population). Report of the Committee for Research on Migration Studies). Warsaw: PAN.

Andall, Jacqueline (2000): *Gender, Migration and Domestic Service: The Politics of Black Women in Italy.* London/New York: Routledge.

Anderson, Bridget (2000): *Doing the Dirty Work? The Global Politics of Domestic Labour.* London: Zed Books.

Anntonen, Anneli and Sipilä, Jorna (1996): European Social Care Services: Is it Possible to Identify Models? In: *Journal of European Policy* 6 (2), pp. 87–100.

Anonymous (2007): *Wohin mit Vater? Ein Sohn verzweifelt am Pflegesystem* (What Can We Do with Father? A Son Despairs at the Care System). Frankfurt am Main: Fischer Verlag.

Anthias, Floya (2012): Transnational Mobilities, Migration Research and Intersectionality. In: *Nordic Journal of Migration Research* (2), pp. 102–10.

Apitzsch, Ursula (2013): Arlie Hochschild. In: Schmidbaur, Marianne; Lutz, Helma; Wischermann, Ulla (eds.): *Klassikerinnen feministischer Theorie*

(Classics of Feminist Théory) Volume 3. Sulzbach/Taunus: Ulrike Helmer, pp. 204–11.

Apitzsch, Ursula and Schmidbaur, Marianne (eds.) (2010): *Care und Migration. Die Ent-Sorgung menschlicher Reproduktionsarbeit entlang von Geschlechter- und Armutsgrenzen* (Care and Migration: The Disposal of Human Reproductive Labour along Gender and Poverty Lines). Opladen & Farmington Hills: Barbara Budrich.

Appelt, Erna and Fleischer, Eva (2014): Familiale Sorgearbeit in Österreich. Modernisierung eines konservativen Care-Regimes? (Family Care Work in Austria. Modernisation of a Conservative Care Regime?). In: Aulenbacher, Brigitte; Riegraf, Birgit; Hildegard Theobald (eds.): *Sorge: Arbeit, Verhältnisse, Regime* (Care: Work, Relations, Regimes). In: *Soziale Welt*, Special Issue 20, pp. 397–415.

Arendt, Hannah (1958): *The Human Condition.* Chicago: University of Chicago Press.

Arendt, Hannah (1960): *Vita Activa oder vom tätigen Leben.* (German translation of *The Human Condition*). München: Piper.

Aulenbacher, Brigitte (2015): Wider die Sorglosigkeit des Kapitalismus. Care und Care Work aus der Sicht feministischer Ökonomie – und Gesellschaftskritik (Against the Carelessness of Capitalism. Care and Care work from the Perspective of Feminist Economics and Social Criticism). In: Aulenbacher, Brigitte; Riegraf, Birgit; Völker, Susanne (eds.): *Feministische Kapitalismuskritik* (Feminist Critique of Capitalism). Münster: Westfälisches Dampfboot, pp. 32–45.

Aulenbacher, Brigitte; Bachinger Almut; Décieux, Fabienne (2015a): Gelebte Sorglosigkeit? Kapitalismus, Sozialstaatlichkeit und soziale Reproduktion am Beispiel des österreichischen "migrant-in-a-family-care" Modells (Lived Carelessness? Capitalism, the Welfare State and Social Reproduction Using the Example of the Austrian "Migrant-in-a-Family-Care" Model). In: *Kurswechsel, Zeitschrift für gesellschafts-, wirtschafts- und umweltpolitische Alternativen* 1, pp. 6–14.

Aulenbacher, Brigitte; Dammayr, Maria; Décieux, Fabienne (2015b): Prekäre Sorge, Sorgearbeit und Sorgeproteste. Über die Sorglosigkeit des Kapitalismus und eine sorgsame Gesellschaft (Precarious Care, Care Work and Care Protests. On the Carelessness of Capitalism and a Caring Society). In: Amacker, Michèle and Völker, Susanne (eds.): *Prekarisierungen. Arbeit, Sorge, Politik* (Precarisation, Work, Care, Politics). Weinheim und Basel: Beltz Juventa, pp. 59–74.

Aulenbacher, Brigitte; Décieux, Fabienne; Riegraf, Birgit (2018): The Economic Shift and Beyond: Care as a Contested Terrain in Contemporary Capitalism. In: *Current Sociology Monograph* (2), 66, pp. 517–30.

Aulenbacher, Brigitte (2020): Auf neuer Stufe vergesellschaftet: Care und soziale Reproduktion im Gegenwartskapitalismus (Socialised at a New Level: Care and Social Reproduction in Contemporary Capitalism). In: Becker, Karina; Binner, Kristina; Décieux, Fabienne (eds.): *Gespannte Arbeits- und Geschlech-*

terverhältnisse im Marktkapitalismus (Tense Labour and Gender Relations in Market Capitalism). Wiesbaden: Springer, pp. 125–47.

Aulenbacher, Brigitte; Leiblfinger, Michael; Prieler, Veronika (2021a): Das umstrittene Selbstständigenmodell – Live-in-Betreuung in Österreich (The Controversial Self-Employment Model – Live-in Care in Austria). In: Aulenbacher, Brigitte; Lutz, Helma; Schwiter, Karin (eds.): *Gute Sorge ohne gute Arbeit?* (Live-in-Care in Deutschland, Österreich und der Schweiz). Beltz Juventa: Weinheim und Basel, pp. 66–78.

Aulenbacher, Brigitte; Leiblfinger, Michael; Prieler, Veronika (2021b): "Das Thema ist, die Menschen wollen zu Hause sein." Zum Nachdenken über Live-in-Care, Gütesiegel, staatliche Förderung und neue Betreuungsformen ("The Issue is that People Want to be at Home." Reflecting on Live-in Care, Quality Seals, State Funding and New Forms of Care). In: Aulenbacher, Brigitte; Lutz, Helma; Schwiter, Karin (eds.): *Gute Sorge ohne gute Arbeit? Live-in-Care in Deutschland, Österreich und der Schweiz* (Good Care Without Good Work? Live-in Care in Germany, Austria and Switzerland). Weinheim und Basel: Beltz Juventa, pp. 212–35.

Aulenbacher, Brigitte; Lutz, Helma; Palenga-Möllenbeck, Ewa; Schwiter, Karin (eds.) (2024): *Home Care for Sale. The Transnational Brokering of Senior Care in Europe*. London: Sage.

Aulenbacher, Brigitte and Prieler, Veronika (2024): The 'Good Agency'? On the Interplay of Formalization and Informality in the Contested Marketisation of Live-in Care in Austria. In: Aulenbacher, Brigitte; Lutz, Helma; Palenga-Möllenbeck, Ewa; Schwiter, Karin (eds.): *Home Care for Sale. The Transnational Brokering of Senior Care in Europe*. London: Sage, pp. 79–94.

Auth, Diana; Brüker, Daniela; Discher, Kerstin; Kaiser, Petra; Leiber, Simone; Leitner, Sigrid; Varnholt, Anika (2020): *Sorgende Angehörige: eine intersektionale Analyse* (Caring Relatives: An Intersectional Analysis). Münster: Westfälisches Dampfboot.

Avato, Johanna; Koettl, Johannes; Sabates-Wheeler, Rachel (2010): Social Security Regimes, Global Estimates, and Good Practices: The Status of Social Protection for International Migrants. In: *World Development* 38 (4), pp. 455–66.

Bachinger, Almut (2009): *Der irreguläre Pflegearbeitsmarkt. Zum Transformationsprozess von unbezahlter in bezahlte Arbeit durch die 24-Stunden-Pflege* (The Irregular Care Labour Market. On the Transformation Process from Unpaid to Paid Work through 24-Hour Care). Dissertation, University of Vienna.

Bachinger, Almut (2010): 24-Stunden-Betreuung – Gelungenes Legalisierungsprojekt oder prekäre Arbeitsmarktintegration? (24-Hour Care – Successful Legalisation Project or Precarious Labour Market Integration?). In: *SWS-Rundschau* 50 (4), pp. 399–412.

Backes, Gertrud M.; Amrhein, Ludwig; Wolfinger, Martina (2008): Gender in der Pflege: Herausforderung für die Politik (Gender in Care: A Challenge for Politics). In: *WISO Diskurs: Expertisen und Dokumentationen zur Wirtschafts- und Sozialpolitik, Arbeitsbereich Frauen- und Geschlechterforschung*, pp. 59–67.

Badinter, Elisabeth (2013): *The Conflict: How Overzealous Motherhood Undermines the Status of Women*. New York: Picador.

Bailey, Jemimah (2015): Understanding Contemporary Fatherhood: Masculine Care and the Patriarchal Deficit. In: *Families, Relationships and Societies* 4 (1), pp. 3–17.

Bal, Mieke (2012): Facing: Intimacy Across Divisions. In: Pratt, Geraldine and Rosner, Victoria (eds.): *The Global and the Intimate: Feminism in Our Time*. New York: Columbia University Press, pp. 119–44.

Baldassar, Loretta and Merla, Laura (2013): Locating Transnational Care Circulation in Migration and Family Studies. In: Baldassar, Loretta and Merla, Laura (eds.): *Transnational Families, Migration and the Circulation of Care: Understanding Mobility and Absence in Family Life*. London/New York: Routledge, pp. 25–58.

Bartmann, Christoph (2016): *Die Rückkehr der Diener. Das Bürgertum und sein Personal* (The Return of Servants. The Bourgeoisie and their Staff). 2nd edition, München: Carl Hanser Verlag.

Beck, Ulrich (2007): The Cosmopolitan Condition: Why Methodological Nationalism Fails. In: *Theory, Culture and Society* 24 (7–8), pp. 286–90.

Becker-Schmidt, Regina (1992): Geschlechterverhältnisse und Herrschaftszusammenhänge (Gender Relations and Contexts of Domination). In: Kulke, Christine; Kopp-Degetoff, Heidi; Ramming, Ulrike (eds.): *Wider das Schlichte Vergessen* (Against Simple Forgetting). Berlin: Orlanda, pp. 216–36.

Beer, Ursula (1990): *Geschlecht, Struktur, Geschichte. Soziale Konstituierung der Geschlechterverhältnisse* (Gender, Structure, History. The Social Constitution of Gender Relations). Frankfurt am Main/New York: Campus.

Benazha, Aranka (2021): Alles rechtens? Rechtliche Rahmenbedingungen der Live-in Betreuung in Deutschland (Everything Legal? The Legal Framework for Live-in care in Germany). In: Aulenbacher, Brigitte; Lutz, Helma; Schwiter, Karin (eds.): *Gute Sorge ohne gute Arbeit? Live-in-Care in Deutschland, Österreich und der Schweiz* (Good Care Without Good Work? Live-in Care in Germany, Austria and Switzerland). Weinheim-Basel: Beltz Juventa, pp. 46–65.

Benazha, Aranka and Lutz, Helma (2019): Intersektionale Perspektiven auf die Pflege: Geschlechterverhältnisse und Migrationsprozesse (Intersectional Perspectives on Care: Gender Relations and Migration Processes). In: Rudolph, Clarissa and Schmidt, Katja (eds.): *Interessenvertretung und Care. Voraussetzungen, Akteure und Handlungsebenen* (The Representation of Interests and Care: Preconditions, Actors and Levels of Action). Münster: Verlag Westfälisches Dampfboot, pp. 146–60.

Benazha, Aranka; Leiblfinger, Michael; Prieler, Versonika; Steiner, Jeniffer (2021): Live-In Care im Ländervergleich (Live-in-Care in a Country Comparison). In: Aulenbacher, Brigitte; Lutz, Helma.; Schwiter, Karin. (eds.): *Gute Sorge ohne gute Arbeit? Live-in-Care in Deutschland, Österreich und der Schweiz* (Good Care Without Good Work? Live-in Care in Germany, Austria and Switzerland). Weinheim und Basel: Beltz Juventa, pp. 20-45.

Behnke, Cornelia and Meuser, Michael (2012): Look Here Mate! I'm Taking Parental Leave for a Year – Involved Fatherhood and Images of Masculinity. In: Oechsle, Mechtild; Müller, Ursula; Hess, Sabine (eds.): *Fatherhood in Late Modernity: Cultural Images, Social Practices, Structural Frames*. Opladen/ Toronto: Barbara Budrich, pp. 129–45.

Bennholdt-Thomsen, Veronika (1988): Die stumme Auflehnung der Bauersfrauen (The Silent Rebellion of Peasant Women). In: Mies, Maria; von Werlhof, Claudia; Bennholdt-Thompsen, Veronika (eds.): *Frauen, die letzte Kolonie. Zur Hausfrauisierung der Arbeit* (Women, the Last Colony. On the Housewifisation of Work). 2nd edition. Reinbek: Rowohlt.

Biao, Xiang (2007): How Far Are the Left-Behind Left behind? A Preliminary Study in Rural China. In: *Population, Space and Place* 13 (3), pp. 179–91.

Bloch, Ernst (1978): *Das Prinzip Hoffnung* (The Principle of Hope). Vol 1. Frankfurt am Main: Suhrkamp.

BMSFJ (no date): Bundesministerium für Familie, Senioren, Frauen und Jugend. (Federal Ministry for Family Affairs, Senior Citizens, Women and Youth). Akuthilfen für pflegende Angehörige inder Covid-19-Pandemie warden verlängert (Acute Support for Family Carers in the COVID-19 Pandemic is Being Extended). https://www.bmfsfj.de/bmfsfj/aktuelles/presse/ pressemitteilungen/akuthilfen-fuer-pflegende-angehoerige-in-der-covid-19-pandemie-werden-verlaengert-160238 [accessed 15 August 2024].

BMSFJ (no date): Vereinbarkeit von Familie und Pflege (Reconciliation of Family and Care). https://www.bmfsfj.de/resource/blob/93370/4eof41fcc10072af375 c9be8241fc339/bessere-vereinbarkeit-von-familie-pflege-und-beruf-flyerdata.pdf [accessed 23 July 2024].

Boatcă, Manuela (2008): Wie weit östlich ist Osteuropa? Die Aushandlung gesellschaftlicher Identitäten im Wettkampf um Europäisierung (How Far East is Eastern Europe? The Negotiation of Social Identities in the Competition for Europeanisation). In: Rehberg, Karl-Siegbert (ed.), *Die Natur der Gesellschaft: Verhandlungen des 33. Kongresses der Deutschen Gesellschaft für Soziologie in Kassel 2006.* (The Nature of Society: Proceedings of the 33rd Congress of the German Sociological Association in Kassel 2006). Vol. 1 and 2, Frankfurt am Main: Campus, pp. 2231–39.

Bock, Gisela and Duden, Barbara (1977): Arbeit aus Liebe – Liebe als Arbeit. Zur Entstehung der Hausarbeit im Kapitalismus (Labour of Love – Love as Labour. The Emergence of Housework Under Capitalism). In: Gruppe Berliner Dozentinnen (eds.): *Frauen und Wissenschaft. Beiträge zur Berliner Sommeruniversität für Frauen* (Women and Science. Contributions to the Berlin Summer University for Women). Berlin: Courage Verlag, pp. 118–99.

Bourdieu, Pierre (1998): *La Domination Masculine* (Male Domination). Paris: Seuil

Boris, Eileen (1993): The Home as a Workplace: Deconstructing Dichotomies. In: *International Review of Social* History 39, pp. 415–28.

Boris, Eileen and Klein, Jeniffer (2012): Front Line Caregivers: Still Struggling. In: *Dissent* 59 (1), pp. 46–50.

Bowlby, John (1958): The Nature of the Child's Tie to his Mother. In: *International Journal of Psychoanalysis* 39, pp. 350–73.

Boyd, Monica (2017): Closing the Open Door? Canada's Changing Policy for Migrant Caregivers. In: Michel, Sonya and Peng, Ito (eds.): *Gender, Migration and the Work of Care: A Multi-Scalar Approach to the Pacific Rim*. Basingstoke: Palgrave Macmillan, pp. 167–89.

Brandth, Berit and Kvande, Elin (1998): Masculinity and Childcare: The Reconstruction of Fathering. In: *Sociological Review* 46 (2), pp. 293–313.

Braun, Lily (1901a): *Frauenarbeit und Hauswirtschaft* (Women's Work and the Domestic Economy). Berlin: Vorwärts.

Braun, Lily (1901b): *Die Frauenfrage. Ihre geschichtliche Entwicklung und ihre wirtschaftliche Seite* (The Women's Question. Its Historical Development and its Economic Aspects). Leipzig: Hirzel.

Brill, Klaus (2014): Von Hexen und Erlösern (Of Witches and Saviours). In: *Süddeutsche Zeitung*, 30 September 2014.

Brüning, Franziska (2010 [2008]): Ausgesetzt im Waisenhaus (Abandoned in the Orphanage). https://www.sueddeutsche.de/panorama/kinder-in-rumaenien-ausgesetzt-im-waisenhaus-1.208295 [accessed 1 May 2024].

Bucher, Barbara (2018): *Rechtliche Ausgestaltung der 24-Stunden Betreuung durch ausländische Pflegekräfte in deutschen Privathaushalten. Eine kritische Analyse* (Legal Regulation of 24-Hour Care by Foreign Caregivers in German Private Households. A Critical Analysis). Baden-Baden: Nomos.

Bundesministerium für Bevölkerungsforschung (BiB) (2015): Rund ein Drittel mehr Pflegebedürftige im 2030 (Around a Third More People in Need of Care in 2030). www.bib.bund.de/DE/Aktuelles/Presse/Archiv/2015/2015_06_pflegebeduerftige.html [accessed 1 May 2024].

Bundesrat (2015): Zweites Gesetz zur Stärkung der pflegerischen Versorgung und zur Änderung weiterer Vorschriften PSG II. (Second Act to Strengthen Nursing Care and Amending Further Regulations). https://www.bundesrat.de/SharedDocs/drucksachen/2015/0501-0600/567-15.pdf%3F__blob%3DpublicationFile%26v%3D1 [accessed 11 July 2024].

Burawoy, Michael (2015): *Public Sociology. Öffentliche Soziologie gegen Marktfundamentalismus und globale Ungleichheit* (Public Sociology Against Market Fundamentalism and Global Inequality). Weinheim: Beltz Juventa.

Bureychak, Tetyana (2011): Masculinities in Soviet and Post-Soviet Ukraine: Models and Their Implications. In: Hankivsky, Olena and Salvykova, Anastasiya (eds.): *Gender, Politics and Society in Ukraine*. Toronto: Toronto University Press, pp. 325–61.

Butler, Judith (2006): *Precarious Life: The Powers of Mourning and Violence*. London/New York: Verso.

Büscher, Monika; Urry, John; Witchger, Katian (2011): Introduction: Mobile Methods. In: Büscher, Monika; Urry, John; Witchger, Katian (eds.): *Mobile Methods*. London/New York: Routledge, pp. 1–20.

Bröckling, Ulrich (2007): *Das unternehmerische Selbst* (The Entrepreneurial Self). Frankfurt a.M.: Suhrkamp.

Chamberlain, Gethin (2007): Suffering Grips Europe's Nation of Orphans. https://www.telegraph.co.uk/news/worldnews/1546651/Suffering-grips-Europes-nation-of-orphans.html [accessed 1 May 2024].

Chernova, Zhanna (2007): Model "sovetskogo" otsovstva: diskursivnye predpisaniya (Model of "Soviet" Fatherhood: Discursive Prescriptions). In: Zdravomyslova, Elena and Temkina, Anna (eds.): *Rossiyskiy gendernyi poryadok: sociologicheskiy podhod* (The Russian Gender Order: A Sociological Approach). St. Petersburg: Publishing House of the European University, pp. 138–68.

Chun, Jennifer Jihye and Gottfried, Heidi (2018): Caring Across Borders: The Transformation of Care and Care Work. In: *Global Dialogue*, July 2018. https://globaldialogue.isa-sociology.org/articles/caring-across-borders-the-transformation-of-care-and-care-work [accessed 15 August 2024].

Ciulei, Thomas and Ott, Peter (2008): "Die Blumenbrücke" (The Flower Bridge). Diskussionsprotokoll Nr. 10, Duisburger Filmwoche, 5 November 2008. https://protokult.de/2008/die-blumenbruecke/ [accessed 1 May 2024].

Cock, Jacklyn (1989): *Maids and Madams: Domestic Workers under Apartheid*. 2nd edition. London: The Women's Press.

Cohen, Stanley (1972): *Folk Devils and Moral Panics*. London: MacGibbon and Kee.

Collins, Patricia Hill (1990): *Black Feminist Thought: Knowledge, Consciousness, and the Politics of Empowerment*. Boston: Unwin Hyman.

Connell, R. (1987): *Gender and Power: Society, the Person and Sexual Politics*. Cambridge: Polity.

Connell, R. (1995): *Masculinities*. Sidney: Allen & Unwin.

Constable, Nicole (2007): *Maid to Order in Hong Kong: Stories of Migrant Workers*. 2nd edition. Ithaca: Cornell University Press.

Coronel, F.K. and Unterreiner, Frederic (2007): Increasing the Impact of Remittances on Children's Rights. Philippines Paper. New York: UNICEF, Division of Policy and Practice. https://www.gfmd.org/sites/g/files/tmzbdl1801/files/documents/gfmd_brussels07_contribution_unicef_philippines_en.pdf [accessed 1 May 2024].

Cortés, Rosalia (2007): Children and Women Left Behind in Labor Sending Countries: An Appraisal of Social Risks. Global Report on Migration and Children. New York: UNICEF, Division of Policy and Practice. https://www.academia.edu/110820248/Children_and_Women_Left_Behind_in_Labor_Sending_Countries_An_Appraisal_of_Social_Risks [accessed 1 May 2024].

Cox, Rosie (ed.) (2015): *Au Pairs' Lives in Global Context: Sisters or Servants?* Basingstoke: Palgrave Macmillan.

Cvajner, Martina (2019): *Soviet Signoras. Personal and Collective Transformations in Eastern European Migration*. Chicago/London: University of Chicago Press.

Dalla Costa, Mariarosa (1973): Die Frauen und der gesellschaftliche Umsturz (Women and the Social Revolution). In: Della Costa, Mariarosa and James, Selma (eds.): *Die Macht der Frauen und der Umsturz der Gesellschaft* (The Power of Women and the Social Revolution). 3rd edition. Berlin: Merve Verlag, pp. 40–43.

Dammert, Matthias (2009): *Angehörige im Visier der Pflegepolitik: Wie zukunftsfähig ist die subsidiare Logik der deutschen Pflegeversicherung* (Relatives in the Focus of Care Policy: How Sustainable Is the Subsidiary Logic of German Care Insurance). Wiesbaden: VS Verlag für Sozialwissenschaften.

Datta, Ayona and Brickell, Katherine (2009): "We Have a Little Bit More Finesse, as a Nation": Constructing the Polish Worker in London's Building Sites. In: *Antipode* 41 (3), pp. 439–64.

Davis, Angela (1982): The Approaching Obsolescence of Housework: A Working-Class Perspective. In: Davis, Angela: *Women, Race and Class*. pp. 222–45. London: The Women's Press Limited.

Dayton-Johnson, Jeff; Katseli, Louka T.; Xenogiani, Theodora (2007): Policy Coherence for Development 2007: Migration and Developing Countries. A Development Centre Perspective. OECD Publishing. www.keepeek. com/Digital-Asset-Management/oecd/development/policy-coherence-for-development-2007_9789264026100-en#.WnGjKucxnIU#page3 [accessed 3 May 2024].

Degiuli, Franscesca (2016): *Caring for a Living: Migrant Women, Ageing Citizens and Italian Families*. Oxford: Oxford University Press.

Delphy, Christine (1984): *Close to Home: A Materialist Analysis of Women's Oppression*. London: Hutchinson and The University of Massachusetts Press.

Deutscher Akademischer Austauschdienst (DAAD) (2017): Ukraine. Daten & Analysen zum Hochschul- und Wissenschaftsstandort (Ukraine: Data and Analyses on the Country's Universities). www.daad.de/medien/der-daad/ analysenstudien/bildungssystemanalyse/ukraine_daad_bsa.pdf [accessed 15 August 2024].

Deutscher Berufsverband für Pflegeberufe e.V. (DBfK) (German Professional Association for Nursing Professions (DBfK)) (2006) Positionspapier des DBfK zur illegalen Beschäftigung in der Pflege (Position Paper of the DBfK on Illegal Employment in the Care Sector). https://www.dbfk.de/media/docs/download/ DBfKPositionen/Position-illegale-Beschaeftigung-2006-10-16.pdf [accessed 15 August 2024].

Deutscher Gewerkschaftsbund (German Trade Union Confederation) (2022): Ergebnisse der Beschäftigtenbefragung zum DGB-Index Gute Arbeit 2022 (Results of the Employee Survey for the DGB Good Work Index 2022). https:// index-gute-arbeit.dgb.de/++co++b20b2d92-507f-11ed-b251-001a4a160123 [accessed 11 July 2024].

Dollinger, Franz-Wilhelm (2008): Von der Schwarzarbeit zur legalen pflegerischen Dienstleistung. Wie wir den Status der osteuropäischen Pflegerinnen legalisieren können (Speech: From Undeclared Work to Legal Care Services. How We Can Legalise the Status of Eastern European Nurses). https://www.kas.de/c/document_library/get_file?uuid=44bff9d7-af9d-3d22-4c91-61f2875be133&groupId=252038 [accessed 2 May 2024].

Donath, Susan (2000): The Other Economy: A Suggestion for a Distinctively Feminist Economics. In: *Feminist Economics* 6 (1) 115–23.

Dörre, Klaus; Ehrlich, Martin; Haubner, Tine (2014): Landnahme im Feld der Sorgearbeit (Lang Grabbing in the Field of Care Work). In: Aulenbacher, Brigitte; Riegraf, Birgit; Theobald, Hildegard (eds.): *Sorge: Arbeit, Verhältnisse, Regime* (Care: Work, Relations, Regimes). In: *Soziale Welt*, Special Issue 20, pp. 107–24.

Doucet, Andrea (2006): *Do Men Mother? Fathering, Care and Domestic Responsibility.* Toronto: Toronto University Press.

Dowling, Emma (2021/2022): *The Care Crises. What Caused It and How Can We End It?* Brooklyn/New York: Verso.

Edmond, Wendy and Fleming, Suzie (eds.) (1975): *All Work and No Pay: Women, Housework and the Wages Due.* Power of Women Collective. Bristol: Falling Wall Press Ltd.

Emunds, Bernhard (2016): *Damit es Oma gut geht: Pflege-Ausbeutung in den eigenen vier Wänden* (Keeping Grandma Well: Care Exploitation at Home). Frankfurt am Main: Westend Verlag.

Emunds, Bernhard; Kocher, Eva; Habel, Simone; Pflug, Rebekka; Tschenker, Theresa; von Deetzen, Verena (2021): Gute Arbeit für Live-In-Care. Gestaltungsoptionen für Praxis und Politik. (Good Work for Live-in Care. Organisation Options for Practice and Policy). https://nbi.sankt-georgen.de/assets/documents/cillas--und_nbi-position-2021_2-live-in-care.pdf [accessed 12 July 2024].

Emunds, Bernhard; Degan, Julian; Habel, Simone; Hagedorn, Jonas (eds.) (2022): *Freiheit – Gleichheit – Selbstausbeutung. Zur Zukunft der Sorgearbeit in der Dienstleistungsgesellschaft.* (Freedom – Equality – Self-exploitation. On the Future of Care Work in the Service Society). Marburg: Metropolis.

Engels, Friedrich (1974 [1884]): *Der Ursprung der Familie, des Privateigentums und des Staates* (The Origin of the Family, Private Property and the State). 3rd edition. Berlin: Dietz Verlag.

England, Paula (2010): The Gender Revolution: Uneven and Stalled. In: *Gender and Society* 24 (2), pp. 149–66.

Erel, Umut; Murji, Karim; Nahaboo, Zaki (2016): Understanding the Contemporary Race-Migration Nexus. In: *Ethnic and Racial Studies* 39 (8), pp. 1339–60.

Esping-Anderson, Gøsta (ed.) (2002): *Why We Need a New Welfare State.* Oxford: Oxford University Press.

Esping-Anderson, Gøsta (2009): *The Incomplete Revolution: Adapting to Women's New Roles.* Cambridge: Polity Press.

European Social Platform (2011): Care. Recommendations for Care that Respects the Rights of Individuals, Guarantees Access to Services and Promotes Social Inclusion. http://www.socialplatform.org/wp-content/uploads/2013/03/20121217_SocialPlatform_Recommendations_on_CARE_EN1.pdf [accessed 2 May 2024].

Fagan, Jay and Barnett, Marina (2003): The Relationship Between Maternal Gate-keeping, Paternal Competence, Mothers' Attitudes About the Father Role, and Father Involvement. In: *Journal of Family Issues* 24 (8), pp. 1020–43.

Faist, Thomas (2000): Das Konzept Transstaatliche Räume (The Concept of Transnational Spaces). In: Faist, Thomas (ed.): *Transstaatliche Räume – Politik, Wirtschaft und Kultur zwischen Deutschland und Türkei* (Trans-State Spaces – Politics, Economy and Culture Between Germany and Turkey). Bielefeld: Transcript, pp. 9–56.

Fassin, Didier (2020): L'illusion dangereuse de l'égalité devant l'épidémie (The Dangerous Illusion of Equality Before the Epidemic). https://www.college-de-france.fr/fr/actualites/illusion-dangereuse-de-egalite-devant-epidemie [accessed 12 July 2024].

Federal Swiss Council (2017): 24-Stunden-Betreuungsarbeit: Neue Regelung bis Mitte 2018.(24-Hour Care Work: New Regulation Until Mid-2018) Bern: SECO.

Federici, Silvia (2012 [1975]): Wages Against Housework. In: Federici, Silvia: *Revolution at Point Zero: Housework, Reproduction, and Feminist Struggle.* Oakland: PM Press, pp. 15–22.

Fedyuk, Olena and Kindler, Marta (2016): Migration of Ukrainians to the European Union: Background and Key Issues. In: Fedyuk, Olena and Kindler, Marta (eds.): *Ukrainian Migration to the European Union: Lessons for Migration Studies.* Imisco Research Series Springer Open, pp. 1–16.

Flaake, Karin (2014): *Neue Mütter – neue Väter. Eine empirische Studie zu veränderten Geschlechterbeziehungen in Familien* (New Mothers – New Fathers. An Empirical Study on Changing Gender Relations in Families). Gießen: Psychosozial-Verlag.

Fodor, Éva (2011): Geschlechterbeziehungen im (Post-)Sozialismus (Gender Relations Under (Post-)Socialism). In: *Aus Politik und Zeitgeschichte* 37–8. www.bpb.de/shop/zeitschriften/apuz/33132/frauen-in-europa (Politics and Contemporary History) [accessed 6 May 2024].

Folbre, Nancy (2006): Demanding Quality: Worker/Consumer Coalitions and High-Road Strategies in the Care Sector. In: *Politics and Society* 34 (1), pp. 1–21.

Foucault, Michel (2014): *Die Regierung des Lebenden* (On the Government of the Living). Frankfurt a.M.: Suhrkamp. For the English translation (2014), see: https://anarch.cc/uploads/michel-foucault/on-the-government-of-the-living.pdf [accessed 14 August 2024].

Fraser, Nancy (1994): After the Family Wage: A Postindustrial Thought Experiment. In: Fraser, Nancy: *Justice Interruptus: Critical Reflections on the "Postsocialist" Condition.* Hoboken: Taylor and Francis, pp. 41–66.

Fraser, Nancy (2013): *Fortunes of Feminism. From State-Managed Capitalism to Neoliberal Crisis*. London: Verso.

Fraser, Nancy (2014): Can Society Be Commodities All the Way Down? Polanyian Reflections on Capitalist Crisis. In: *Economy and Society* 43 (4), pp. 541–58.

Fraser, Nancy (2022): *Cannibal Capitalism: How our System is Devouring Democracy, Care, and the Planet and What We Can Do About It*. London: Verso.

Furedi, Frank (1994): A Plague of Moral Panics. In: *Living Marxism 73*. web. archive.org/web/20000614173221/http://www.informinc.co.uk/LM/LM73/LM73_Frank.html [accessed 6 May 2024].

Furedi, Frank (2013): Using Children as a Moral Shield. https://www.spiked-online.com/2013/01/14/using-children-as-a-moral-shield/ [accessed 6 May 2024].

Fussek, Claus and Loerzer, Sven (2007): *Alt und abgeschoben: Der Pflegenotstand und die Würde des Menschen* (Old and Abandoned: The Care Crisis and the Dignity of the Human Being). Freiburg: Herder Verlag.

Fussek, Claus and Schober, Gottlob (2013): *Es ist genug! Auch alte Menschen haben Rechte* (Enough is Enough! Old People Have Rights Too). München: Knaur Taschenbuch.

Fuszara, Malgorzata (2000): New Gender Relations in Poland in the 1990s. In: Gal, Susan and Kligman, Gail (eds.): *Reproducing Gender: Politics, Publics, and Everyday Life After Socialism*. Princeton: Princeton University Press, pp. 259–85.

Gamburd, Michele R. (2000): *The Kitchen Spoon's Handle: Transnationalism and Sri Lanka's Migrant Housemaids*. Ithaca/London: Cornell University Press.

Gather, Claudia; Geißler, Birgit; Rerrich, Maria S. (eds.) (2002): *Weltmarkt Privathaushalt. Bezahlte Hausarbeit im globalen Wandel* (World Market Private Household: Paid Domestic Work in Global Transformation). Münster: Westfälisches Dampfboot.

Gassner, Sonja (2020): Bodies and Boundaries: On the Possibility of a Politics of Affirmatively Shared Vulnerability. In: *Zeitschrift für Praktische Philosophie* 7 (2), 2020, pp. 417–42.

Geissler, Birgit (2010): Haushaltsdienstleistungen: Unsichtbar und "dirty"? (Household Services: Invisible and "Dirty"?). In: Becke, Guido; Bleses, Peter; Ritter, Wolfgang; Schmidt, Sandra (eds.): *"Decent Work": Arbeitspolitische Gestaltungsperspektive für eine globalisierte und flexibilisierte Arbeitswelt* ("Decent Work": Perspectives for Shaping the Politics of Work in a Globalised and Flexibilised World of Work). Wiesbaden: VS Verlag, pp. 209–19.

Gerasimova, Ekaterina and Chuikina, Sofia (2004): Obshchestvo remonta (A Society of Renovation). In: *Neprikosnovennyi zapas* (Reserve Stock) 34 (2), pp. 70–7.

Giddens, Anthony (1991): *Modernity and Self-Identity. Self and Society in the Late Modern Age*. Stanford: Stanford University Press.

Giordano, Chiara (2020): The Professionalisation of Domiciliary Care for the Elderly: A Comparison Between Public and Private Care Service Providers in Belgium. In: *International Journal of Sociology and Social Policy*, 41 (9/10), pp. 1072–88.

Giordano, Chiara (2021): Freedom or Money? The Dilemma of Migrant Live-in Elderly Carers in Times of COVID-19. In: *Gender, Work & Organization* 28, pp. 137–50.

Giza-Poleszczuk, Anna (2007): Rodzina i system społeczny (Families and the Social System). In: Marody, Mirosława (ed.): *Wymiary życia społecznego. Polska na przełomie XX i XXI wieku.* (Dimensions of Social Life. Poland at the Turn of the Twentieth and Twenty-First Centuries). Warsaw: Wydawnictwa Uniwersytetu Warszawskiego, pp. 272–301.

Goffman, Erving (1952): *The Presentation of Self in Everyday Life.* New York: Bantam Doubleday Dell Publishing Group.

Golinowska, Stanisława (2010): The Long-Term Care System for the Elderly in Poland. ENEPRI Research Report 83. www.ceps.eu/publications/long-term-care-system-elderlypoland [accessed 7 May 2024].

Goode, Erich and Nachman, Ben-Yehuda (1994): *Moral Panics: The Social Construction of Deviance.* Oxford: Blackwell.

Goven, Joanna (1993): Gender Politics in Hungary: Autonomy and Anti-Feminism. In: Funk, Nanette and Mueller, Magda (eds.): *Gender Politics and Post-Communism: Reflections from Eastern Europe and the Former Soviet Union.* New York: Routledge, pp. 224–40.

Graff, Agnieszka (2014): Report from the Gender Trenches: War Against "Genderism" in Poland. In: *European Journal of Women's Studies* 21 (4), pp. 431–42.

Gropas, Ruby, Bartolini, Laura and Triandaffyllidou, Anna (2015): Country Report Italy. https://www.researchgate.net/publication/312586156_Country_Report_-_ITALY_ITHACA_Research_Report_N_22015 [accessed 7 May 2024].

Haffert, Ingeborg (2014): *Eine Polin für Oma. Der Pflegenotstand in unseren Familien* (A Polish Woman for Grandma. The Care Crisis in Our Families). 2nd edition Berlin: Econ Verlag.

Haidinger, Bettina (2013): *Hausfrau für zwei Länder sein. Zur Reproduktion des transnationalen Haushalts* (A Housewife for Two Countries. On the Reproduction of the Transnational Household). Münster: Westfälisches Dampfboot.

Hall, Stuart; Critcher, Chas; Jefferson, Tony; Clarke, John; Roberts, Brian (1978): *Policing the Crisis: Mugging, the State and Law and Order.* London/Basingstoke: Macmillan.

Harten, Hans-Christian (1996): *De-Kulturation und Germanisierung. Die nationalsozialistische Rassen- und Erziehungspolitik in Polen 1939-1945* (De-Culturation and Germanisation. The National Socialist Racial and Educational Policy in Poland 1939–1945). Frankfurt am Main/New York: Campus.

Hartigan, John (1999): *Racial Situations: Class Predicaments of Whiteness in Detroit.* Princeton: Princeton University Press.

Hartmann, Heidi (1981): The Unhappy Marriage of Marxism and Feminism: Towards a More Progressive Union. In Sargent, Lydia (ed.): *Women & Rev-*

olution. A Discussion of the Unhappy Marriage of Marxism and Feminism. Montréal: Black Rose Books, pp. 1–42.

Harvey, David (2004): The "New Imperialism": Accumulation by Dispossession. In: *Actuel Marx* Volume 35 (1), pp: 71 – 90.

Haug, Frigga (2011): Das Care-Syndrom. Ohne Geschichte hat die Frauenbewegung keine Perspektive (The Care Syndrome. Without History, the Women's Movement Has No Perspective). In: *Das Argument* 292 (3), pp. 345–64.

Hayden, Dolores (1981): *The Grand Domestic Revolution: A History of Feminist Design for American Homes, Neighborhoods, and Cities.* Cambridge: MIT Press.

Hays, Sharon (1996): *The Cultural Contradictions of Motherhood.* Yale: Yale University Press.

Hearn, Jeff (1987): *The Gender of Oppression: Men, Masculinity and the Critique of Marxism.* Brighton: Wheatsheaf.

Henau, Jerome de; Himmelweit, Susan; Łapniewska, Zofia; Perrons, Diane (2016): Investing in the Care Economy. A Gender Analysis of Employment Stimulus in Seven OECD Countries. International Trade Union Confederation. https://www.ituc-csi.org/IMG/pdf/care_economy_2_en_web.pdf [accessed 7 May 2024].

Henau, Jerome de; Himmelweit, Susan; Perrons, Diane (2017): Investing in the Care Economy. Simulating employment Effects by Gender in Countries in Emerging Economies. International Trade Union Confederation. https://www.researchgate.net/publication/344402077_Investing_in_the_Care_Economy_A_gender_analysis_of_employment_stimulus_in_seven_OECD_countries [accessed 15 July 2024].

Hess, Sabine (2009): *Globalisierte Hausarbeit. Au-pair als Migrationsstrategie von Frauen aus Osteuropa* (Globalised Domestic Work. Au Pair Work as a Migration Strategy for Women from Eastern Europe) 2nd edition. Wiesbaden: VS Verlag.

Hielscher, Volker; Kirchen-Peters, Sabine; Nock, Lukas (2017): *Pflege in den eigenen vier Wänden: Zeitaufwand und Kosten* (Care in One's Own Four Walls: Time Requirements and Cost). Study 363, Hans-Böckler-Stiftung. https://www.boeckler.de/pdf/p_study_hbs_363.pdf [accessed 7 May 2024].

Himmelweit, Susan (1995): The Discovery of "Unpaid Work": The Social Consequences of the Expansion of Work. In: *Feminist Economics* 1 (2), pp. 1–19.

Hochschild, Arlie R. (2000): Global Care Chains and Emotional Surplus Value. In: Giddens, Anthony and Hutton, Will (eds.): *On the Edge: Living with Global Capitalism.* London: Jonathan Cape, pp. 130–46.

Hochschild, Arlie R. (2001): Emotion Work, Feeling Rules, and Social Structure: In Branaman, Ann (ed.): *Self and Society.* London: Blackwell Publishers, pp. 138–55.

Hochschild, Arlie R. (2003): *The Managed Heart: The Commercialization of Human Feeling.* 2nd edition. Berkeley: University of California Press.

Hochschild, Arlie R. (2010): The Backstage of a Global Free Market: Nannys and Surrogates. In: Apitzsch, Ursula and Schmidbaur, Marianne (eds.): *Care und Migration. Die Ent-Sorgung menschlicher Reproduktionsarbeit entlang von Geschlechter- und Armutsgrenzen*. (Care and Migration. The Dis-supply of Human Reproductive Labour Along Gender and Poverty Lines). Opladen & Farmington Hill: Verlag Barbara Budrich, pp. 23–40.

Hochschild, Arlie R. (2012): *The Outsourced Self: Intimate Life in Market Times*. New York: Metropolitan Press.

Hochschild, Arlie R. and Ehrenreich, Barbara (2003): *Global Woman: Nannies, Maids and Sex Workers in the New Economy*. New York: Metropolitan Books.

Holch, Christine (2006): Die 24-Stunden-Polin (The 24-Hour Polish Woman). *Chrismon. Das evangelische Magazin* 11, pp. 41–8. https://chrismon.de/artikel/593/24-stunden-polin [accessed 7 May 2024].

Hondagneu-Sotelo, Pierrette and Avila, Ernestine (1997): I'm Here, but I'm There: The Meanings of Latina Transnational Motherhood. In: *Gender and Society* 11 (5), pp. 548–71.

Hondagneu-Sotelo, Pierrette (2001): Doméstica: *Immigrant Workers Cleaning and Caring in the Shadows of Affluence*. University of California Press: Berkeley.

Hrycak; Alexandra (2005): Coping with Chaos: Gender and Politics in a Fragmented State. In: *Problems of Postcommunism* 52 (5), pp. 69–81.

Hryciuk, Renata Ewa and Korolczuk, Elzbieta (2013): At the Intersection of Gender and Class: Social Mobilisation Around Mothers' Rights in Poland. In: Jacobsson, Kerstin and Saxonberg, Steven (eds.): *Beyond NGO-isation: The Development of Social Movements in Central and Eastern Europe*, London: Ashgate, pp. 49–70.

Hrženjak, Majda (ed.) (2011): *Politics of Care*. Ljubljana: Peace Institute.

Hunin, Jan (2008): Eurowees, achtergelaten met broertje, hond en schildpad (Euro-orphan, Abandoned with Little Brother, Dog and Turtle. *De Volkskrant* 11 July 2008. www.volkskrant.nl/buitenland/eurowees-achtergelaten-met-broertje-honden-schildpad~a915382/ [accessed 15 August 2024].

Illouz, Eva (2007): *Cold Intimacies: The Making of Emotional Capitalism*. London: Polity Press.

Imre, Anikó (2001): Gender, Literature and Film in Contemporary East Central European Culture. CLCWeb: *Comparative Literature and Culture* 3, 1. docs.lib.purdue.edu/clcweb/vol3/iss1/6/ [accessed 15 August 2024].

International Labour Organisation (ILO) (2013): Domestic Workers Across the World: Global and Regional Statistics and the Extent of Legal Protection. Geneva: ILO. https://webapps.ilo.org/wcmsp5/groups/public/---dgreports/---dcomm/---publ/documents/publication/wcms_173363.pdf [accessed 7 May 2024].

International Labour Organisation (ILO) (2015a): ILO Global Estimates on Migrant Workers. Results and Methodology. Special Focus on Migrant Domestic Workers. Geneva: ILO. www.ilo.org/wcmsp5/groups/public/@dgreports/@dcomm/documents/publication/wcms_436343.pdf [accessed 7 May 2024].

International Labour Organisation (ILO) (2015b): World Employment and Social Outlook. www.futureofworkhub.info/allcontent/2015/5/19/world-employment-social-outlook-thechanging-nature-of-jobs [accessed 7 May 2024].

International Labour Organisation (ILO) (2022): Care at Work: Investing in Care Leave and Services for a More Gender Equal World of Work. https://www.ilo.org/publications/major-publications/care-work-investing-care-leave-and-services-more-gender-equal-world-work. [accessed 15 July 2024].

IOM UN Migration (2016): Migration Health Annual Review 2016. https://publications.iom.int/books/migration-health-annual-review-2016 [accessed 21 July 2024].

IOM (2021): World Migration Report 2022. https://publications.iom.int/books/world-migration-report-2022 [accessed 21 July 2024].

Isfort, Michael (2009): Versorgung in Familien mit mittel- und osteuropäischen Haushaltshilfen. (Care in Families with Central and East European Household Employees). Pressemitteilung der DIP, Deutsches Institut für angewandte Pflegeforschung e.V. www.dip.de/presse/pressemitteilungen/pressemitteilung/?tx_ttnews%5Bpointer%5D=8&tx_ttnews%5BbackPid%5D=62&tx_ttnews%5Btt_news%5D=46&cHash=a428eea8869657b4dde37fb697f94092 [accessed 7 May 2024].

Jagger, Alison M. and McBride, William L. (1985): Reproduction as Male Ideology. In: *Hypatia: A Journal of Feminist Philosophy (Women's Studies International Forum)* 8 (3), pp. 185–96.

Janisch, Wolfgang and Stadler, Rainer (2021): Urteil verteuert die häusliche Pflege (Judgement Makes Home Care More Expensive). In: *Süddeutsche Zeitung*, Issue June 24.

Jäger, Siegfried: (2012): *Kritische Diskursanalyse: Eine Einführung* (Critical Discourse Analysis. An Introduction). 6th edition. Münster: Unrast.

Jenson, Jane (2017): The New Maternalism: Children First; Women Second. In: Ergas, Yasmine; Jenson, Jan; Michel, Sonya (eds.): *Reassembling Motherhood: Procreation and Care in a Globalized World*. New York: Columbia University Press, pp. 269–86.

Joseph, Gloria (1981): The Incompatible Ménage à Trois: Marxism, Feminism, and Racism. In: Sargent, Lydia (ed.): *Women & Revolution: A Discussion of the Unhappy Marriage of Marxism and Feminism*. Montréal: Black Rose Books, pp. 91–107.

Jurczyk, Karin and Lange, Andreas (2009): Vom ewigen Praktikanten zum "Reflexiven Vater"? Eine Einführung in aktuelle Debatten um Väter (From Eternal Intern to "Reflective Father"? An Introduction to Current Debates About Fathers). In: Jurczyk, Karin (ed.): *Vaterwerden und Vaterschaft heute: Neue Wege – neue Chancen!* (Becoming a Father and Fatherhood Today: New Ways – New Opportunities!). Gütersloh: Verlag Bertelsmann-Stiftung, pp. 13–45.

Kałwa, Dobrochna (2007): "So wie zu Hause". Die private Sphäre als Arbeitsplatz ("Just Like at home". The Private Sphere as a Workplace). In: Nowicka, Magdalena (ed.): *Von Polen nach Deutschland und zurück. Die Arbeitsmigration und ihre Herausforderungen für Europa* (From Poland to Germany and Back. Labour Migration and its Challenges for Europe). Bielefeld: Transcript Verlag, pp. 205–25.

Kałwa, Dobrochna (2008): Commuting Between Private Lives. In: Metz-Göckel, Sigrid; Morokvasic, Mirjana; Münst, Senganata A. (eds.): *Migration and Mobility in an Enlarged Europe: A Gender Perspective*. Leverkusen: Barbara Budrich Verlag, pp. 121–40.

Karakayali, Juliane (2010): *Transnational Haushalten. Biographische Interviews mit "care workers" aus Osteuropa* (Transnational Households: Biographical Interviews with Care Workers from Eastern Europe). Wiesbaden: VS Verlag.

Kastner, Bernd (2008): Gesetzlose Hilfeleistung (Unlawful Assistance). In: *Süddeutsche Zeitung*, 25 January 2008, p. 41.

Kaufmann, Jean-Claude (1999): *Mit Leib und Seele: Theorie der Haushaltstätigkeit* (With Body and Soul: Theory of Domestic Work). Konstanz: Universitäts-Verlag.

Kelly, Philip and Lusis, Tom (2006): Migration and the Transnational Habitus: Evidence from Canada and the Philippines. In: *Environment and Planning A: Economy and Space* 38 (5), pp. 831–47.

Keryk, Myroslava (2004): Labour Migrant: Our Saviour or Betrayer? Ukrainian Discussions Concerning Labour Migration. *Migration Online*. https://scholar.google.se/citations?view_op=view_citation&hl=sv&user=_TGR_BcAAAAJ&citation_for_view=_TGR_BcAAAAJ:20sOgNQ5qMEC [accessed 10 May 2024].

Keryk, Myroslava (2010): "Caregivers with a Heart Needed": The Domestic Care Regime in Poland after 1989 and Ukrainian Migrants. In: *Social Policy and Society* 9 (10), pp. 431–44.

Kindler, Marta; Kordasiewicz, Anna; Szulecka, Monika (2016): *Care Needs and Migration for Domestic Work: Ukraine–Poland*. Geneva: International Labor Office.

Kicinger, Anna and Weinar, Agnieszka (eds.): *State of the Art of the Migration Research in Poland*. CMR Working Papers, No. 26/84. https://www.econstor.eu/bitstream/10419/140810/1/573872252.pdf [accessed 23 July 2024].

Kis, Oksana (2007): "Beauty Will Save The World!": Feminine Strategies in Ukrainian Politics and the Case of Yulia Tymoshenko. In: *spacesofidentity* 7 (2). https://soi.journals.yorku.ca/index.php/soi/article/view/7970/16906 [accessed 10 May 2024].

Klaveren, Maarten van; Tijdens, Kea; Hughie-Williams, Melanie; Ramos Martin, Nuria (2010): Ukraine – An Overview of Women's Work, Minimum Wages and Employment. Decisions for Life MDG3 Project Country Report. https://wageindicator.org/about/wageindicatorcountries/country-report-ukraine [accessed 10 May 2024].

Klenner, Christina and Leiber, Simone (2009): Wohlfahrtsstaaten und Geschlechterungleichheit im Transformationsprozess (Welfare States and Gender Inequality in Transformation). In: Klenner, Christina and Leiber, Simone:

Wohlfahrtsstaaten und Geschlechterungleichheit in Mittel- und Osteuropa. Kontinuität und postsozialistische Transformation in den EU-Mitgliedsstaaten (Welfare States and Gender Inequality in Central and Eastern Europe: Continuity and Post-Socialist Transformation in the EU Member States). Wiesbaden: VS Verlag, pp. 11–31.

Klinger, Cornelia (2012): Leibdienst – Liebesdienst – Dienstleistung (Body Service – Love Service – Service). In: Dörre, Klaus; Sauer, Dieter; Wittke, Volker (eds.): *Kapitalismustheorie und Arbeit. Neue Ansätze soziologischer Kritik* (Theory of Capitalism and Work: New Sociological–Critical Approaches). Frankfurt am Main/New York: Campus, pp. 259–72.

Kocher, Eva (2012): Hausarbeit als Erwerbsarbeit: Der Rechtsrahmen in Deutschland. Voraussetzungen einer Ratifikation der ILO-Domestic Workers Convention durch die Bundesrepublik Deutschland (Domestic Work as Gainful Employment: The Legal Framework in Germany. Prerequisites for Ratification of the ILO Domestic Workers Convention by the Federal Republic of Germany). Report for the Hans Böckler Foundation. https://www.kok-gegen-menschenhandel.de/fileadmin/user_upload/Hausarbeit_als_Erwerbsarbeit_ILO.pdf [accessed 11 July 2024].

Kocher, Eva (2014): Die Ungleichbehandlung von Hausangestellten in der 24-Stunden-Pflege gegenüber anderen Arbeitnehmerinnen und Arbeitnehmern – eine Frage des Verfassungsrechts (The Unequal Treatment of Domestic Workers in 24-Hour Care Compared to Other Employees – A Question of Constitutional Law). In: Scheiwe, Kirsten and Krawietz, Johanna (eds.): *Keine Arbeit wie jede andere. Die Regulierung von Arbeit im Privathaushalt* (Not a Job Like Any Other. The Regulation of Work in the Private Household). Berlin: De Gruyter, pp. 85–110.

Kofman, Eleonore (2012): Rethinking Care Through Social Reproduction: Articulating Circuits of Migration. In: *Social Politics: International Studies in Gender, State & Society* 19 (1), pp. 142–62.

Kollontai, Alexandra (1977 [1909]): The Social Basis of the Woman Question. In: Kollontai, Alexandra: *Selected Writings of Alexandra Kollontai*. London: Allison & Busby. www.marxists.org/archive/kollonta/1909/social-basis.htm [accessed 10 May 2024].

Kontos, Maria (2013): Negotiating Social Citizenship Rights of Migrant Domestic Workers: The Right to Family Reunification and Family Life in Policies and Debates. In: *Journal of Ethnic and Migration Studies* 39, pp. 409–24.

Korolczuk, Elzbieta and Hryciuk, Renata Ewa (2010): In the Name of the Family and Nation. Framing Father's Activism in Contemporary Poland. https://www.researchgate.net/profile/Elzbieta-Korolczuk/publication/322444963_In_the_name_of_the_family_and_nation_Framing_fathers%27_activism_in_contemporary_Poland/links/5a92cc8145851535bcd92eb0/In-the-name-of-the-family-and-nation-Framing-fathers-activism-in-contemporary-Poland.pdf [accessed 21 July 2024].

Koshulap, Iryna (2007): Images of Fatherhood in Ukraine: Past and Present. In: Hankivsky, Olena and Salvykova, Anastasiya (eds.): *Gender, Politics and Society in Ukraine*. Toronto: Toronto University Press, pp. 364–84.

Koven, Seth and Michel, Sonya (1990): Womanly Duties: Maternalist Politics and the Origins of Welfare States in France, Germany, Great Britain, and the United States, 1880–1920. *The American Historical Review* 95(4), pp. 1076–108.

Koven, Seth and Michel, Sonya (1993): Introduction. In: Koven and Michel (eds.): *Mothers of a New World. Maternalist Politics and the Origins of Welfare States.* London: Routledge, pp. 1–42.

Krawietz, Johanna (2014): *Pflege grenzüberschreitend organisieren. Eine Studie zur transnationalen Vermittlung von Care-Arbeit* (Organising Care Across Borders. A Study on the Transnational Mediation of Care Work). Frankfurt am Main: Mabuse Verlag.

Krzyzkowski, Janusz and Mucha, LuKasz (2012): Aging in Poland at the Dawn of the 21st Century. In: *Polish Sociological Review* 2, pp. 247–260.

Kuhlmey, Adelheid and Budnick, Andrea (2023): *Pflegende Angehörige in Deutschland: Vereinbarkeit von Pflege und Erwerbstätigkeit (Informal Caregivers* in Germany: Achieving Work–Life Balance). In: Bundesgesundheitsblatt – Gesundheitsforschung – Gesundheitsschutz 66(2). https://www.research-gate.net/publication/370085611_Pflegende_Angehorige_in_Deutschland Vereinbarkeit_von_Pflege_und_ErwerbstätigkeitInformal_caregivers_in_ Germany_achieving_work-life_balance [accessed 21 July 2024].

Kurz-Scherf, Ingrid (1996): Vom guten Leben. Feministische Perspektiven jenseits der Arbeitsgesellschaft (The Good Life. Feminist Perspectives Beyond the Labour Society). In: Knapp, Ulla (ed.): *Beschäftigungspolitik für Frauen in der Region: Überarbeitete Tagungsbeiträge* (Employment Policy for Women in the Region: Revised Conference Contributions). Opladen: Leske und Budrich, pp. 79–97.

Lan, Pei-Chia (2006): *Global Cinderellas: Migrant Domestic Workers and Newly Rich Employers in Taiwan.* Durham/London: Duke.

Leiber, Simone and Rossow, Vera (2017): Zwischen Vermarktlichung und Europäisierung: Die wachsende Bedeutung transnational agierender Vermittlungsagenturen in der häuslichen Pflege in Deutschland (Between Marketisation and Europeanisation: The Growing Importance of Transnationally Operating Placement Agencies in Home Care in Germany). In: *Sozialer Fortschritt* (Social Progress) 66 (3/4), pp. 285–302.

Leiber, Simone; Rossow, Verena; Österle, August; Timm Frerk (2020): Yet Another Black Box: Brokering Agencies in the Evolving Market for Live-in Migrant Care Work in Austria and Germany. In: *International Journal of Care and Caring* 5 (2), pp. 187–208.

Leiblfinger, Michael; Prieler, Veronika; Schwiter, Karin; Steiner, Jennifer; Benazha, Aranka; Lutz, Helma (2020): *Impact of the COVID-19 Pandemic on Live-in Care Workers in Germany, Austria, and Switzerland.* London: London School of Economics and Political Science (LSE). https://journal.ilpnetwork.

org/articles/51/files/submission/proof/51-1-430-1-10-20201008.pdf [accessed 17 July 2024].

Lenin, Vladimir I. (1961 [1919]): *The Tasks of the Proletarian Women's Movement in the Soviet Republic.* https://www.marxists.org/archive/lenin/works/1919/sep/23a.htm [accessed 10 May 2024].

Leon, Margarita (ed.) (2014): *The Transformation of Care in European Societies.* Basingstoke: Palgrave Macmillan.

Lessenich, Stephan (2020): Leben machen und sterben lassen: Die Politik mit der Vulnerabilität (Make Life and Let Die: The Politics of Vulnerability). In: *WISI Mitteilungen* 06/2020, pp. 454–61.

Libanova, Ella; Levenets, Yuri; Makarova, Elena; Kotyhorenko, Victor; Cherenko, Ludmila; Khmelevska, Oksana; Tkachenko, Lydia; Balakirev, Olga (2011): Національну Доповідь про людський розвиток 2011 Україна: на шляху до соціального залучення, Представництво Програми розвитку ООН в Україні [Natsional'nu Dopovid' pro lyuds'kyy rozvytok 2011 Ukrayina: na shlyakhu do sotsial'noho zaluchennya, Predstavnytstvo Prohramy rozvytku OON v Ukrayin] (National Human Development Report 2011 Ukraine: Towards Social Inclusion, UNDP Representative in Ukraine). https://issuu.com/undpukraine/docs/ua_2011_ukr [accessed 10 May 2024].

Lister, Ruth and Williams, Fiona (2007): *Gendering Citizenship in Western Europe: New challenges for Citizenship Research in a Cross-National Context.* Bristol: Bristol University Press.

Lutz, Helma (2007a): "Die 24-Stunden-Polin". Eine intersektionelle Analyse transnationaler Dienstleistungen ("The 24-hour Polish woman". An Intersectional Analysis of Transnational Services). In: Klinger, Cornelia; Knapp, Gudrun-Axeli; Sauer, Birgit (eds.): *Achsen der Ungleichheit. Zum Verhältnis von Klasse, Geschlecht und Ethnizität* (Axes of Inequality: On the Relationships Between Class, Gender and Ethnicity). Frankfurt am Main/New York: Campus, pp. 210–34.

Lutz, Helma (2007b): The "Intimate Others" – Migrant Domestic Workers in Europe. In: Berggren, Erik; Likic-Brboric, Branka; Toksöz, Gülay; Trimikliniotis,Nicos (eds.): *Irregular Migration, Informal Labour and Community: A Challenge for Europe.* Maastricht: Shaker Publishing 2007, pp. 226–41.

Lutz, Helma (2008): Introduction: Migration and Domestic Work. In: Lutz, Helma (ed.): *Migration and Domestic Work: A European Perspective on a Global Theme.* Aldershot: Ashgate, pp. 1–10.

Lutz, Helma (2010): Gender in the Migratory Process. In: *Journal of Ethnic and Migration Studies* 36, (10), pp. 1647–63.

Lutz, Helma (2011): *The New Maids: Transnational Women and the Care Economy.* London: Zed Books.

Lutz, Helma (2015): Myra's Predicament: Motherhood Dilemmas for Migrant Care Workers. In: *Social Politics* 22 (3), pp. 341–59.

Lutz, Helma (2016): "Good Motherhood" – A Dilemma for Migrant Women from Eastern Europe. In: Amelina, Anna; Horvath, Kenneth; Meeus, Bruno (eds.): *An Anthology of Migration and Social Transformation: European Perspectives*. Heidelberg/New York/Dordrecht/London: Springer, pp. 245–58.

Lutz, Helma (2017a): Euro-Orphans and the Stigmatisation of Migrant Motherhood. In: Ergas, Yasmine; Jenson, Jane; Michel, Sonya (eds.): *Reassembling Motherhood: Procreation and Care in a Globalised World*. New York: Columbia University Press, pp. 247–68.

Lutz, Helma (2017b): Care as a Fictitious Commodity: Reflections on the Intersections of Migration, Gender and Care Regimes. In: *Migration Studies* 5 (3), pp. 356–68.

Lutz, Helma (2018a): Intersektionelle Biographieforschung (Intersectional Biographical Research). In: Lutz, Helma; Schiebel, Martina; Tuider, Elisabeth (eds.): *Handbuch Biographieforschung* (Handbook of Biographical Research). Wiesbaden: Springer, pp. 139–50.

Lutz, Helma (2018b): Care Migration: The Connectivity of Transnational Social Inequalities. In: Aulenbacher, Brigitte; Lutz, Helma; Riegraf, Birgit (eds.): Global Sociology of Care and Care Work. Care Migration: The Connectivity between Care Chains, Care Circulation and Transnational Social Inequality. In: *Current Sociology Monograph*, 66 (4), pp. 577–89. https://www.researchgate. net/publication/324709668_Care_migration_The_connectivity_between_ care_chains_care_circulation_and_transnational_social_inequality. [accessed 15 August 2024].

Lutz, Helma (2018c): Masculinity, Care and Stay-Behind Fathers: A Postsocialist Perspective. In: *Critical Sociology*, 44 (7–8), pp. 1061–76.

Lutz, Helma and Benazha, Aranka (2022): Transnationale soziale Ungleichheit. Migrantische Care und Haushaltsarbeit (Transnational Social Inequalities: Migrant Care and Housework). In: Biele Mefebue, Astrid; Bührmann, Andrea; Sabine Grenz (eds.): *Handbuch Intersektionalitätsforschung* (Handbook of Intersectionality Research). Wiesbaden: Springer, pp. 289–334.

Lutz, Helma and Benazha, Aranka (2024): At Home with the Employer? Contradictory Notions of the Care Clients' Home as a Workplace and Living Space. In: Aulenbacher, Brigitte; Lutz, Helma; Palenga-Möllenbeck, Ewa; Schwiter, Karin (eds.): *Home Care for Sale*. London: Sage, pp. 221–32.

Lutz, Helma and Gawarecki, Kathrin (eds.) (2005): *Kolonialismus und Erinnerungskultur. Die Kolonialvergangenheit im kollektiven Gedächtnis der deutschen und niederländischen Einwanderungsgesellschaft* (Colonialism and the Culture of Remembrance. The Colonial Past in the Collective Memory of the German and Dutch Immigration Society.) Münster/New York/ München/Berlin: Waxmann. https://www.waxmann.com/index.php?eID= download&buchnr=1491 [accessed 15 August 2024].

Lutz, Helma and Palenga-Möllenbeck, Ewa (2010): Care Work Migration in Germany: Semi-Compliance and Complicity. In: *Social Policy and Society* 9 (3), pp. 419–30.

Lutz, Helma, and Palenga-Möllenbeck, Ewa (2011a): Das Care-Chain-Konzept auf dem Prüfstand. Eine Fallstudie der transnationalen Care-Arrangements polnischer und ukrainischer Migrantinnen (Putting the Care Chain Concept to the Test. A Case Study of the Transnational Care Arrangements of Polish and Ukrainian Migrant Women). In: Metz-Göckel, Sigrid and Bauschke Urban, Carola (eds.): *Transnationalisierung und Gender*. Special Issue: Gender. 3 (1), pp. 9–27.

Lutz, Helma and Palenga-Möllenbeck, Ewa (2011b): Care, Gender and Migration: Towards a Theory of Transnational Domestic Work Migration in Europe. In: *Journal of Contemporary European Studies* 19 (3), pp. 349–64.

Lutz, Helma and Palenga-Möllenbeck, Ewa (2012): Care Workers, Care Drain, and Care Chains: Reflections on Care, Migration, and Citizenship. In: *Social Politics* 19 (1), pp. 15–37.

Lutz, Helma and Palenga-Möllenbeck, Ewa (2014): Care-Migrantinnen im geteilten Europa. Verbindungen und Widersprüche in einem transnationalen Raum (Care Migrants in a Divided Europe. Connections and Contradictions in a Transnational Space). In: Aulenbacher, Brigitte; Riegraf, Birgit; Theobald, Hildegard (eds.): *Sorge: Arbeit, Verhältnisse, Regime* (Care: Work, Relations, Regimes). In: *Soziale Welt*, Special Issue 20, pp. 217–31.

Lutz, Helma and Palenga-Möllenbeck, Ewa (2015): Care-Arbeit, Gender und Migration: Überlegungen zu einer Theorie transnationaler Migration im Haushaltssektor in Europa (Care Work, Gender and Migration: Reflections on a Theory of Transnational Migration in the Household Sector in Europe). In: Meier-Gräwe, Uta (ed.): *Die Arbeit des Alltags. Gesellschaftliche Organisation und Umverteilung* (The Work of Everyday Life. Social Organisation and Redistribution). Wiesbaden: Springer, pp. 181–200.

Lutz, Helma and Palenga-Möllenbeck, Ewa (2016): *Global Care Chains*. In: Triandafyllidou, Anna (ed.): *Routledge Handbook of Immigration and Refugee Studies*. Abingdon/New York: Taylor and Francis, pp. 139–44.

Lutz, Helma and Schwiter, Karin (2024): Umkämpfte Formalisierung und Normalisierung der Live-in- Betreuung. Zur Vermarktlichung von Care- Arbeit im "sorglosen Kapitalismus" (The Contested Formalisation and Normalisation of Live-in Care. On the Marketisation of Care Work in "Carefree Capitalism"). In: Atzmüller, Roland; Binner, Kristina; Décieux, Fabienne; Deindl, Raphael; Grubner, Johanna; Kneissel, Katharina (eds.): *Gesellschaft in Transformation. Sorge, Kämpfe und Kapitalismus* (Society in Transformation. Care, Struggles and Capitalism). Wiesbaden: Beltz-Juventa, pp.68–78.

Lutz, Helma; Schiebel, Martina; Tuider, Elisabeth (eds.): *Handbuch Biographieforschung* (Handbook of Biographical Research). Wiesbaden: Springer, pp. 139–50.

Lutz, Helma; Herrera-Vivar, Maria Teresa; Supik, Linda (2011): Framing Intersectionality: An Introduction. In: Lutz, Helma; Herrera-Vivar, Maria Teresa; Supik, Linda (eds.): *Framing Intersectionality: Debates on a Multi-Faceted Concept in Gender Studies*. London/New York: Routledge, pp. 1–22.

Luxemburg, Rosa (1912): *Women's Suffrage and Class Struggle*. In: Luxemburg, Rosa. *Political Writings*. New York: Monthly Review Press. www.marxists.org/archive/luxemburg/1912/05/12.htm [accessed 13 May 2024].

Luxemburg, Rosa (1971 [1912]): *On the Fallen Women of Liberalism*. https://www.marxists.org/archive/luxemburg/1912/misc/fallen-women-liberalism.htm. [accessed 21 July 2024].

Luxemburg, Rosa (2003 [1913]): *The Accumulation of Capital: A Contribution to the Economic Explanation of Capitalism*. London/New York: Routledge.

Macdonald, Cameron Lynne (2010): *Shadow Mothers: Nannies, Au Pairs, and the Micropolitics of Mothering*. Berkeley/Los Angeles: University of California Press.

Madianou, Mirca and Miller, Danny (2011): Mobile Phone Parenting: Reconfiguring Relationships Between Filipina Mothers and Their Left-Behind Children. In: *New Media and Society* 13 (3), pp. 457–70.

Madörin, Mascha (2011): Das Auseinanderdriften der Arbeitsproduktivitäten: Eine feministische Sicht (The Drifting Apart of Labour Productivity: A Feminist View). In: *Jahrbuch Denknetz* 11, pp. 56–70. https://www.denknetz.ch/wp-content/uploads/2017/07/Madorin_Das_Auseinandertriften_der_Arbeitsproduktivitäten.pdf [accessed 21 July 2024].

Majchrzyk-Mikuła, Joanna (2008): *Eurosieroctwo (Euro-Orphan): Materiał Sygnalny* (Euro-Orphan: Signature Material). Warsaw: Studium Prawa Europejskiego.

Marx, Karl and Engels, Friedrich (1990 [1846]): *The German Ideology*. https://www.marxists.org/archive/marx/works/download/Marx_The_German_Ideology.pdf [accessed 15 August 2024].

Mazierska, Ewa (2008): *Masculinities in Polish, Czech and Slovak Cinema: Black Peters and Men of Marble*. Oxford/New York: Berghahn Books.

McKay, Deirdre (2007): "Sending Dollars Shows Feeling": Emotions and Economics in Filipino Migration. In: *Mobilities* 2 (2), pp. 175–94.

Medici, Gabriela (2015): *Migrantinnen als Pflegehilfen in Schweizer Privathaushalten. Menschenrechtliche Vorgaben und staatliche Handlungspflichten* (Migrant Women as Care Workers in Swiss Private Households. Human Rights Requirements and State Obligations to Act). Zürich: Schulthess.

Mendel, Annekatrein (1993): *Zwangsarbeit im Kinderzimmer. "Ostarbeiterinnen" in deutschen Familien von 1939-1945* (Forced Labour in the Nursery. "Eastern labourers" in German Families 1939–1945). Frankfurt am Main: DIPA Verlag.

Menschik, Jutta and Leopold, Evelyn (1974): *Gretchens rote Schwestern. Frauen in der DDR* (Gretchen's Red Sisters. Women in the GDR). Frankfurt am Main: Fischer.

Meuser, Michael (2014): Care und Männlichkeit in modernen Gesellschaften: Grundlegende Überlegungen illustriert am Beispiel involvierter Vaterschaft (Care and Masculinity in Modern Societies: Fundamental Considerations Illustrated by the Example of Involved Fatherhood). In: Aulenbacher, Brigitte;

Riegraf, Birgit; Theobald, Hildegard (eds.): *Sorge: Arbeit, Verhältnisse, Regime* (Care: Work, Relations, Regimes). In: *Soziale Welt*, Special Issue 20, pp. 159–74.

Mezey, Naomi and Pillard, Cornelia T.L. (2012): Against the New Maternalism. In: *Michigan Journal of Gender & Law* 18, pp. 229–96.

Michel, Sonya (1999): *Children's Interests/Mothers' Rights: The Shaping of America's Child Care Policy*. New Haven: Yale University Press.

Michel, Sonya (2012): Maternalism and Beyond. In: Van der Klein, Marina; Plant, Rebecca Jo; Sander Nichole; Weintrob, Lori (eds.): *Maternalism Reconsidered: Motherhood, Welfare and Social Policy in the Twentieth Century*. New York: Berghan, pp. 22–37.

Michel, Sonya and Peng, Ito (2012): All in the Family? Migrants, Nationhood, and Care Regimes in Asia and North America. In: *Journal of European Social Policy* 22 (4), pp. 406–18.

Michel, Sonya and Peng, Ito (2017): *Gender, Migration and the Work of Care: A Multi-Scalar Approach to the Pacific Rim*. Basingstoke: Palgrave Macmillan.

Michoń, Piotr (2009): "Bleib zu Hause, Liebling" – Mütter, Arbeitsmärkte und staatliche Politik in Polen und den baltischen Ländern ("Stay at Home, Darling" – Mothers, Labour Markets and State Policy in Poland and the Baltic Countries). In: Klenner, Christiane and Leiber, Simone (eds.): *Wohlfahrtsstaaten und Geschlechtergerechtigkeit im Transformationsprozess* (Welfare States and Gender Justice in the Transformation Process). Wiesbaden: VS Verlag, pp. 163–92.

Mills, Wright C. (1951): *White Collar: The American Middle Classes*. Oxford: Oxford University Press.

Mimiko, Nahzeem Oluwafemi (2012): *Globalisation: The Politics of Global Economic Relations and International Business*. Durham: Carolina Academic Press.

Minijob-Zentrale (2011): *Trendreport Alltag statt Luxus* (Everyday Life Instead of Luxury Trend Report). Essen: In-house publication.

Mosse, George L. (1996): *The Image of the Man: On the Construction of Modern Masculinity*. Oxford: Oxford University Press.

Mulinari, Diana and Neergaard, Anders (2013): We are Sweden Democrats Because We Care for Others: Exploring Racisms in the Swedish Extreme Right. In: *European Journal of Women's Studies* 21 (1), pp. 43–56.

Mundlak, Guy and Shamir, Hila (2008): Between Intimacy and Alienage: The Legal Construction of Domestic and Care Workers in the Welfare State. In: Lutz, Helma (ed.): *Migration and Domestic Work: A European Perspective on a Global Theme*. Farnham Surrey: Ashgate, pp. 161–76.

Müller, Beatrice (2016): *Wert-Abjektion. Zur Abwertung von Care Arbeit im patriarchalen Kapitalismus – am Beispiel der ambulanten Pflege* (Value Devaluation. On the Devaluation of Care Work in Patriarchal Capitalism – Using the Example of Outpatient Care). Münster: Westfälisches Dampfboot.

Müller, Tanja and Skeide, Annekatrin (2018): Grounded Theory und Biographieforschung (Grounded Theory and Biographical Research). In: Lutz, Helma;

Schiebel, Martina; Tuider, Elisabeth (eds.): *Handbuch Biographieforschung* (Handbook of Biographical Research). Wiesbaden: Springer, pp.49–62.

Neckel, Sighard (2006): Vorwort (Preface). In: Hochschild, Arlie R.: *Das gekaufte Herz. Die Kommerzialisierung der Gefühle* (The Purchased Heart. The Commercialisation of Feelings). Frankfurt am Main/New York: Campus, pp. 13–24.

Nicholas, Tekla (2008): Remittances, Education, and Family Reunification: Transnational Strategies of Haitian Immigrant Families in South Florida. In: *African & African Diaspora Studies Program Graduate Student Scholarly Presentations* 7. https://digitalcommons.fiu.edu/africana_student_pres/7/ [accessed 13 May 2024].

Nieswand, Boris (2011): *Theorising Transnational Migration: The Status Paradox of Migration*. London/New York: Routledge.

Novikova, Irina (2012): Fatherhood in Postsocialist Contexts: Lost in Translation? In: Oechsle, Mechtild; Müller, Ursula; Hess, Sabine (eds.): *Fatherhood in Late Modernity: Cultural Images, Social Practices, Structural Frames.* Opladen/Berlin/Toronto: Barbara Budrich, pp. 95–112.

Nullmeier, Frank (2004): Vermarktlichung des Sozialstaats. (Marketisation of the Welfare-State). In: *WSI Mitteilungen* 9, pp. 495–500.

Olcon-Kubicka, Marta (2009): *Indywidualizacja a nowe formy wspólnotowości* (Individualisation and New Forms of Community). https://www.academia.edu/3410953/Indywidualizacja_a_nowe_formy_wsp%C3%B3lnotowo%C5%9Bci_Individualization_and_New_Forms_of_Community_ [accessed 22 July 2024].

Ostner, Ilona (2002): A New Role for Fathers? The German Case. In: Hobson, Barbara (ed.): *Making Men into Fathers – Men, Masculinities and the Social Politics of Fatherhood.* Cambridge: Cambridge University Press, pp. 67–150.

Organisation for Economic Co-Operation and Development (OECD) (1997): *Beyond 2000. The New Social Policy Agenda.* OECD Working Paper 5 (43). Paris: OECD.

Organisation for Economic Co-Operation and Development (OECD) (2017): Education at a Glance: OECD Indicators. Paris: OECD-Publishing (also online at www.oecdilibrary. org/education/education-at-a-glance-2017/summary/german_fo679baf-de [accessed 13 May 2024].

Orloff, Ann S. (2006): From Maternalism to Employment for All: State Politics to Promote Women's Employment Across the Affluent Democracies. In: Levy, Jonah D. (ed.): *The State after Statism: New State Activities in the Age of Liberalisation.* Cambridge: Harvard University Press, pp. 230–68.

Österle, August (2014): Care-Regime in den neuen EU-Wohlfahrtstaaten (Care Regimes in the New EU Welfare States). In: Aulenbacher, Brigitte; Riegraf, Birgit; Theobald, Hildegard (eds.): *Sorge: Arbeit, Verhältnisse, Regime* (Care: Work, Relations, Regimes). In: *Soziale Welt*, Special Issue 20, pp. 363–98.

Österle, August and Bauer, Gudrun (2016): The Legalization of Rotational 24-Hour Care Work in Austria: Implications for Migrant Care Workers. In: *Social Politics* 23 (2), pp. 192–213.

Palenga-Möllenbeck, Ewa (2010): *Migrationsdiskurse in Polen* (Migration Discourses in Poland). Unpublished Research Report.

Palenga Möllenbeck, Ewa (2013): New Maids, New Butlers? Polish Domestic Workers in Germany and the Commodification of Social Reproductive Work. In: *Equality, Diversity and Inclusion: An International Journal* 32 (6), pp. 557–74.

Palenga Möllenbeck, Ewa (2016): Unequal Fatherhoods: Citizenship, Gender, and Masculinities in Outsourced "Male" Domestic Work. In: Gullikstad, Berit; Korsnes Kristensen, Guro; Ringrose, Priscilla (eds.): *Paid Domestic Labour in a Changing Europe: Questions of Gender Equality and Citizenship*. London: Palgrave Macmillan, pp. 217–43.

Palenga-Möllenbeck, Ewa and Lutz, Helma (2016): Fatherhood and Masculinities in Postsocialist Europe: The Challenges of Transnational Migration. In: Kilkey, Majella and Palenga-Möllenbeck, Ewa (eds.): *Family Life in an Age of Migration and Mobility: Global Perspectives Through the Life Course*. Basingstoke: Palgrave Macmillan, pp. 213–36.

Palenga-Möllenbeck, Ewa (2018): "Unsichtbare ÜbersetzerInnen" in der Biographieforschung: Übersetzung als Methode ("Invisible Translators" in Biographical Research: Translation as a Method). In: Lutz, Helma; Schiebel, Martina; Tuider, Elisabeth (eds.): *Handbuch Biographieforschung* (Handbook of Biographical Research). Wiesbaden: Springer, pp. 669–80.

Palenga-Möllenbeck, Ewa (2022): Making Migrants' Input Invisible: Intersections of Privilege and Otherness from a Multilevel Perspective. In: *Social Inclusion* 10 (1), pp. 184–93.

Palenga-Möllenbeck, Ewa (2024): Care Markets, Care Provision, Working Conditions and the Role of the Brokering Agencies. In: Aulenbacher, Brigitte; Lutz, Helma; Palenga-Möllenbeck, Ewa; Karin Schwiter (eds.): *Home Care for Sale*. London: Sage, pp. 21–36.

Parreñas, Rhacel S. (2001): *Servants of Globalisation: Women, Migration, and Domestic Work*. Stanford: Stanford University Press.

Parreñas, Rhacel S. (2005): *Children of Global Migration: Transnational Families and Gendered Woes*. Stanford: Stanford University Press.

Peng, Ito (2009): *The Political and Social Economy of Care in the Republic of Korea*. Geneva: UN Research Institute for Social Development.

Peng, Ito (2017): Explaining Exceptionality: Care and Migration Policies in Japan and South Korea. In: Michel, Sonya and Peng, Ito (eds.): *Gender, Migration and the Work of Care: A Multi-Scalar Approach to the Pacific Rim*. Basingstoke: Palgrave Macmillan, pp. 191–216.

Peng, Ito (2019): The Care Economy: A New Research Framework. Sciences Po LIEPP Working paper 89. https://sciencespo.hal.science/hal-03456901/document [accessed 21 July 2024].

Pfau-Effinger, Birgit (2005): Culture and Welfare State Policies: Reflections on a Complex Interrelation. In: *Journal of Social Policy* 34 (1), pp. 3–20.

Phoenix, Ann (2009): Idealisierung emotionaler Bindung oder materielle Versorgung? Transnationale Mutterschaft und Kettenmigration (Idealisation of Emotional Attachment or Material Provision? Transnational Motherhood and Chain Migration). In: Lutz, Helma (ed.): *Gender-Mobil? Geschlecht und Migration in transnationalen Räumen* (Gender-mobile? Gender and Migration in Transnational Spaces). Münster: Westfälisches Dampfboot, pp. 86–101.

Pierson, Chris (2001): The Welfare State into the Twenty-First Century. In: *Hitotsubashi Journal of Social Studies* 33 (1), pp. 37–43.

Pissin, Annika (2013): *The Global Left-Behind Child in China: "Unintended Consequences" in Capitalism.* Working Paper 39. Centre for East and South-East Asian Studies. Lund University, Sweden. https://www.academia.edu/5666198/ The_global_left_behind_child_in_China. [accessed 13 May 2024].

Pistrol, Florian (2016): *Vulnerabilität: Erläuterungen zu einem Schlüsselbegriff im Denken Judith Butlers* (Vulnerability: Explanations of a Key Concept in Judith Butler's Thought). In: *Zeitschrift für Praktische Philosophie*, 3, 1, pp. 233–72.

Pleck, Joseph (2010): Fatherhood and Masculinity In: Michael E. Lamb (ed.): *The Role of the Father in Child Development.* London: Wiley, pp. 32–66.

Poeze, Miranda and Mazzucato, Valentina (2014): Ghanaian Children in Transnational Families. Understanding the Experiences of Left-Behind Children Through Local Parenting Norms. In: Baldassar, Loretta and Merla, Laura (eds.): *Transnational Families and the Circulation of Care.* New York/Abingdon: Routledge, pp. 149–69.

Polanyi, Karl (1978 [1944]): *The Great Transformation. Politische und gesellschaftliche Ursprünge von Gesellschaften und Wirtschaftssystemen.* Frankfurt am Main: Suhrkamp.

Pongratz, Hans and Voß, Günter G. (1998): Der Arbeitskraftunternehmer. Eine neue Grundform der Ware Arbeitskraft? (The Labour Entrepreneur. A New Basic Form of Commodity Labour?) In: *Kölner Zeitschrift für Soziologie und Sozialpsychologie* (Cologne Journal of Sociology and Social Psychology) 1, pp. 131–58.

Pratt, Geraldine (2012): *Families Apart: Migrant Mothers and the Conflicts of Labour and Love.* Minneapolis: University of Minnesota Press.

Randeria, Shalini (2009): Malthus versus Condorcet – Population Policy, Gender and Culture from an Ethnological Perspective. In: Berking, Sabine and Zolkos, Magdalena (eds.): *Between Life and Death: Governing Populations in the Era of Human Rights.* Frankfurt am Main: Peter Lang, pp. 25–46.

Ratha, Dilip, Mohapatra, Sanket and Silwa, Ani (2011): Migration and Remittances Factbook 2011. Washington DC: The International Bank for Reconstruction and Development/The World Bank. https://elibrary.worldbank.org/doi/ abs/10.1596/978-0-8213-8218-9 [accessed 13 May 2024].

Redaktion Pflegeinstitut.eu (n.d.): Ukrainische Pflegekräfte in Deutschland (Caregivers from Ukraine in Germany) Pflegeinstitut.pl/de/news/ukrainische-pflegekraefte-deutschland.html [accessed 15 August 2024].

Rerrich, Maria S. (2012): Migration macht Schule. Herausforderungen für Care in einer rumänischen Gemeinde (Migration Becomes Accepted. Challenges for Care in a Romanian Community). In: *Mittelweg 36*, 5, pp. 73–93.

Riegraf, Birgit and Reimer, Romy (2014): Wandel von Wohlfahrtsstaatlichkeit und neue Care- Arrangements. Das Beispiel der Wohn-Pflege-Gemeinschaften (Changes in the Welfare State and New Care Arrangements. The Example of Residential Care Communities). In: Aulenbacher, Brigitte; Riegraf, Birgit; Theobald, Hildegard (eds.): *Sorge: Arbeit, Verhältnisse, Regime* (Care: Work, Relations, Regimes). In: *Soziale Welt*, Special Issue 20, pp. 293–309.

Rohde, Caterina (2014): *Au-pair Migration. Transnationale Bildungs- und Berufsmobilität junger Frauen zwischen Russland und Deutschland* (Au Pair Migration. Transnational Educational and Professional Mobility of Young Women Between Russia and Germany). Opladen: Barbara Budrich Academic Press.

Romero, Mary (1992): *Maid in the USA. New* York: Routledge.

Romero, Mary (2013): Nanny Diaries and Other Stories: Immigrant Women's Labor in the Social Reproduction of American Families. In: *Revista des Estudios Sociales* 45, pp. 186–97.

Rossow, Verena (2021): *Der Preis der Autonomie: Wie sorgende Angehörige Live-in-Arbeitsverhältnisse ausgestalten* (The Price of Autonomy: How Caring Relatives Organise Live-in Working Relationships). Opladen: Budrich Academic Press.

Rossow, Verena and Leiber, Simone (2017): Zwischen Vermarktlichung und Europäisierung. Die wachsende Bedeutung transnational *agierender* Vermittlungsagenturen in der häuslichen Pflege in Deutschland (Between Marketisation and Europeanisation. The Growing Importance of Transnationally Operating Placement Agencies in Home Care in Germany). In: *Sozialer Fortschritt* 66 (3–4), pp. 285–302.

Rotkirch, Anna (2000): *The Man Question: Loves and Lives in Late 20th Century Russia*. Helsinki : University of Helsinki. https://www.academia.edu/2643465/The_Man_Question_Loves_and_lives_in_late_20th_century_Russia [accessed 13 May 2024].

Rüffer, Anita (2015): Wenn Pflegekräfte aus Osteuropa sich um Demenzkranke kümmern. Interview mit Prof. Dr. Thomas Klie (When East European Care Workers Look After Dementia Patients. Interview with Prof. Dr. Thomas Klie). www.badische-zeitung.de/freiburg/wenn-pflegekraefte-aus-osteuropa-sich-um-demenzkranke-kuemmern--111625773.html [accessed 13 May 2024].

Safuta, Anna (2018): Fifty Shades of White: Eastern Europeans' Peripheral Whiteness in the Context of Domestic Services Provided by Migrant Women. In: *Tijdschrift voor Genderstudies* 21, 3, pp. 217–23. https://www.researchgate.net/publication/327773024_Fifty_shades_of_white_Eastern_Europeans'_eripheral_whiteness'_in_the_context_of_domestic_services_provided_by_migrant_women

Safuta, Anna and Degavre, Florence (2013): What has Polanyi got to do with it? Undocumented Migrant Domestic Workers and the Usages of Reciprocity. In: Oso, Laura and Ribas Mateos, Natalia (eds.): *The International Handbook on Gender, Migration and Transnationalism: Global and Development Perspectives.* Cheltenham: Edward Elgar Publishing, pp. 420–38.

Safuta, Anna; Kordasiewicz, Anna; Urbańska, Sylwia (2016): Verpasste Kreuzung: Polen als Herkunft- und Zielland für migrantische Pflege- und Haushaltskräfte (Missed Crossroads: Poland as a Country of Origin and Destination for Migrant Care and Domestic Workers). In: Weicht, Bernhard and Österle, August (eds.): *Im Ausland zu Hause pflegen: Die Beschäftigung von MigrantInnen in der 24 Stunden Pflege* (Caring at Home Abroad. The Employment of Migrants in 24-Hour Care). Münster: LIT Verlag, pp. 247–70.

Safuta, Anna and Noack, Kristin (2020): A Magnifying Glass for Precarity and Unfulfilled Care Needs: The Effects of the Coronavirus Pandemic on Migrant Care Workers in Germany https://www.fes.de/themenportal-gender-jugend-senioren/gender-matters/gender-blog/beitrag-lesen/a-magnifying-glass-for-precarity-and-unfulfilled-care-needs [accessed 13 May 2024].

Samarasinghe, Vidyamali (1998): The Feminization of Foreign Currency Earnings: Women's Labor in Sri Lanka. In: *The Journal of Developing Areas* 32 (3), pp. 303–26.

Sassen, Saskia (1991): *The Global City.* Princeton: Princeton University Press.

Sassen, Saskia (1998): *Globalization and its Discontents: Essays on the Mobility of People and Money.* New York: New Press.

Satola, Agnieszka (2015): *Migration und irreguläre Pflegearbeit in Deutschland. Eine biographische Studie* (Migration and Irregular Care Work in Germany. A Biographical Study). Stuttgart: Ibidem Verlag.

Sawulski, Jakub (2017): Is Poland a Welfare State? IBS Policy Paper. https://ibs.org.pl/wp-content/uploads/2022/12/IBS_Policy_Paper_02_2017_en.pdf [accessed 21 July 2024].

Saxonberg, Steven and Szelewa, Dorota (2007): The Continuing Legacy of the Communist Legacy? The Development of Family Policies in Poland and the Czech Republic. In: *Social Politics,* 14 (3), pp. 351–79.

Scheiwe, Kirsten and Krawietz, Johanna (2010): *Transnationale Sorgearbeit: Rechtliche Rahmenbedingungen und gesellschaftliche Praxis* (Transnational Care Work: Legal Framework Conditions and Social Practice). Wiesbaden: VS Verlag.

Scheiwe, Kirsten (2014): Menschenwürdige Arbeit für Hausangestellte. Zur Bedeutung des ILO-Übereinkommens 189 für Deutschland (Decent Work for Domestic Workers. On the Significance of ILO Convention 189 for Germany). In: Meier-Gräwe, Uta (ed.): *Die Arbeit des Alltags. Gesellschaftliche Organisation und Umverteilung* (Everyday Work. Societal Organisation and Redistribution). Wiesbaden: VS Verlag, pp. 37–56.

Scheiwe, Kirsten (2021): Domestic Workers, EU Working Time Law and Implementation Deficits in National Law – Change in Sight? In: *ZIAS*, 1 (35). pp. 1–128.

Schenk, Dieter (1990): "…unerwünschte polnische Elemente sind zu entfernen." Die Aktion zur Vernichtung der polnischen Intelligenz im Raum Danzig-Westpreußen und die Nichtverfolgung der NS-Täter in Deutschland nach 1945 ("Unwanted Polish Elements are to be Removed." The Action to Exterminate the Polish Intelligentsia in the Danzig-West Prussia Region and the Non-Prosecution of the Nazi Perpetrators in Germany After 1945). Manuscript, lecture at University of Lodz. www.dieter-schenk.info/publikationen.html [accessed August 15 2024].

Schier, Michaela and Jurcyk, Karin (2007): Familie als Herstellungsleistung in Zeiten der Entgrenzung (Family as a Production Service in Times of Dissolution of Boundaries). In: *Politik und Zeitgeschichte* 34., pp. 10–17.

Schilliger, Sarah and Schilling, Katharina (2017): Care-Arbeit politisieren: Herausforderungen der (Selbst-)Organisierung von migrantischen 24h-Betreuerinnen (Politicising Care Work: Challenges of (Self-)Organising Migrant 24h Caregivers). In: *Femina Politica*, 26(2), pp. 101–11.

Scholz, Sylka (2004): *Männlichkeit erzählen. Lebensgeschichtliche Identitätskonstruktionen ostdeutscher Männer* (Narrating Masculinity. Life-Historical Identity Constructions of East German Men). Münster: Westfälisches Dampfboot.

Schwiter, Karin; Berndt, Christian; Truong, Jasmine (2018): Neoliberal Austerity and the Marketisation of Elderly Care. In: *Social & Cultural Geography* 19 (3), pp. 379–99.

SECO Staatssekretariat für Wirtschaft (2022): Eckwerte Rahmen Arbeitsverträge in der Betreuung durch Live- Ins bei den Klienten zuhause (Key Values Framework Employment Contracts for Live-in Support at the Client's Home) Bern. https://www.seco.admin.ch/seco/de/home/Arbeit/Arbeitsbedingungen/Arbeitnehmerschutz/live-in-betreuung.html [accessed 22 July 2024].

Segal, Lynne (1990): *Slow Motion: Changing Masculinities, Changing Men*. New Brunswick: Rutgers University Press.

Sen, Amartya (1993): Capability and Well-Being. In: Nussbaum, Martha and Sen, Amartya (eds.): *The Quality of Life*. Oxford: Clarendon Press, pp. 31–53.

Shire, Karen (2015): State Policies Encouraging the Outsourcing of Personal and Household Labour in Germany: Familialism and Women's Employment in Conservative Welfare States. In: Carbonnier, Clément and Morel, Nathalie. (eds.): *The Political Economy of Household Services in Europe. Work and Welfare in Europe*. London: Palgrave Macmillan, pp. 102–26.

Shutes, Isabel (2021): Gender and Migration and the Inequality of Care. In: Mora, Claudia and Piper, Nicola (eds.): *The Palgrave Handbook of Gender and Migration*. London: Palgrave Macmillan, pp. 107–20.

Sikorska, Małgorzata (2009): Nowa matka, nowy ojciec, nowe dziecko. O nowym układzie sił w Polskich rodzinach (New Mother, New Father, New Child. About the New Balance of Power in Polish Families). Warsaw: WAiP. https://www.publio.pl/files/samples/f4/69/93/48181/Nowa_matka_nowy_ojciec_demo.pdf [accessed 15 August 2024].

Skocpol, Theda (1992): *Protecting Mothers and Soldiers: The Political Origins of Social Policy in the United States.* Cambridge: Harvard University Press.

Slany, Krystina and Ślusarczyk, Magdalena (2013): Migracje zagraniczne Polaków w świetle NSP 2011: Trendy i charakterystyki socjo-demograficzne (Migration Abroad of Poles in the Light of the Population Census 2011: Trends and Socio-Demographic Characteristics). Lecture at Młoda polska emigracja w UE jako przedmiot badań psychologicznych, socjologicznych i kulturowych, EuroEmigranci.PL, Cracow.

Slaughter, Anne-Marie (2016): The Work that Makes Work Possible. Atlantic Magazine. www.theatlantic.com/business/archive/2016/03/unpaid-caregivers/474894/ [accessed 13 May 2024].

Smith, Adam (1999): *The Wealth of Nations.* Skinner, Andrew (ed.): London: Penguin Books Ltd.

Solari, Cinzia D. (2017): *On the Shoulders of Grandmothers: Gender, Migration and Post-Soviet State-State Building.* London/New York: Routledge.

SPD et al. (2021): Mehr Fortschritt Wagen. Bündnis für Freiheit Gerechtigkeit und Nachhaltigkeit. Koalitionsvertrag 2021-2025 (Dare to Make More Progress. Alliance for Freedom Justice and Sustainability. Coalition Agreement 2021–2025). https://www.spd.de/fileadmin/Dokumente/Koalitionsvertrag/Koalitionsvertrag_2021-2025.pdf [accessed 21 July 2024].

Spies, Tina (2018): Biographie, Diskurs und Artikulation (Biography, Discourse and Articulation). In: Lutz, Helma; Schiebel, Martina; Tuider, Elisabeht (eds.): *Handbuch Biographieforschung* (Handbook of Biographical Research). Wiesbaden: Springer, pp. 537–47.

Środa, Magdalena (2009): *Kobiety i Wladza* (Women and Power). Warsaw: WAB.

Statistisches Bundesamt (2015): Arbeitszeit von Frauen: Ein Drittel Erwerbsarbeit, zwei Drittel unbezahlte Arbeit (Women's Working Hours: One Third Employment, Two Thirds Unpaid Work). https://www.destatis.de/DE/Presse/Pressemitteilungen/Frueher/PD15_179_63931.html [accessed 13 May 2024].

Stan, Sabina and Roland Erne (2023): Pursuing an Overarching Commodification Script Through Country-Specific Interventions? The EU's New Economic Governance Prescriptions in Healthcare (2009–2019). *Socio-Economic Review,* https://academic.oup.com/ser/advance-article/doi/10.1093/ser/mwad053/7330460 [accessed 15 May 2024].

Statistisches Bundesamt (2017): Pflegestatistik 2015. Pflege im Rahmen der Pflegeversicherung. Deutschlandergebnisse (Long-Term Care Statistics 2015. Long-Term Care Within the Framework of Long-Term Care Insurance. German results) https://www.destatis.de/DE/Themen/Gesellschaft-Umwelt/Gesundheit/Pflege/_inhalt.html [accessed 14 May 2024].

Steiner, Jennifer (2020): "Guter Lohn für gute Arbeit?" Legitimation und Kritik im Regulierungsprozess der "Rund-um -die-Uhr" Betreuung betagter

Menschen in Schweizer Privathaushalten ("Good Pay for Good Work?" Legitimation and Criticism in the Regulatory Process of "Round-the-Clock" Care for Elderly People in Swiss Private Households). In: *Swiss Journal of Sociology* 46 (2), pp. 281–303.

Steiner, Jennifer, Prieler, Veronika, Leiblfinger, Michael and Benazha, Aranka (2019): Völlig legal!? Rechtliche Rahmung und Legalitätsnarrative in der 24h-Betreuung in Deutschland, Österreich und der Schweiz (Completely Legal? Legal Framing and Legality Narratives in 24-Hour care in Germany, Austria and Switzerland). In: *Österreichische Zeitschrift Soziologie* 44, pp. 1–19.

Steffen, Margaret (2015): …raus aus der Schwarzarbeit. Gute Arbeit in Privathaushalten (…Out of Undeclared Work. Good Work in Private Households). https://gesundheit-soziales-bildung.verdi.de/service/publikationen/++co++a158df38-c6a3-11e6-ac89-525400b665de [accessed 14 May 2024].

Synak, Brunon (ed.) (2002): Polska starość (Old Age in Poland). Gdańsk: Wydawnictwo Uniwersytetu Gadańskiego.

Szelewa, Dorota and Polakowski, Michal P. (2008): Who Cares? Changing Patterns of Childcare in Central and Eastern Europe. In: *Journal of European Social Policy* 18 (2), pp. 115–31.

Sztompka, Pjotr (2000): The Ambivalence of Social Change. Triumph or Trauma? WZB Discussion Paper. https://www.econstor.eu/bitstream/10419/50259/1/330535307.pdf [accessed 14 May 2024].

Tarkowska, Elžbieta (2007): Badanie, ubóstwa w krjach postkomunistycznych I kategoria underclass (Survey, Poverty in Post-Communist Countries. The Category of the Underclass). In: Golinowska, Stanisława; Tarkowska, Elžbieta; Topińska, Irena (eds.): *Ubóstwo, wy kluczezezenic społeczne. Badania, metody, wyniki* (Poverty in Post-Communist Countries. Research, Methods, Results). Warsaw: Instytut Pracy I Spraw Socjalnych.

Teo, Youyenn (2016): Not Everyone has "Maids": Class Differentials in the Elusive Quest for Work-Life Balance. In: *Gender, Place & Culture* 23 (8), pp. 1164–78.

Theobald, Hildegard and Luppi, Mario (2018): Elderly Care in Changing Societies: Concurrences in Divergent Care Regimes – A Comparison of Germany, Sweden and Italy. In: *Current Sociology* 66 (4), pp. 629–42.

Thiessen, Barbara (2004): *Reformulierung des Privaten: Professionalisierung personenbezogener haushaltsbezogener Dienstleistungsarbeit* (Reformulation of the Private Sphere: Professionalisation of Personal Household-Related Service Work). Wiesbaden: VS Verlag.

Todorova, Maria (1997): *Imagining the Balkans*. New York/Oxford: Oxford University Press.

Toupin, Louise (2018): *Wages for Housework. A History of an International Feminist Movement, 1972–77*. London: Pluto Press.

Trzebiatowska, Marta (2013): Beyond Compliance and Resistance: Polish Catholic Nuns Negotiating Femininity. In: *European Journal of Women's Studies* 20 (2), pp. 204–18.

Tuttle, William M., Jr. (1995): Rosie the Riveter and Her Latchkey Children: What Americans Can Learn about Child Day Care from the Second World War. In: *Child Welfare* 74 (1), pp. 92–114.

Urbańska, Sylwia (2015): *Matka Polka na odległość. Z doświadczeń migracyjnych robotnic 1989–2010* (The Polish Mother at a Distance. From the Migration Experience of Female Workers 1989–2010). Toruń: Wydawnictwo UMK.

van Haer, Nicholas and Nyber Sørensen, Nina (eds.) (2003): *The Migration-Development Nexus*. Geneva: International Organization for Migration. https://publications.iom.int/system/files/pdf/migration_dev_nexus.pdf [accessed 21 July 2024].

Verdery, Katherine (1994): From Parent-State to Family Patriarchs: Gender and Nation in Contemporary Eastern Europe. In: *East European Politics and Societies* 8 (2), pp. 225–55.

VHBP Bundesverband für häusliche Betreuung und Pflege (Federal association for home care) (2020a and b; 2021, 2022, 2023): https://www.vhbp.de/ [accessed 30 May 2024].

Voss, Günter G. (1998): Die Entgrenzung von Arbeit und Arbeitskraft. Eine subjektorientierte Interpretation des Wandels der Arbeit (The Dissolution of Boundaries between Work and Labour. A Subject-Oriented Interpretation of the Transformation of Labour). In: *Mitteilungen aus der Arbeitsmarkt- und Berufsforschung*. 3, pp. 473–87. https://doku.iab.de/mittab/1998/1998_3_MittAB_Voss.pdf [accessed 23 July 2024].

Walczak, Bartłomiej (2008): Społeczne, edukacyjne i wychowawcze konsekwencje migracji rodziców i opiekunów prawnych uczniów szkół podstawowych, gimnazjalnych i ponadgimnazjalnych (Social, Educational and Upbringing Consequences of Migration. Parents and Legal Guardians of Elementary, Middle and High School Students). Pedagogikum. Wyższa szkoła pedagogiki resocjalizacyjnej Warszawie.

Weber, Max (1895): Antrittsvorlesung. Der Nationalstaat und die Volkswirtschaftspolitik (Inaugural Lecture. The Nation State and Economic Policy). www.deutschestextarchiv.de/book/show/weber_nationalstaat_1895 [accessed 14 May 2024].

Weeks, Kathi (2007): Life Within and Against Work: Affective Labor, Feminist Critique, and Post-Fordist Politics. In: *Ephemera – Theory and Politics in Organization* 7 (1), pp. 233–49.

Weeks, Kathi (2011): In der Arbeit gegen die Arbeit Leben. Affektive Arbeit, feministische Kritik und postfordistische Politik (Living in Labour Against Labour. Affective Labour, Feminist Critique and Post-Fordist Politics). In: *Grundrisse, Zeitschrift für linke Theorie und Debatte* 38, pp. 13–27.

Weicht, Bernhard (2010): Embodying the Ideal Carer. In: *International Journal of Ageing and Later Life* 5 (2), pp. 17–52.

Weicht, Bernhard and Österle, August (eds.) (2016): *Im Ausland zu Hause pflegen. Die Beschäftigung von MigrantInnen in der 24-Stunden-Betreuung* (Caring at Home Abroad. The Employment of Migrants in 24-Hour Care). Vienna: LIT Verlag.

Werlhof, Claudia von (1978): Frauenarbeit. Der blinde Fleck der politischen Ökonomie (Women's Labour. The Blind Spot of Political Economy). In: *Beiträge zur feministischen Theorie und Praxis* 1, pp. 18–32.

Wichterich, Christa (2019): Care Extractivism and the Reconfiguration of Social Reproduction in Post-Fordist Economies. ICDD Working Papers 25, April 2019. https://ideas.repec.org/p/ajy/icddwp/25.html.

Widding Isaksen, Lise, Sambasivan, Uma Devi and Hochschild, Arlie R. (2009): Die globale Fürsorgekrise (The Global Care Crisis). In: *WestEnd – Neue Zeitschrift für Sozialforschung* 6 (2), pp. 56–79.

Williams, Fiona (2010): Migration and Care: Themes, Concepts and Challenges. In: *Social Policy and Society* 9 (3), pp. 385–96.

Williams, Fiona (2014): Making Connections Across the Transnational Political Economy of Care. In: Anderson, Bridget and Shutes, Isabel (eds.): *Migration and Care Labour: Theory, Policy and Politics*. Basingstoke: Palgrave Macmillan.

Williams, Fiona (2018): Care: Intersections of Scales, Inequalities and Crises. In: Aulenbacher, Birgitte; Lutz, Helma; Riegraf, Birgit (eds.): The Global Sociology of Care and Care Work. *Current Sociology Monograph* 66 (4), p. 547.

Wimmer, Andreas and Glick Schiller, Nina (2003): Methodological Nationalism, the Social Sciences, and the Study of Migration: An Essay in Historical Epistemology. In: *International Migration Review* 37 (3), pp. 576–610.

Winker, Gabriele (2015): *Care Revolution. Schritte in eine solidarische Gesellschaft* (Care Revolution, Steps Towards a Society Based on Solidarity). Bielefeld: transcript.

Winkler, Ulrike (2000): "Hauswirtschaftliche Ostarbeiterinnen". Zwangsarbeit in deutschen Haushalten. ("Domestic Labourers from the East". Forced Labour in German households). In: Winkler, Ulrike (ed.): *Stiften gehen. NS Zwangsarbeit und Entschädigungsdebatte* (Leaving for Good. The NS Forced Labour and Compensation Debate). Köln: Papy Rossa Verlag, pp. 148–69.

Wirz, Yevgeniya (2009): Migration and Care in the Ukrainian press. Unpublished research report.

Wirz, Yevgeniya/Eugenia (2021): *Care-Arbeit und Familie International. Rekonstruktionen ukrainischer Arbeitsmigrantinnen* (Care Work and Family International. Reconstructions of Ukrainian Female Migrant Workers). Wiesbaden: Springer VS.

Wissenschaftliche Dienste des Deutschen Bundestages (2016): 24-Stunden-Pflege in Privathaushalten durch Pflegekräfte aus Mittel- und Osteuropa. Rechtslage in ausgewählten EU-Mitgliedsstaaten (24-Hour Care in Private Households by Care Workers from Central and Eastern Europe. The Legal Situation in Selected EU Member States). https://www.bundestag.de/resource/blob/480122/e1e7b32064927dbba950d380980b6c3f/wd-6-078-16pdf-data.pdf [accessed 14 May 2024].

World Bank (2007): Ukraine: Poverty Update. World Bank: Washington DC.

World Bank (2010): Remittances Data Inflows. World Bank: Washington DC.

Yavorska, Mariana and Petrenko, Lyubomyr (2007): Соціальні сироти: виходу з проблеми поки не знайдено [Sotsial'ni syroty: vykhodu z problemy poky ne] (Social Orphans. Still No Solution to the Problem). Deutsche Welle. www. dw-world.de/dw/article/0,2144,2541921,00.html [accessed 14 May 2024].

Yeates, Nicola (2009): *Globalising Care Economies and Migrant Workers: Explorations in Global Care Chains*. Basingstoke: Palgrave Macmillan.

Yeates, Nicola and Pillinger, Jane (2013): *Human Resources for Health Migration: Global Policy Responses, Initiatives, and Emerging Issues*. Open University: Milton Keynes.

Yuval-Davis, Nira (1997): *Gender and Nation*. London: Sage.

Zdravomyslova, Elena and Temkina, Anna (2007): Sovetskie gendernye kontrakty i ikh transformatsyia v sovremennoi Rossii (Soviet Gender Orders and Their Transformation in Modern Russia). In: Zdravomyslova, Elena and Temkina, Anna (eds.): *Rossiyskiy gendernyi poryadok: Sociologicheskiy podhod* (The Russian Gender Order: A Sociological Approach). St Petersburg: Publishing House of the European University, pp. 169–200.

Zentgraf, Kristine M. and Chinchilla, Norma S. (2012): Transnational Family Separation: A Framework for Analysis. In: *Journal of Ethnic and Migration Studies* 38 (2), pp. 345–66.

Zetkin, Clara (1901): Die Wirtschaftsgenossenschaft III. (The Economic Co-operative). In: *Die Gleichheit* 11 (15), pp. 113–114.

Zhurzhenko, Tatjana (2001): Free Market Ideology and New Women's Identities in Post-Socialist Ukraine. In: *European Journal of Women's Studies* 8 (1), pp. 29–49.

Zhurzhenko, Tatjana (2004): *Strong Women, Weak State: Family Politics and Nation Building in Post-Soviet Ukraine*. Washington DC: Woodrow Wilson Center Press/ The Johns Hopkins University Press.

Zimmerer, Jürgen (2004): Von Windhuk nach Warschau. Die rassische Privilegiengesellschaft in Deutsch Südwestafrika, ein Modell mit Zukunft? (From Windhoek to Warsaw. The Racial Privilege Society in German South West Africa, a Model with a Future?). In: Becker, Frank (ed.): *Rassenmischehen-Mischlinge-Rassentrennung. Zur Politik der Rasse im deutschen Kolonialreich* (Mixed-Race Marriages – Half-Castes – Racial Separation. On the Politics of Race in the German Colonial Empire). Stuttgart: Franz-Steiner Verlag, pp. 97–123.

FILMOGRAPHY

Bauer, Nora (2016): *Wa(h)re Engel. Pflegekräfte aus Osteuropa* (True Angels. Caregivers from Eastern Europe. Podcast Deutschlandfunk. www. deutschlandfunkkultur.de/pflegekraefte-aus-osteuropa-wa-h-reengel.1001. de.html?dram:article_id=367079 [accessed 14 May 2024].

Büchner, Christiane (2016): *Die alte Dame und die Pflegerin* (The Old Lady and the Caregiver). MDR, ARTE, Lava Films. Köln: Büchner Filmproduktion GdR.

Büchner, Christiane and Schwarze, Herbert (2016): *Family Business*. MDR, ARTE, Lava Films. Köln: Büchner Filmproduktion GdR.

Ciulei, Thomas (2008): *The Flower Bridge*. Bucharest: Europolis Films.

Dell, Ingo (2017): *Die Karawane der Pflegerinnen* (The Caravan of Carergivers). MDR. Leipzig/Berlin/Greifwald: Hoferichter & Jacobs GmbH; www.youtube.com/watch?v=kxFDz1GXC2s [accessed 14 May 2024].

Kulozik, Diana and Everwien, Andrea (2017): *Moderne "Haussklaverei"* (Modern "Domestic Slavery"). ARD, Kontraste. Berlin: RBB.

Not specified. (2007): *Mutter – Stiefmutter* (Mother and Stepmother). www.youtube.com/watch?v=23j6jpaZFEE [accessed 14 May 2024].

Redaktion Monitor ARD (2013): *Ausgebeutet und allein gelassen. Ausländische Pflegekräfte in deutschen Haushalten* (Exploited and Abandoned. Foreign Caregivers in German households). Köln: WDR: www.youtube.com/watch?v=7Samn6qKKSo [accessed 14 May 2024].

Redaktion Deutsche Welle (Polnische Redaktion) (2014): *Jerzy. Opiekun osób starszych w Niemczech* (Jerzy. Caregiver for the Elderly in Germany). www.youtube.com/watch?v=SwQjKxyJJrw [accessed 14 May 2024].

Rieker, Ariane (2017): *Der Pflegeaufstand* (The Care Rebellion). MDR. Leipzig/Berlin/Greifswald: Hoferichter & Jacobs GmbH: www.youtube.com/watch?v=oqTMuTKoPUM [accessed 14 May 2024].

World Vision (2009): *Price of Hearts: Romania's Home Alone Children*. Frontline Focus: www.youtube.com/watch?v=PpJ2J1NMzqk [accessed 14 May 2024].

Index